THE PATTERN OF SINO-AMERICAN CRISES

Political-Military Interactions in the 1950s

J. H. KALICKI

International Affairs Fellow with the Council
on Foreign Relations, New York

Prepared under the auspices of the
Centre for International Studies, London School of
Economics and Political Science, and the
Center of International Studies, Princeton University

CAMBRIDGE UNIVERSITY PRESS

Published by the Syndics of the Cambridge University Press
Bentley House, 200 Euston Road, London NW1 2DB
American Branch: 32 East 57th Street, New York, N.Y. 10022

© Cambridge University Press 1975

Library of Congress Catalogue Card Number: 74-12967

ISBN: 0 521 20600 6

First published 1975

Printed in the United States of America by
Vail-Ballou Press, Inc., Binghamton, N.Y.

This book was prepared prior to the author's joining the staff of the US
Arms Control and Disarmament Agency and the Policy Planning Staff of
the Department of State. It represents only his personal views and not those
of any department or agency of the United States Government, nor those
of the Council on Foreign Relations.

Robert Manning Strozier Library

B+T

JUL 16 1976

Tallahassee, Florida

To Nina and Mireya

CONTENTS

ILLUSTRATIONS

PREFACE

The preparation of this book has been generously supported by both a three-year Ford Foundation graduate studentship at the Centre for International Studies, London School of Economics and Political Science, starting in October 1968, and two travel grants for research in US archives and university libraries and for interviews of former American officials in 1970, provided by the LSE Centre and the US Arms Control and Disarmament Agency through the US National Academy of Sciences – National Research Council. Finally, a Research Associateship at the Center of International Studies, Princeton University, gave the original doctoral dissertation prepared for the University of London that indispensable push toward conversion into its present published form.

It is a pleasure to acknowledge the help and encouragement which I have received in England and America. The major theoretical influence on this study has been the crisis theory of Coral Bell, my former supervisor at LSE. I am also indebted to Cyril Black, John Gittings, Geoffrey Goodwin, Leon Gordenker, Geoffrey Hudson, Klaus Knorr, Michael Leifer, Fred Northedge, Donald Puchala and Oran Young for their helpful advice and comments on portions of this work, and to the Cambridge University Press for their kind assistance and counsel in the production of this book. I owe special gratitude to the former government officials who gave so generously of their time to put the flesh and bones on the written record of this period.

Thanks are also due to Elisabeth Campbell, Dorothy Hamerton and their staffs at Chatham House for their unflagging support, as well as to Geoffry Allen of the British Library of Political and Economic Science, John Ma and David Tseng of the Hoover Institution's East Asian Collection, Wanda Randall of Princeton

University's Dulles Library, and Edwin Thompson of the Eisenhower Library for their personal interest and often overwhelming assistance to my research. Any surviving defects are entirely my own.

The lioness's share of the credit belongs to my editor and wife, Anne, without whose watchful eye and constant encouragement this book would not have been possible.

J.H.K.

Harwich Port
September 1973

ACKNOWLEDGMENTS

Permission to quote in all editions is gratefully acknowledged: John Foster Dulles Library of Diplomatic History, Princeton University Library, Princeton, New Jersey, and the Dwight D. Eisenhower Presidential Library, Abilene, Kansas; Sherman Adams, Robert R. Bowie, Arleigh Burke, Chung Il Kwon, Eleanor L. Dulles, John S. D. Eisenhower, James C. Hagerty, Neil McElroy, Livingston T. Merchant, Robert D. Murphy, Arthur W. Radford, Matthew B. Ridgway, Nathan F. Twining, and George K. C. Yeh; Council on Foreign Relations for Richard Stebbins, *The United States in World Affairs, 1954* (New York: Harper and Row) copyright 1956; Farrar, Straus and Giroux for Richard Rovere, *Affairs of State*, copyright 1956; *Foreign Affairs* for John Foster Dulles, 'Policy for Security and Peace', April 1954; Foreign Policy Research Institute for William Kintner *et al.*, *A Study on Crisis Management*, copyright 1965; Harper and Row Publishers for Sherman Adams, *First Hand Report*, copyright 1961 and Matthew B. Ridgway, *Soldier*, copyright 1956; Houghton Mifflin Company for McGeorge Bundy, *The Pattern of Responsibility*, copyright 1952 and Harold Hinton, *Communist China in World Politics*, copyright 1966; The Hudson Institute for Herman Kahn and Anthony Wiener, *Crisis and Arms Control*, copyright 1962; Little, Brown and Company for *Khrushchev Remembers*, with an Introduction, Commentary and Notes by Edward Crankshaw, Translated and Edited by Strobe Talbott, copyright 1970; Macmillan Publishing Co. for Glenn Paige, *The Korean Decision*, copyright 1968, Allen Whiting, *China Crosses the Yalu*, copyright 1960, and James Robinson, 'Crisis', *International Encyclopedia of the Social Sciences* edited by David L. Sills, copyright 1968; Charles E. Merrill Publishing Co. for Joseph de Rivera, *The Psychological Dimension of Foreign Policy*, copyright 1968; W. W. Norton, New York and Hamish Hamilton, London for Dean Acheson, *Present at the Creation, My Years in the State Department*, copyright 1969 by Dean Acheson; Princeton University Press for Oran

Young, *The Politics of Force, Bargaining During International Crises,* copyright 1968; The RAND Corporation for Alice Hsieh, *Communist China's Strategy in the Nuclear Era,* copyright 1962; Sage Publications for Charles A. McClelland, 'Decisional Opportunity and Political Controversy: The Quemoy Case', *The Journal of Conflict Resolution* vol. vi, no. 3 (Sept. 1962); The Society for General Systems Research for Charles McClelland, 'Systems and History in Internation Relations', *General Systems Yearbook,* copyright 1958; Time Inc. for James R. Shepley, 'How Dulles Averted War', *Life,* copyright 1956; University of Chicago Press for Tang Tsou, *America's Failure in China,* copyright 1963; University of Pennsylvania Press for Carl Berger, *The Korean Knot,* copyright 1957; University of Washington Press for Karl Rankin, *China Assignment,* copyright 1964; and Yale University Press for Thomas Schelling, *Arms and Influence,* copyright 1966.

ABBREVIATIONS

ANZUS	Australia–New Zealand–United States
BBC/FE	*BBC Summary of World Broadcasts (Far East)*
CB	*Current Background*
CCP	Chinese Communist Party
CDSP	*Current Digest of the Soviet Press*
CINCFE	Commander-in-Chief, Far East
CINCUNC	Commander-in-Chief, UN Command
CPR	Chinese People's Republic (PRC)
CPSU	Communist Party of the Soviet Union
CPV	Chinese People's Volunteers
DSB	Department of State *Bulletin*
DPRK	Democratic People's Republic of Korea
DRV	Democratic Republic of Vietnam
ECMM	*Extracts from China Mainland Magazines*
EDC	European Defence Community
GRC	Government of the Republic of China
ICBM	Inter-Continental Ballistic Missile
ITV	Independent Television
JCS	Joint Chiefs of Staff
KPLA	Korean People's Liberation Army
KVC	Korean Volunteer Corps
MDT	Mutual Defense Treaty
NATO	North Atlantic Treaty Organisation
NCNA	New China News Agency
NEATO	Northeast Asia Treaty Organisation
NKSPA	North Korean Supreme People's Assembly
NSC	National Security Council
OHC	Oral History Collection
OHP	Oral History Project
PLA	People's Liberation Army
PRC	People's Republic of China
ROC	Republic of China on Taiwan

ROK	Republic of Korea
SCMP	*Survey of the China Mainland Press*
SEATO	Southeast Asia Treaty Organisation
SFRC	Senate Foreign Relations Committee
UKPF	United Korean Patriotic Front
UN	United Nations
UNC	UN Command
UNCK	UN Commission on Korea
UNCURK	UN Commission for the Unification and Rehabilitation of Korea
UNTCK	UN Temporary Commission on Korea
UK	United Kingdom
US	United States
USSR	Union of Soviet Socialist Republics
VPA	Vietnam People's Army
WFTU	World Federation of Trade Unions

Introduction

The chain of developments since President Nixon's February 1972 visit to the People's Republic of China [a] seems to have aroused a keen and enduring interest among press and informed publics in the problems and prospects of Sino-American relations. And yet talk of table tennis and acrobatic troupes or even attention to eye-catching encounters of Nixon and Kissinger with Mao and Chou, should not obscure the slower but more fundamental changes which have been occurring recently in the relations between the two states.

In the economic sphere, the US trade embargo has been relaxed to such an extent that it is no longer unrealistic to talk about bilateral trade in hundred-million-dollar terms. In the strategic sphere, both the Shanghai Communiqué and the Indochina peace accords have signalled the defusing of Taiwan and Indochina as sources of tension between Peking and Washington. And in the diplomatic sphere, it would not be going too far to suggest that the two powers are building a 'co-operative adversary' relationship with increasingly parallel positions on Asian security questions – ranging from such specific instances as the similar stances over the 1971 Indo-Pakistani War to such general postures as opposition to hegemony and avoidance of conflict.

Indeed, the Chinese have shown more and more responsiveness to US intimations that there is ample room for progress in the relationship between the two nations, especially since the President's 1970 'state of the world' message to Congress highlighted his shift in emphasis toward accentuating negotiation rather than confrontation.

What I choose to call the 'diplomatic' view of Sino-American relations seems to differentiate sharply between the confronta-

[a] Unless explicitly identified with the Republic of China on Taiwan (ROC), 'China' will always refer to the People's Republic of China (PRC). Peking, Taipei, Washington, Moscow and other capitals will often stand as shorthand for their respective governments or states.

tion of the past and the hoped-for negotiation of the future. In the past, this view has emphasised the negative aspects of US/PRC confrontation, such as the absence both of diplomatic recognition and of trade relations in the two decades following the Chinese Communist Revolution of 1949. For the future, the diplomatic approach highlights the potential for positive change inherent in the Nixon Doctrine and in the hopefully successful accommodation with a China after Mao, in the context of the evolving US-USSR-PRC triangular relationship.

The diplomatic approach has made many valuable contributions, but it has tended to offer a one-sided image of Sino-American relations in the 1950s and 1960s, an image of two peoples, once friends and then strangers, taking separate roads leading in quite different directions. Moreover, many an analysis, when taken to its logical conclusion, gives the reader the impression that opportunities for Sino-American co-operation in those years could have been seized or created, if only this fatal post-war divergence in policies and courses of action had been arrested soon after 1949.

The strategic approach

The 'strategic' approach adopted here is intended to draw attention away from the largely sterile consideration of diplomatic and commercial impasse in the relationship of China and America since 1949, and to redirect it to the (paradoxically) far more positive record of crisis interactions between the two states, in the first decade of their ideological and strategic confrontation. This is a record of over-all progress from the dysfunctional crises of the Korean War to the moderately functional 1958 crisis in the Taiwain Straits. It is also a record of widening American and Chinese commitments to the defence of opposing positions on the Asian rimland, and hence of increasing stability for the uneasy balance of power in the Far East. Finally, it is a record of growing sophistication in the crisis behaviour of both Chinese and American decision-makers, as they became more creative, flexible and oriented to crisis control in their strategic relationship.

This study of Sino-American crises in the 1950s sets out, then, to define the most prominent crisis system in the Far East in terms of the crisis behaviour of the United States and the People's

Republic of China and of the crisis interactions occurring between them. By comparative case study, it demonstrates how Sino-American crises have functioned in Korea, Indochina and the Taiwan Straits; by cumulative case study, it elucidates the pattern of strategic interactions evolving through these crises over time.

Definitions

A short pause to elucidate the terms in this discussion is perhaps in order at this stage, although the more historically-minded reader need not tarry long over this section. As suggested in Lewis Coser's 1956 treatise, *The Functions of Social Conflict*, conflicts can be said to be 'functional' to the extent that violence and mutual disadvantage dominate such a relationship – making for a decrease rather than an increase 'in the adaptation or adjustment of particular social relationships or groups'.[1]

A more difficult problem is presented when one attempts to identify that range of conflict represented by the rather vague term 'crisis'. James Robinson was no doubt right when he observed that ' "Crisis" is a lay term in search of a scholarly meaning.' [2] As a lay term, it often arises in the context of personal, small group and organisational experiences. A common denominator for all of these levels of individual and social experience seems to be that they are taken to be periods of intense danger entailing a threat to the existing state of affairs, but beyond this common denominator, the number and variety of interpretations of the term abound.

Accepting the original, Greek meaning of 'crisis' as a turning point between a favourable and an unfavourable outcome, I propose to adopt as a working definition the one formulated by Kintner and Schwartz in 1965, instead of adding one more idiosyncratic contribution to the plethora which already exists. For our purposes, an international crisis is 'a hostile confrontation of two or more nations arising from conflicting policies toward a geographic or problem area which, by virtue of the use or suggested use of force, engenders a critical increase in tension'.[3] It should be understood, however, that while a 'critical increase in tension' is the immediate consequence of a crisis, in the longer term it can lead to an over-all decrease in tension, and

[1] Numbered references are for notes appearing between pages 219–42.

a stabilisation of relationships resulting from the effective handling of the confrontation.

I will also adopt the list of crisis characteristics proposed by Kahn and Wiener in 1962, which I have reorganised in the interest of greater consistency. An inter-state crisis is understood to be a situation in which

> events converge;
> interrelations among actors are changed (intra- and international); and
> international tensions increase.

The crisis actors perceive turning points and receive threats, warnings or promises. They become acutely aware that

> time pressures increase;
> uncertainties increase;
> information may become more inadequate;
> control of events is decreased; and nevertheless decisions and actions are required;
> the outcome will shape the future.[4]

In analytical terms, I am interested in assessing both how China and the United States came to confront each other in a series of East Asian situations and also to what extent they pressed their conflicting policies as opposed to co-operating in order to control conflict. My focus is on the evolving strategic relationship between the two states, as manifested in their crisis interactions throughout the 1950s, rather than on the decision-making processes of each state *per se*, although I consider the latter insofar as they do affect Sino-American crisis interactions.

Another relevant distinction is that between 'adversary' crises, which occur between enemies, and 'intramural' crises, which occur between allies. I am concerned primarily with adversary crises between China and America, but intramural problems are considered when they significantly influence the course of a Sino-American crisis, as is the case with Anglo-American relations during the Indochina crisis and with Sino-Soviet relations during the second Taiwan Straits crisis. Most importantly, however, the crisis experience and interactions of Peking and Washington, in and of themselves, will be seen to develop a pattern of threats and counter-threats, actions and reactions which define both the character and the extent of their commitments in the post-1949 international system in the Far East.

Sino-American crises and crisis theory

After establishing a historical and strategic context for the Korean conflict, I examine two crisis sequences in it – from the US intervention against the North Korean attack to the Chinese intervention, and then from direct Sino-American confrontation to impasse – which occur over a prolonged period from June 1950 to June 1951. Whereas the Korean crises are characterised first by relatively independent crisis behaviour by each side (leading belatedly to inter-dependent initiatives and responses) and second by direct confrontation, the Indochina crisis of March–April 1954 is characterised by inter-dependent and indirect crisis interactions throughout. Both Peking and Washington are seen to become more sophisticated in their crisis handling, in that they have learned [b] to communicate more effectively, respond more relevantly, and rely on the Viet Minh, the Associated States and France to act as *proxies*, that is, agents and strategic intermediaries. This hypothesis corresponds with Charles McClelland's view of a crisis as a 'learning situation in which the protagonists have to search for ways to disengage unless one or more parties intend to intensify and widen the violence of the conflict'.[6]

My analysis of the two Taiwan Straits crises – from September 1954 to April 1955 and from August to October 1958 – reveals an increasing inter-dependence in the crisis behaviour of China and America and a growing sophistication in their alternation between direct and indirect involvement, on the models of Korea and Indochina. In short, I argue that both sides learn from crisis to crisis,[c] in the sense that their leaders acquire information and experience which enable them to handle successive crises more effectively, less dangerously, and even with greater poise than was the case at the outset of the 1950s.

Nothwithstanding the arguments of some social psychologists that creativity, efficiency, productivity and morale are reduced

---

[b] In cybernetic terms, learning can be seen as a function of feedback, in which Actor A's cognition of Actor B's response to its action either corrects or reinforces its predisposition to act in the same way in similar circumstances in the future.[5]

[c] What may be a crisis for one party may not be a crisis for the other: it may simply be perceived as a dispute or a strategic/diplomatic challenge, or it may be perceived as a relatively unlimited conflict. Indochina 1954 is a good case in point: as will be seen, it was a crisis for the United States, a war for France, the Associated States and the Viet Minh, a strategic challenge for China and a diplomatic challenge for Britain and the USSR.

to a minimum at times of acute crisis,[7] I argue that – at least in the case of the crises which are considered here – all of these factors are optimised under high stress. The ingenuity and resourcefulness of American and Chinese 'crisis handlers' were at a peak when they faced the gravest threats, whereas both sterile diplomatic intercourse and bureaucratic inertia combined to deter any major progress in Sino-American relations in conditions of reduced stress.

The results which emerge from this study underscore the contribution which Sino-American crisis analysis can make to crisis interaction theory and to conflict theory in general. They extend crisis theory in two principal directions, by providing (1) an analysis of intra-war crises (in Korea) in addition to extra-war crises [d] (in Indochina and the Taiwan Straits) and (2) an application of crisis theory to a single dyad over time, instead of taking cases that are unrelated with regard to participants in and continuity of crises. Furthermore, the results emphasise the applicability of crisis management' principles and techniques, suitably modified, to areas outside the Soviet-American relationship, by far the favourite subject of a modern-day crisis analysts.

[d] Oran R. Young offers a useful diagram (Fig. 1) showing the place of crisis in international politics. 'Here the zone of crisis, labelled B, covers a highly coercive but intermediate level of political interaction falling between ordinary activities and open warfare. From this perspective, it is logically possible to have movement toward warfare (C) either through a

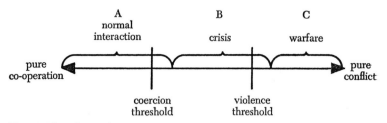

Fig. 1. The place of crisis in international politics

period of crisis (B) or by means of a direct jump from normal interaction (A) to open warfare (C) . . . wars seem more often to begin through a progression from B to C than from A to C without B. Also, crises do *not* necessarily lead to open warfare. On the contrary . . . a shift from A to B often generates increased concern over the dangers of a situation and the consequent need for caution.' [8] Two further points about this diagram are in order. First, the poles of 'co-operation' and 'pure conflict' are ideal types and are not encountered in real-life situations. Second, this is a diagram of extra-war crises and can be modified to represent intra-war crises. Fig. 2

They serve to broaden the scope of crisis theory to include partially functional areas which may, at first sight, have appeared totally dysfunctional in character.

Prospectus

Three broad categories to be considered in this book are (1) the structure and dynamics of each crisis; (2) the over-all pattern of Sino-American crises; and (3) the relationship between the crises and Sino-American relations as a whole.

The first set concerns the nature of each Sino-American crisis in the 1950s. In each case, the crisis is dissected in order to identify the pattern of actions and reactions which result in phases of escalation, declension and de-escalation, the principal components of a crisis life cycle. *Escalation,* or the aggravation of a crisis, is characterised by an intensification of conflictual, as opposed to co-operative, interactions, the dominance of the crisis system over the crisis actors, and an increased risk and threat of war or (in the case of intra-war crisis) of less restricted and more violent warfare. *Declension,*[e] or the stabilisation of a crisis, is

is one possible version which I have designed with 1950–1 Korean crises in mind. The first limiting pole, *antebellum* crisis, is commonplace in

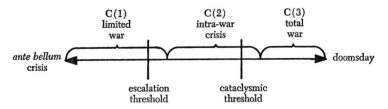

Fig. 2. The place of crisis during wartime

international politics; the second, doomsday, is thankfully a hypothetical type. The zone of intra-war crisis, labelled C(2), covers a violent but still intermediate level of strategic interaction falling between limited and total war. The crisis thresholds mediate between the crisis, on the one hand, and more or less limited warfare, on the other. The problem for both Peking and Washington was to keep their ends of the Korean crises below the 'cataclysmic threshold'.

[e] This term, devised by Coral Bell, is more appropriate than 'decision point', normally used in the literature: to Bell's more accurate implication that stabilisation occurs over a period of time, I would add that the declension phase is a function of the interactions *between* crisis actors, rather than of the unilateral attempt of any single actor to control the crisis system.

characterised by the balancing of conflictual by co-operative interactions, an assertion of the influence of the crisis actors over the crisis system, and a reduced risk and threat of war or a lowered level of violence.

I establish when, how and why the crisis develops a momentum of its own during the escalation phase, and when and how the national actors assert enough control to arrest the escalation of the crisis and usher in a phase of declension. I then consider the techniques – such as the orchestration of physical and verbal actions, the transmission of signals, and the use of clear or ambiguous threats and commitments – which are used to manipulate or manage the crisis interactions and establish a phase of crisis *de-escalation,* or defusing of a crisis. This phase is characterised by an intensification of co-operative as opposed to conflictual interactions, the domination of crisis actors over the crisis system, and a minimised risk and threat of war or an increasing possibility of cease-fire.

The second category concerns the pattern of Sino-American crises through the 1950s. Through a method of comparative and cumulative case study, I investigate the extent to which each succeeding crisis established, on the level of the dyad, areas of commitment and resolve or left areas susceptible to subsequent probes. On the actor level, I consider the extent to which decision-makers can be said to learn from crisis to crisis, whether some of the lessons might have been counter-productive, and whether a learning curve of crisis management can be detected in the Sino-American case.

The third set concerns the interaction between the *acute* crises which constitute the case studies and the decade-long *chronic* crisis which makes up the context in which they occur. The chronic crisis is defined both by the net effect of the preceding acute crises on the international climate – demarcating spheres of commitment and/or of contest – and by the inherent incompatibility of the US presence on, and the PRC aspirations for, pre-eminence over the rimlands of Asia. While the chronic crisis is essentially static, reflecting the level of tension set by successive acute crises, the latter are essentially dynamic: relatively intensive strategic interactions occur among Peking, Washington, proxies and intermediaries, which dominate their crisis behaviour until they become stabilised or partially resolved through a sufficiently strong unilateral initiative or through joint co-ordination.

The format for dealing with these issues consists essentially of an alternation between crisis and inter-crisis periods, on a chronological basis, linked to three general phases of development – namely, the establishment of Sino-American confrontation from 1949 to 1953, its elaboration in 1954 and 1955 and its ultimate management in the remainder of the decade. I begin by discussing the state of US/PRC relations at the start of the decade and by establishing the connection between post-War events in Korea and the course of Sino-American crises thereafter. I analyse the Korean crises in chapter 3, the Indochina crisis in chapter 5, and the two Taiwan Straits crises in chapters 6 and 8. In chapters 4 and 7, I establish the context of chronic bilateral crisis by discussing the inter-crisis periods of 1951–4 and 1955–8.

Fig. 3. The Far East

Part One: The foundations of confrontation

1: Sino-American relations at the turn of the decade

The Chinese Communist Revolution of 1949 marked a watershed in Sino-American relations. It was the point of departure for a period of increasingly bitter hostility between the giants of America and Asia who had, on the whole, befriended each other for almost two centuries. The decade from 1949 to 1959 saw the rise of four major confrontations between the United States and China – one each over Korea and Indochina, and two over the Taiwan Straits – which were symptomatic of the underlying tense relationship between the two powers.

And yet there were few *a priori* reasons for the 1950s to be a decade of Sino-American hostility. After the débâcle in which the Kuomintang recipients of massive American military and economic aid melted away to their island refuge of Formosa (Taiwan), which they held along with the Pescadores and a series of smaller off-shore islands, Secretary of State Dean Acheson announced, in transmitting his 1949 White Paper on China, that the United States would neither interfere in the Chinese civil war in the future nor continue to support Generalissimo Chiang Kai-shek.

The White Paper, appearing at a time of defeat for the US China policy of the 1940s, was to usher in a ten-month period of denunciation of past policy and recrimination among politicians. Major General Patrick Hurley, US Ambassador to China in 1944–5, called the document 'a smooth alibi for the pro-Communists in the State Department who had engineered the overthrow of our ally . . . and aided in the Communist conquest of China'. A joint statement by the future Senate leaders of the China Lobby stigmatised it as 'a 1,054-page white-wash of a wishful, do-nothing policy which has succeeded only in placing Asia in danger of Soviet conquest'. This comment found a strange echo in one reported from Mao himself, who called the White Paper 'a bucket of cold water, particularly for those who believe that everything American is good and hope that China will model herself on the United States'.[1]

This bitter criticism of past mistakes was to be a key factor in the disoriented US approach to China in the period which followed. After the People's Republic of China was proclaimed on 21 September 1949, Washington had tried to maintain an open-minded attitude on recognition of the new government in Peking. After a majority of State Department consultants on the Far East reportedly recommended withdrawal of recognition from the Nationalist government, recognition of the Communist government, and establishment of trade relations with the PRC, Secretary Acheson asserted in his 12 October press conference that Peking would have to exercise effective control over China, recognise its international obligations, and govern with popular consent before US recognition could follow. Although this declaration did call for a certain degree of moral approbation – a traditional US approach to questions of recognition – the test for popular consent was left open to subsequent interpretation. The stance was a far cry from the later dogmatism of Secretary Dulles. More immediately, it did nothing to prevent a total defeat of Chiang's forces, a defeat which was by then regarded as the inevitable outcome of the string of Communist victories on the mainland following the crossing of the Yangtze on 20 April.

In December, the State Department told its diplomats to expect the fall of Formosa and to represent it to world opinion as unrelated to US security. This circular was promptly leaked by General MacArthur's headquarters in Tokyo, a well-known focus of support of Generalissimo Chiang Kai-shek, and resulted in a Congressional uproar over the apparent US betrayal of the Chinese Nationalists. Secretary Acheson later defended his Department's action as representing 'the only attitude which will have the desired effect, which is to minimise the damage to the prestige of the United States and the morale of others should Formosa fall'.[2] Acheson's point was pressed further home on 5 January, when President Truman announced, in his presence, that the United States would 'not provide military aid or advice to Chinese forces on Formosa',[3] in spite of increasing Republican resistance to a desertion of the Chinese Nationalists.

The Truman administration, recognising that the primary communist goal was the total reunification of China under their rule, seemed to acquiesce as the PLA followed up their take-over of Hainan Island in the southwest with an occupation of the off-shore islands, leading to a projected final victory over Chiang in Formosa and the Pescadores. Thus the basis seemed established for US disengagement from Chinese affairs but, as will be seen, commitment to the PRC's neighbours.

The PRC looks to its security needs

Although no mere band of agrarian reformers or social democrats (as some had alleged in the mid-1940s), the Chinese Communist Party (CCP) had for a time formed a united front with the Kuomintang during the war against Japan and had co-operated in limited ways with General Marshall in the latter's attempts to find a political solution to the Chinese civil war. In an ironic fashion (of which Mao was well aware), the Chinese Communists owed the speed of their victory to the American military supplies captured from the escaping Nationalists. Perhaps the most relevant point about the Communist success was that it was due fundamentally to an indigenous guerrilla insurgency depending for its strength on active rural support. Hence, the CCP was beholden to no external power for its assumption of power. Indeed, the Soviet Union was in the particularly uncomfortable position of being second only to the United States in siding with Chiang Kai-shek. Moscow signed a nonaggression treaty with Nationalist China in 1945, moved its embassy south with each Kuomintang retreat, and even urged the Chinese comrades to defer the final offensive, labelling it premature. Stalin's advice was disregarded; victory was gained.

Although a Far Eastern Yugoslavia was theoretically conceivable up to the autumn of 1949,[a] domestic requirements and the current state of the Cold War were to guard against Mao's taking a Titoist line in the world communist movement. Domestically, economic and technical assistance were essential to long-term development and the USSR remained the major aid donor most likely to support socialist reconstruction in China. Circumstances related to Cold War history, moreover, must have persuaded Mao to reject either a neutralist policy or aid from the West and

[a] As early as 1936, Mao Tse-tung had declared to Edgar Snow that 'We are certainly not fighting for an emancipated China in order to turn the country over to Moscow!' [4] Yet in his November 1948 essay *On Internationalism and Nationalism*, Liu Shao-ch'i gave total support to the Soviet Union, asserting that 'American imperialism has become the bastion of all the reactionary forces in the world, while the Soviet Union has become the bastion of all progressive forces'.[5]

instead to align with the Soviet bloc. The winter of 1949–50, which Mao and a high-level CCP delegation spent in Moscow negotiating a Sino-Soviet treaty to replace the old Soviet pact with the Kuomintang, was a time of tightening bipolarity in the international system. The East-West confrontation was being forged over the heat of the 1948–9 Berlin crisis. The Soviet empire in Eastern Europe was being consolidated; the North Atlantic Treaty Organisation had been formed in April 1949. Russia exploded its first atomic bomb in August, ushering in the era of the balance of terror. Mao Tse-tung could ill afford to ignore so powerful a neighbour, even had he wanted to.

Furthermore, it is possible to identify distinct factors which would serve to reinforce concretely the instinctive Chinese distrust of American post-war policy in the Far East. In the first place, the United States was in the process of negotiating a peace treaty with Japan, independently of the Soviet Union. It is not surprising that Peking readily viewed the American occupation as the succcessor to and partly the inheritor of Japanese imperialism,[6] and that it viewed the negotiation of the end of that occupation by John Foster Dulles – the hard-line Republican diplomat both favoured by Chiang and denounced by Stalin – with not a few misgivings. Nor is it surprising that Peking, especially during the unstable period after the seizure of power, would fear a resurgent Japanese imperialism under American instigation and control, considering MacArthur's firm hand during the occupation.[7] The USSR was able to capitalise on this fear – and on its exclusion from the negotiations with Japan – by signing the 1950 Sino-Soviet Treaty of Friendship, Alliance and Mutual Assistance, which guaranteed the PRC against attack from Japan or any of the latter's allies. Moreover, the existence of such an external threat, real or imagined, could be exploited for the purpose of reducing internal opposition and generating support for the new regime.

In the second place, a Chinese Communist *tour d'horizon* would reveal serious confrontations already in existence on China's southwest and eastern flanks. To the southwest, a guerrilla war against the French was entering its fourth year; to the east, tension levels between the northern and southern sections of Korea were steadily increasing. In Indochina, Chinese aid to the Viet Minh, which had been granted in small amounts by the Nationalists, was continued and increased at crucial points by the Communists, whose commitment was further secured by the presence of Kuomintang forces in Vietnam.[8] This rendered south-west China vulnerable both to Kuomintang raids and later to Franco-American reprisals, which became a serious threat in 1954. The confrontation between North and South Korea, over-shadowed by their Soviet and American allies, threatened even more immediately the Chinese industrial heartland in Man-churia. As for Korea, inferences could be and were easily drawn by Peking from historical precedents set by Japan several times before, in which that peninsula was the key to aggression against Chinese territory. Thus geopolitical factors were bound to force a new, and as yet insecure, PRC Government to maintain a friendly political and ideological relationship with its large nu-clear neighbour.

In the third place, although the Chinese Nationalist forces were forced to take refuge across the Taiwan Straits, they were the remaining challenge to the authority and internal stability of the Communist regime and the remaining obstacle to Chinese reunification. As early as 15 March 1949, the Chinese Commu-nists had declared that they intended to 'liberate' Formosa be-cause otherwise it would serve the United States as 'a spring-board for future aggression' against the mainland. Their primary objective remained the victorious consummation of the civil war and an eradication of the threat to their maritime flank.

In the context of the new China, therefore, American power was perceived as a principal barrier both to Mao's instatement of jurisdiction throughout China and to a reassertion of Chinese influence in East and Southeast Asia – in spite of the fact that American policy at the turn of the decade was, as observed ear-lier, characterised by a desire to disengage from Chinese (but not Asian) affairs. Soviet power, on the other hand, remained only a potential obstacle to China until the late 1950s: although there were difficulties in Sino-Soviet relations, they would be obscured by Peking's perception of a Western threat, and would in fact become pre-eminent only as Chinese power came to chal-lenge the status quo of the area, and to put into question the stability of the Soviet-American stalemate and succeeding dé-tente.

American ambivalence in response to Mao's China

To look at the other side of the Asian security coin, the main problem for American policy in the Far East became the construction of sufficient political, economic, and military strength to balance that of the New China – that is, the formation of an Asian balance of power favourable to the remaining American interests in the area. This entailed a major change from past policy, in that China could no longer be considered the friendly foundation for such a US-oriented system; rather, American statesmen were forced, as time passed by, to rely less and less on decreasingly imperial – and decreasingly influential – Britain and France, and instead to look to such countries as Japan and, more reluctantly, India, as well as to such artificial collective-security coalitions as ANZUS and SEATO. That such a re-orientation was difficult to accept became apparent as Dulles and his colleagues made the vain attempt to link security questions in the West with those in the East (as in the case of Korea and NATO, Indochina and the EDC) as well as to link China with Russia as a monolithic enemy. Talk of the 'loss' of the old China was followed by a refusal to envisage the permanent existence of the new. What John Foster Dulles wrote in 1950 reflected the wide-spread Administration view at the time:

Communism will have a hard time regimenting the Chinese people. Its armies in China have had some success in arousing a sense of social responsibility and in imposing discipline on its supporters. But it would be a miracle if Communism were quickly to master the under-lying sense of separateness; to impose a pattern of conformity upon a people that is individualistic; to produce and distribute the food neces-sary to allay unrest; and to maintain order where disorder has been chronic.

This will be more difficult for the Chinese Communist regime be-cause its ally and backer is a country – the Soviet Union – which *takes from* its associates rather than a country like the United States which *gives to* its associates.[9]

This passage from his book *War or Peace* seems to reflect the complex, bitter-sweet mixture of regret about the old China, re-luctant respect for the new, uncertain anticipation of the future difficulties of Moscow and Peking, and apprehension about the future power of the Sino-Soviet bloc.

More generally, the over-all distribution of forces in the Far East at the beginning of the 1950s caused both sides to relin-quish their traditional foreign policy approaches and to assume positions on ground not entirely of their own choosing. China, a land power, had not yet developed a successful strategy for over-coming challenges from the sea, in spite of the century-old challenge from that direction on the part of the West. A power which for millennia was the primary (and in its eyes, the only) cultural and political force in the Far East, China was still in the throes of a fundamental transition from relations with tributaries to relations with equals.

The United States, which had either basked in Fortress America or played the role of international maverick before the Second World War, found that in the post-war period it was becoming more and more an essential component of the power balance in Europe and Asia. And yet in spite of this rapidly increasing external US commitment, it did not seem inevitable to the experts who wrote the China White Paper in 1949 that conflict would follow between the United States and China. In a top-secret memorandum in July 1949, Secretary Acheson directed Philip C. Jessup to review US China policy on the basis of accepting communist control over the mainland but of preventing 'further extension of Communist domination on the continent of Asia or in the Southeast Asia area'.[10] Moreover, up to the spring of 1950, the Truman Administration was prepared to develop a *modus vivendi* with the new Chinese rulers, not so much because they might maintain a certain distance from Stalin as because they constituted the effective government of the day.[11]

Unfortunately, this pragmatic attitude would be short-lived in the face of domestic reaction (be it Taftite or McCarthyist), the Administration's hardening of its own national security policies and, most directly, North Korea's attack on the South in June 1950. Having glanced briefly at China and the United States in the international setting of 1949–50, let us now turn to the background and occurrence of this seminal attack and its effect on subsequent crisis behaviour.

2: Korean genesis [a]

In retrospect the year 1950 was the natural time for the first test of East–West resolve in Asia, in spite of President Truman's view, stated in June, that 'the world was closer to peace than at any time since 1945'.[1] It was a time for tight bipolarity, when the ideological and power-political conflict between the United States and the Soviet Union assumed global proportions and made the maximum demand on national allegiances. In Europe, the consolidation of Western and Soviet blocs and the stand-off resulting from the Berlin blockade had defined an uneasy *modus vivendi,* which the United States and the Soviet Union were forced to accept at least for the short term. The nuclear stalemate was to ensure a longer-term preservation of the status quo.

Korea as a likely target

In Asia, however, neither the commitments nor the resolve of the Great Powers to defend them were by any means as well defined and secured, although the re-alignment of China with the Soviet bloc was widely interpreted as a movement of the central balance of power in Moscow's favour. Even allowing for the benefit of hindsight, Korea was for many reasons a likely target for a Soviet-authorised attack in the early 1950s. The first reason was the inherent instability of post-war Korea itself: this instability will be traced over three two-year phases (1945–6, 1947–8, 1949–50). The second was the power vacuum created by the US failure to appear credibly committed to the defence of

[a] Historical narrative is not an end either of this chapter or of the over-all study; it is rather a means toward a further understanding of the nature of Sino-American crisis interactions. The discussion has been broadened at this stage to suggest – through historical background and the wider political context – both the explanation for the linking of Korea, Taiwan and Indochina by the US Administration, and also the explanation for the shift from a retrocessive to an escalating Chinese Communist commitment to North Korean defence.

the South after the middle (1947–8) phase. The third was the great extent of Russian control over the North, especially during the third phase, and therefore over the conduct of an attack across the 38th Parallel dividing the two zones.

1945–6. The instability of Korea, in both political-economic and military terms, increased steadily between 1945 and 1950. In spite of the promise made by Roosevelt, Churchill and Chiang Kai-shek at the 1943 Cairo Conference that 'Korea shall become free and independent' after the War, neither Russia nor America was prepared to let the other dominate the peninsula. The US Military Command refused to recognise the People's Republic of Korea and established instead a post-war military government. On the other hand, the Soviet military command, which had occupied northern Korea on 12 August 1945 as a result of Russia's declaration of war against Japan, chose to exercise its power through local and provincial 'People's Committees'. The joint occupation, formalised in Moscow in December 1945, was re-named a 'trusteeship', to be administered by a US–USSR Joint Commission for up to five years.

1947–8. By the summer of 1947, the Commission had proved a failure, for both sides had proposed measures ostensibly designed to place Korea on a fully independent footing but in fact planned so as to secure control of the whole peninsula – a critical link for control of either the Asian heartland or the rimlands of the West Pacific, as a century of great power rivalry had shown.

The US Government, having rejected a Soviet proposal designed to exclude leading South Koreans from a provisional government,[b] placed the Korean problem on the agenda of the General Assembly on 23 September 1947. That body subsequently rejected two Soviet resolutions, inviting 'elected representatives of the two parts of Korea to take part in the discussion of the Korean question' and recommending the simultaneous withdrawal of occupying troops by the beginning of 1948; it adopted the amended American draft on 14 November, which established the UN Temporary Commisson on Korea, which was to observe elections throughout the country by the end of March and to ad-

[b] The USSR insisted that all socio-political organisations which opposed the trusteeship should be excluded from the provisional government. Since leading South Koreans opposed the system, Molotov would have thereby come close to entrenching the Korean Communists in positions of power.

vise the elected representatives on establishing a National Government. The Russians refused to co-operate, and general elections were consequently held only in the South under UNTCK supervision on 10 May. The Republic of Korea (ROK) constitution was promulgated on 17 July. The Russians sponsored elections for the North Korean Supreme People's Assembly on 25 August, and this body duly ratified the constitution of the Democratic People's Republic of Korea (DPRK) on 3 September. On 21 September, the UNTCK reported to the General Assembly that the results of the 10 May elections were 'a valid expression of the free will of the electorate in South Korea', and on 12 December the UN recognised the ROK as the legal government of all of Korea.

The 1947–8 phase of post-war Korean history had ended, then, with the establishment of the Republic of Korea under the aegis of the United Nations – which recognised Seoul as the seat of the legal government of both Koreas. A rival government was established, under the protection of the Soviet Union, in the northern capital of Pyongyang.

1949–50. The third phase, which would last two years until 10 May 1950, would be characterised by (1) the withdrawal of American and Russian occupying forces, (2) the polarisation of the internal setting, and (3) the steady increase of Russian influence over Pyongyang, to a certain extent at the expence of Chinese influence.

(1) *Withdrawal from Korea.* In spite of the failure of efforts toward peaceful unification, the existence of thousands of well-trained guerrillas and political agents in the South, and the resulting South Korean opposition to American withdrawal, the only American forces remaining in Korea by the end of June 1949 were a Military Advisory Group of five hundred men. The American decision to withdraw from the South was certainly influenced both by the Soviet withdrawal in the North, completed by the end of the year (although not under the supervision of the UN Commission on Korea, as in the South), and by the establishment of the ROK Government, but it was above all the consequence of the US Government's strategic review in the late 1940s which had implicitly excluded the Asian mainland from the American defence perimeter. In a March 1949 interview, General Douglas MacArthur himself had explicitly excluded South Korea from US protection:

Now the Pacific has become an Anglo-Saxon lake and our line of defence runs through the chain of islands fringing the coast of Asia. It starts from the Philippines and continues through the Ryukyu archipelago which includes its main bastion, Okinawa. Then it bends back through Japan and the Aleutian Island chain to Alaska.[2]

As one of many countries remaining outside this strictly delimited sphere of US protection, the ROK was aware of MacArthur's and later of Secretary of State Acheson's warning – in his 12 January speech to the National Press Club – that it would have to depend for its defence upon its own efforts backed 'by the commitments of the entire civilised world under the Charter of the United Nations'.[3]

The importance of this speech, in terms of the probable effect that it had on decision-making in Moscow and Pyongyang, cannot be underestimated. In it, Acheson reasserted that the American defence perimeter in the Pacific ran from the Aleutians to Japan, the Ryukyus and the Philippines. The Secretary's thesis was that the United Nations 'so far has not proved a weak reed' and would be able to help 'any people who are determined to protect their independence against outside aggression' but are not directly defended by the United States.[4] This speech was made in spite of the lack of armed units permanently at the disposal of the UN and in spite of the paralytic effect of the Soviet veto (except during the period of Soviet boycott) in the Security Council – making the two organs more suited to political debate than to resolution of international issues dividing the great powers.

In justice to the Secretary, he did also say that 'no person can guarantee these areas [outside the US defence perimeter] against attack', and he was later to justify his position by pointing to the fact that the UN *did* respond to North Korean aggression. This does little, however, to counter the main criticism that US leaders were to blame for encouraging Moscow and Pyongyang to attempt aggression in the first place and that it was substantially the US intervention which saved South Korea. Acheson claimed, moreover, that accusations that his 12 January speech encouraged the attack on South Korea were 'specious', because 'Australia and New Zealand were not included either, and the first of all our mutual defence agreements was made with Korea'. The Russians 'would have been more impressed by the two years' agitation for withdrawal of combat forces from Korea, the defeat in Congress of a minor aid bill for it, and the increasing discussion of a peace treaty with Japan'.[5] These were all substantial considerations which could not fail to have influenced the enemy, but this is so precisely because there was ambivalence not only in American words but also in American actions.

For example, in aid terms, limited funds were authorised for South Korean defence under the Mutual Defence Assistance Act of 1949 and a US–ROK agreement under it signed on 6 January 1950, but Congress delayed appropriating $10 970 000 until 15 March. Of this, South Korea actually received only a few hundred dollars' worth of signal equipment by June. In the interim, Seoul had to make do with the equipment transferred to it when the American occupation troops left in 1948 and 1949, a situation which both the US Military Assistance Group and the Administration felt was consistent with the need to put the ROK Army on a defensive and not an offensive footing. To put it mildly, the US failure to supply the South Koreans with tanks, heavy artillery, or supporting combat aircraft contrasted unfavourably – and, in the test, catastrophically – with the superior offensive equipment supplied by the Russians to the North Koreans.[6]

(2) *Polarisation of internal setting.* No sooner had the American troops withdrawn from South Korea (June 1949) than there was an increase of North Korean raids across the 38th Parallel. Carl Berger maintains that 'These skirmishes and firefights provided the North Korean armies with invaluable combat experience, as well as military intelligence on the capabilities of the South Korean Constabulary.'[7] In the beginning of August 1949, an estimated 6000 North Korean troops invaded Ongjin peninsula. On 14 October, the North Korean government strongly implied that it would reunite Korea by force if necessary. In letters to the Secretary-General and the President of the UN General Assembly, it declared that

should the United Nations ignore in the future the will and strivings of the Korean people, considering only the selfish interest of a small group of traitors and betrayers of the Korean people, the Korean people will not abandon the struggle and will reserve for itself the right to continue by measures at its disposal the struggle for removal of UNCK and for final unification of the country by its own forces into a united democratic state.[8]

Throughout the winter of 1949–50, Pyongyang radio urged the South Koreans to rise in rebellion. The North Korean authorities hoped to use their 'United Korean Patriotic Front' (UKPF) as a vehicle for revolt and continually reported Communist partisan activities in the South.

At the same time, Syngman Rhee was eager to achieve reunification under his own government and was not bashful about pursuing this aim. He was to find a ready supporter in General MacArthur, who not only attempted to conquer the North in the fall of 1950 but also gave Rhee tacit support at the beginning of that year. On New Year's Day, the General indicated that Japan might have to be rearmed – a step which could entail altering Article IX of the Japanese Constitution prohibiting offensive military forces. On 12 January, Secretary Acheson specifically included Japan in the US defence perimeter. In February, MacArthur was visited by Rhee, who announced on his return that the Republic of Korea would have allies in effecting an early reunification. The unfortunate coincidence of these developments with top-level Sino-Soviet consultations in Moscow was to augur ill for the future stability of Northeast Asia, especially in view of accentuated Chinese and Korean fears of a renewal of Russo–Japanese rivalry in the area.

(3) *Increasing Russian influence.* The final characteristic of this third historical phase was the low level of Chinese influence over the DPRK leadership – and thus of Chinese participation in the crisis period preceding the 25 June attack. This is a highly important element in the framework surrounding the crisis, especially after 10 May, a possible date for the Communist decision to actually begin southward military movement.[c] For had American decision-makers accurately identified the enemy, they might not have intervened so precipitously in the Taiwan Straits and Indochina (assuming, that is, that they were not merely looking for any likely pretext to take these steps) and might have avoided the 'entirely new war' following the Chinese crossing of the Yalu.

[c] On this date the South Korean Defence Minister declared that 'North Korean troops were moving in force toward the 38th Parallel and that there was imminent danger of invasion from the North'. The American intelligence services confirmed this general spring build-up by the South Korean forces, although their reports became embroiled in a later controversy over the reasons for their being discounted by General MacArthur and General Willoughby, his chief of intelligence (G-2 of the Far East Command).[9] Nevertheless, the joint weekly intelligence cable from the Commander-in-Chief, Far East, noted on 10 March 1950: 'Report received that People's Army will invade South Korea in June 1950.'[10]

The theory that a Sino-Soviet conspiracy had master-minded the 25 June attack was (and still is) steadfastly held, however; the threats directed against Peking, resulting from this supposition, were to become essential components in the logic of Sino-American crisis escalation between June and November. It is therefore important to evaluate the status of the USSR–PRC–DPRK strategic triangle at that time; the effect that this set of relationships had on the decision to invade South Korea; and the interplay between these ties and the declaratory US policy of an Asian defence perimeter, discussed earlier.

The USSR-PRC-DPRK strategic triangle

Mao Tse-tung made his first trip abroad, to Moscow, on 16 December 1949, was joined by Chou En-lai and others on 21 January 1950, and only departed, after ten weeks of talks, on 4 March. He told TASS during his stay that

The length of my sojourn here depends in part upon the amount of time which it will take to solve the questions of interest to the People's Republic of China. Among them, first of all, are such questions as the existing treaty of friendship and alliance between China and the USSR, the question of Soviet credits to the PRC, the question of trade and a trade agreement between our two countries, and others.[11]

Mao's reference to the 1945 Sino–Soviet treaty, concluded between Stalin and Chiang Kai-shek, touched on perhaps the most important matter under discussion. While the 1945 document provided for mutual military assistance against a potential Japanese attack, the 1950 treaty was significantly to amend it to include attack 'by Japan or any state allied with it' – a provision specifically directed against American 'imperialism'. It is clear from the previous chapter that both China and the USSR viewed the American presence in the Far East as the successor to the Japanese imperial sphere of influence. For these two allies, American hostility to the Chinese Revolution of 1949, the defeats of the Japanese Communist Party in parliamentary elections in the same year, and American willingness to conclude a separate peace treaty with the conservative Yoshida government, could only have made for a highly charged predecisional context.

In addition to its interest in strengthening the Sino-Soviet alliance as a result both of Mao's famous 'lean to one side policy' of 1949 and of the external threat of a Japanese-American alliance, the new Chinese leadership was vitally interested in consolidating its territorial strength, not only in the outlying provinces of Tibet and Sinkiang but in the central and coastal areas as well. After General Lin Piao's Fourth Army overcame Nationalist resistance in Hainan Island in April 1950 and General Su Yu's Third Field Army seized the Chushan Islands near Shanghai, the People's Liberation Army was entrusted with the task of securing final victory over the Kuomintang in Taiwan. In May, the authoritative *Jen-min Jih-pao* (*People's Daily*) hailed both victories as the beginning of 'the last battle in completing the liberation and unification of our country'.[12]

Mao's foreign policy has often been described as a mixture of traditional Chinese and revolutionary Communist components. Peking, the self-proclaimed leader of national liberation movements in Asia, was insisting that only affiliation with the Soviet bloc could bring independence from forces of imperialism and neo-colonialism. *Jen-min Jih-pao*, in an editorial for Anti-Colonialism Day (16 February 1950), was to ridicule those who relied on the United States, which 'talks with great hypocrisy about "national independence" for the "backward countries" '.[13] Chou En-lai underscored the Chinese leadership's suspicions about US intentions when he noted that America 'seized control over Japan and South Korea after World War II, but is also attempting to control China, Indonesia, Viet-Nam, Thailand, Burma, and India'.[14]

The best way to determine the rôle of China in the pre-crisis period from 10 May to 25 June is to examine the known movements of troops into Manchuria and the cases in which the state of PRC-DPRK relations had become manifest during the same period. In April, the Fourth Field Army was redeployed to its starting point in Northeast China. Between the middle of May and the end of June, more than 60 000 troops entered the Northeast Region, bringing total strength to around 180 000.

Allen Whiting has suggested that the redeployment 'placed Peking's best troops in a position to backstop Pyongyang, in the event North Korean plans went awry'.[15] As will be seen, however, the state of PRC-DPRK relations indicates that the Chinese redeployment was restricted to unexpected contingencies (which were later to commit Chinese forces across the Yalu), and did not represent any joint day-to-day decision-making between the countries. Peking's attention was concentrated elsewhere: on the developments in Japan – the country which had obsessed Chinese decision-makers since it invaded Manchuria in the 1930s – and on Taiwan, the stronghold of Chiang Kai-shek, Mao's enemy since the 1920s. Korea was clearly a peripheral area in the Chinese view of Asia in the 1940s, although it is still noteworthy that it was mentioned at least formally on 16 November 1949 in the Peking conference of the World Federation of Trade Unions (WFTU), by Vice-Chairman Liu Shao-ch'i: 'The movement of the Korean people against Syngman Rhee, puppet of American imperialism, and for the establishment of a unified people's democratic republic of Korea cannot be halted.' [16]

That Peking's relations with Pyongyang were correct but distant, progressing very slowly in spite of geographical proximity, is indicated by the fact that Pyongyang and Peking had just emerged from a dispute concerning allocation of hydroelectric power from the Suphong Dam, forty miles north of Antung on the Yalu River. On the diplomatic level, moreover, North Korea's first envoy to China did not arrive in Peking until 28 January 1950, after the Soviet and Czech representatives. The Chinese took even more time to send their own ambassador, who presented his credentials in Pyongyang as late as 13 August – well after the start of the War. The Soviet Union had sent its ambassador to Pyongyang on 1 January 1949, and the Korean ambassador arrived in Moscow on the 27th. In fact, the only available clue as to material Chinese support for the North Korean build-up was its transfer back to Korea of 12 000 Korean troops [d] that had fought in the Chinese civil war as the People's Liberation Army (PLA) 164th Division. Upon arriving in Korea, the unit was redesignated the Korean People's Liberation Army (KPLA) Fifth Division and assigned to an advance position near the 38th Parallel. As Allen Whiting has concluded about the state of Sino-Korean relations,

Specific Chinese interest in matters pertaining to its territory adjoining Korea was undoubtedly coupled with general Communist concern for the viability of the neighbouring regime. There is little evidence, however, that the Chinese commitments in North Korea compared in any way with those of the Soviet Union. In particular, there is no clear evidence of Chinese participation in the planning and preparation of the Korean War.[18]

The available evidence indicates rather that the USSR was the principal supporter of the North Korean attack. This was natural

[d] The Department of State had suggested an apparently inflated figure of 40 000; [17] Whiting's more recent estimate appears the more reasonable.

in view of the Soviet 'liberation' of Korea in 1945 and its responsibility for establishing the DPRK in Pyongyang in 1948. In February 1949, Kim Il-sung headed a high-ranking North Korean delegation to Moscow, which resulted in a ten-year agreement on economic and cultural co-operation, but interestingly enough no general treaty of friendship and mutual assistance. There was a strong possibility that the USSR wanted to avoid a public commitment to North Korean defence, which might have proved difficult to maintain if there were a conflict with the ROK backed by the United States.

Yet the possibility of such a conflict must have appeared markedly smaller to the Soviets as a result of their interpretation of American conduct in 1949–50. The pronouncements of MacArthur and Acheson on the US defence perimeter seemed to leave the way open to a forcible reunification of Korea and of China; the US economic and military aid commitments appeared to be phantoms left over from the 1940s: over two thousand million dollars were spent on China alone between 1945 and 1949. Washington had provided an opening for the attainment of ends that were at the core of national interests as conceived in Peking and Pyongyang and of international interests as conceived in Moscow. In the circumstances, one could not expect many arguments, on the Communist side, in favour of looking the gift horse in the mouth, even if the horse might prove to be Trojan. Indeed, we are told in *Khrushchev Remembers* that Mao opined to Stalin that 'the USA would not intervene since the war would be an internal matter which the Korean people would decide for themselves'.[19]

It remains impossible to determine the precise extent of Soviet control over the DPRK in this period. Yet it is possible to arrive at a fairly close approximation of the degree of Soviet influence. Except for the Chinese transfer of the PLA 164th Division, all equipment and training of DPRK troops were Russian. Approximately ten thousand North Korean troops were trained in Siberia during 1949 alone. Soviet control was expressed by an advisory system at every level of the KPLA. Petrol supplies were repeatedly kept down to one-month levels with reserves retained in the USSR. It appears that Pyongyang shared Seoul's eagerness to attack the other side,[e] and the Russians may very well have

---

[e] Syngman Rhee, despite the weakness of the ROK armed forces, insisted that it was only American pressure and the fear of precipitating world war which stopped him from over-running the North.[20]

been a source of restraint at least before they gave Pyongyang the go-ahead. In fact, large Russian deliveries of tanks, lorries, and heavy artillery in April and May 1950 made possible the June invasion.

Whiting notes that 'possible points of Chinese influence appear to have been systematically eliminated during the post-War years'.[21] When the Manchuria-based Korean Volunteer Corps (KVC) was combined with the KPLA in 1946, it seemed to have declined in status vis-à-vis groups from Russian-controlled areas. Much of the KPLA leadership in the Korean War turned out to be Russian-trained, including the Commander-in-Chief (Kim Il-sung), the Chief of Staff and of the Security Agency (Nam Il), and the Chief of Military Intelligence (Lee Sang-jo, who arrived from Russia a few weeks before the outbreak of the war). Korean Communists from Yenan, having formed the Korean Independence Alliance, won only secondary positions in the Korean Labour Party. ('During the following years, purges and demotions persistently weeded out those Koreans who had returned from China.') [22]

Nevertheless, the North Korean role in the attack was obviously important, if only in terms of its execution; it was DPRK units that crossed the Parallel on 25 June (26 June in Korea). Pyongyang had preceded the attack by declaratory moves. Immediately after the South Korean elections were held in May 1950, the Central Committee of the UKPF met and published on 7 June an appeal to the people of the South, which was broadcast intensively by Radio Pyongyang on the 7th, 8th and 9th. In it, the Front dismissed the May elections as unfree and proposed new Korea-wide elections to convene a new legislature in Seoul on 15 August. After receiving no response, the UKPF demanded the merger of the North and South Korean legislatures; by 15 August, (1) 'national traitors' were to be arrested, (2) the army and police were to be reorganised on 'democratic' foundations, and (3) the UNCK would leave Korea at once.

This final document constituted an ultimatum – 15 August was to be the deadline for Korean unification. The Soviet press gave considerable coverage to the activities of the UKPF in May and June and, in particular, to the 19 June document. Viewed in combination with the southward advance of North Korean troops since 10 May, the declarations of the UKPF are the last North Korean overture for peace on their own terms, disguised by propagandistic references to 'unification', 'freedom', and 'democracy'.[f] Even if Pyongyang did expect a positive reaction to its series of overtures, it appears that North Korean agents in the South had assurred their superiors that a full-scale invasion would be required to touch off mass revolts against the government of Syngman Rhee.[24]

It therefore seems reasonable to conclude, first, that Chinese influence on the decisions and events leading up to the 25 June attack was limited in 1949 and was steadily declining in 1950 and, second, that Soviet influence was the principal factor in permitting the North Koreans to launch their attack. Third, the instability of post-war Korea can be seen as the catalyst for the escalating interaction between the future protagonists of the Korean War, the United States and Communist China. Finally, if Soviet influence was a sufficient condition for such an attack, the low credibility of the American commitment to the South – which appeared non-existent except for the small military assistance group and the promise of limited economic assistance – was the necessary precondition for the conceivable success of such an attack.

The US initiative: regional implications

It is unlikely that Moscow and Pyongyang bargained on prompt American intervention in Korea on a large scale. Indeed, had President Truman held a narrower view of the powers of his office, he would have asked the US Senate for a declaration of war; in addition, he might have consulted the UN General Assembly instead of presenting it with a *fait accompli*. Instead, between 25 and 27 June 1950, Truman employed vigorous executive initiative – labelling the task at hand a 'police action', dispatching an expeditionary force, and confronting the United Nations with a ready-made test of the principle of collective security.

Alongside Washington's immediate and unexpected response to the North Korean attack, another surprise decision reached at the earliest stage of the War was the decision to send the Seventh Fleet into the *Taiwan Straits*. This decision undoubtedly came as a surprise to Peking and probably to Moscow as well.

[f] Another interpretation of the June moves of the UKPF, to which Carl Berger subscribes, is that they were diversionary. 'Early in June 1950, the North Koreans undertook a last-minute, farcical manoeuvre to mask their plans.' [23]

From Washington's point of view at the time, the move served two purposes: to prevent a Communist attack on Taiwan and to prevent a Nationalist attack, militarily impossible at the time, on the mainland. The Korea and Formosa issues were thought to be further de-coupled at the time by Truman's reluctant refusal, on strong advice from the Joint Chiefs of Staff and Secretary Acheson, of Chiang Kai-shek's offer of 33 000 Chinese Nationalist troops to fight in Korea. Truman favoured the offer because he wanted the widest possible participation in the UN force. The military doubted the combat effectiveness of the troops and hesitated to divert air and sea carriers to transport them to Korea. Acheson disliked taking away the 'natural defenders' of Formosa while maintaining US responsibilities for ROC security (although the Seventh Fleet had already pre-empted the issue of American commitment) and feared that the Chinese Communists would be more likely to intervene if the offer were accepted.[25] The Administration's success in resisting persistent pressures from General MacArthur and the China Lobby to employ Chinese Nationalist troops in Korea – or even to permit ROC attacks on the PRC – is certainly further evidence of the separation of the Korean and Formosan theatres. In this respect, Dean Acheson was correct when he said that Truman

interposed the Seventh Fleet to prevent any attack from either Chinese side upon the other, the purpose being to quarantine the fighting within Korea, not to encourage its extension. When General MacArthur toyed with undercutting this policy, by suggesting, as some Republican senators had, using Chiang's refugee army in the Korean fighting, he was sharply rapped over the knuckles.[26]

In spite of the claim of good intentions, however, the President's 27 June initiative served, in the long run, more to link than to de-couple the Korean and Formosan issues. Although the long-term consequences of that decision probably could not have been fully anticipated at that stage, President Truman's decision to 'neutralise' Formosa would only have the effect of frustrating Chinese Communist plans to invade and occupy the island – and of encouraging them to retaliate if, when and where they could. Small wonder, then, that the Chinese Communists came to view this linkage as part of an over-all anti-Chinese campaign. In Lin Piao's historical account, 'Shortly after the founding of the Chinese People's Republic, American imperialism unleashed the war of aggression in Korea and, in the meantime, encroached upon our territory of Taiwan in an attempt to strangle the newly born Chinese People's Republic after first occupying Korea.' [27] Chinese fears were not likely to be assuaged with the passing of time, for the 'neutralisation' of Formosa in 1950 was to serve as a major precedent for Dulles' efforts to build a defence chain for Western interests in Asia and the Pacific.

As far as Truman was concerned, there was a cause-and-effect relationship between the DPRK attack on Korea and Sino-Soviet designs elsewhere,[g] for he declared on 27 June 1950 that

The attack upon Korea makes it plain beyond all doubt that communism has passed beyond the use of subversion to conquer independent nations and will now use armed invasion and war. It has defied the orders of the Security Council of the United Nations issued to preserve international peace and security. In these circumstances, the occupation of Formosa by communist forces would be a direct threat to the peace and security of the Pacific area and the United States forces performing their lawful and necessary functions in that area.[h] [29]

A possible hypothesis concerning Truman's decision to relate the defence of Korea to that of the other Asian rimlands, is that the Korean War provided the necessary excuse for implementing a decision relating to both Formosa and Indochina that might have been taken some time before. The most that the evidence would seem to suggest, however, is growing American willingness, in the spring of 1950, to take concerted action against a PRC perceived as increasingly hostile and threatening to the United States.

As we have seen, the US Administration had conveyed the impression – in McGeorge Bundy's words – that US policy at the turn of the decade 'was based on a determination to avoid, so far as possible, any entanglement that might give grounds for anti-American feeling in China'.[30] A Presidential release on 5

[g] Harold Hinton makes the dubious argument that a North Korean attack on the south was to be co-ordinated with a Chinese Communist attack on Taiwan and a Viet Minh attack on Hanoi – all with Stalin's consent. He claims that the fact that the 'United States was aware that all three were threatened at that time' tends to prove 'that a co-ordinated attack in all three areas was planned by the Communist side'.[28] The evidence certainly undercuts his hypothesis.

[h] It is interesting that any official hint of a further commitment of the United States to the defence of Nationalist-held islands off-shore the mainland – the best-known of which are Quemoy and Matsu – would have to wait until 1954. (See chapter 6.)

January 1950 set forth unequivocally a policy of US non-interference in Chinese affairs:

> The United States has no predatory designs on Formosa or on any other Chinese territory. The United States has no desire to obtain special rights or privileges or to establish military bases on Formosa at this time. Nor does it have any intention of utilising its armed forces to interfere in the present situation. The United States Government will not pursue a course which will lead to involvement in the civil conflict in China.[31]

Truman even went so far as to prohibit US 'military aid or advice' to the Chinese Nationalists. This impression of US non-intervention was further strengthened when Secretary Acheson met with the press on the afternoon following the release, 'to make the policy clear to the most perverse intelligence' by recapitulating the release point by point, adding that when the United States takes a position, it sticks to that position and does not change it by reason of transitory expediency or advantage on its part'. Finally, in his National Press Club speech of 12 January, he declared outright that 'anyone who violates the integrity of China is the enemy of China and is acting contrary to their own interest'.[32]

So strong was this impression at the end of June that American leaders freely acknowledged and their Chinese Communist counterparts angrily denounced an abrupt change of US policy in the Far East; the US Government in fact did not adhere to the position proclaimed in January, which was making it possible for the PLA to prepare for a final assault on remnant Kuomintang forces. In mid-February, General Su Yu, Vice Commander of the Third Army, made an important speech in Shanghai, in which he asserted that liberation of Taiwan was in sight, despite formidable difficulties. The factors of low morale and dispersion of enemy forces, combined with local Formosan resistance, would enable the PLA to 'carry out the glorious task of liberating the whole of China', overcoming naval difficulties as they had in the Hainan campaign.[33] (This determination to 'liberate' Taiwan – as well as Tibet – was confirmed at a high political level, in the May Day address of Liu Shao-ch'i.)

That the Chinese Communists could seriously continue with their not-so-unrealistic plans to defeat the Nationalists is a fair indication of how limited the US commitment to Taiwan and to the Nationalist-held off-shore islands had appeared to them in the first half of 1950, and of how abrupt the US intervention could appear at the end of June.

Yet the change, in retrospect, was more gradual than abrupt. Even the January Presidential release – which Acheson characterised as having 'so crisp and brutally frank a manner as to end further propaganda and speculation' from both Left and Right [34] – was not so very water-tight. It is true that the last sentence in the section quoted from the release had an unequivocal air about it, but then again the phrases 'at this time' and 'in the present situation' indicated that circumstances might well change in the future – a possibility which Acheson half-conceded in telling the press, on 5 January, that 'in the unlikely and unhappy event that our forces might be attacked in the Far East, the United States must be completely free to take whatever action in whatever area is necessary for its own security'.[35] By mid-March, a shift in US perceptions had become quite clear. In a speech to the San Francisco Commonwealth Club on 15 March, Secretary Acheson warned the Chinese people that 'whatever happens within their own country, they can only bring grave trouble on themselves and their friends, both in Asia and beyond, if they are led by their new rulers into aggressive or subversive adventures beyond their borders'.[36]

The Commonwealth Club speech signified no operational change in the American 'hands off' policy as regards Taiwan and the mainland, but it began to alter the impression of US nonintervention given by the National Press Club speech in January – a point often conveniently overlooked by Acheson's critics. As far as the Chinese were concerned, they did not fail to respond to the speech, although they did not translate it into any effective veto on their plans for Formosa, the Pescadores and the offshore islands. Rather, Chou En-lai rejected Acheson's warning – that the Sino-Soviet Treaty was 'hostile to the interests of the US' as well as to those of China – as the vain attempt of a 'mosquito trying to shatter the fortress of world peace [i.e., the Sino-Soviet alliance]', and he advised the US Administration to 'Cool down and look at the map! The affairs of the Asian peoples must be settled by the Asian peoples themselves and must never be interfered with by such American imperialists as Acheson and company on the other side of the Pacific Ocean!' [37] Acheson's warning, such as it was, to America's antagonists was accompanied by an attempt to reassure America's Asian friends, but unaccompanied by any appreciable increase in US aid. Ambassador

Dulles, for instance, visited Seoul in late June, in order to assure the South Koreans both publicly that 'You are not alone', and privately that the US would give all the support it could and 'will never abandon the Korean people', according to the account of a high-ranking Korean observer.[38]

The altered US perceptions of China tended to make the Truman Administration's determination to keep 'hands off' China more muted and their receptivity to the idea of supporting Taipei greater, as their patience with the Communists diminished and the McCarthyist attacks on the Administration increased. Nevertheless, even two days before the North Korean attack, Secretary Acheson assured his news conference that the President's 5 January policy remained unchanged, thereby denying rumours that the Asian inspection tour of Secretary Johnson and General Bradley, which had centred on talks with General MacArthur, foreboded a change in US China policy. If a predisposition to become involved in the Taiwan Straits in fact existed, if only subconsciously, it would crystallise into a series of concrete American moves on the periphery of China during the Korean crises. In the case of the neutralisation of the Taiwan Straits, what might have been dismissed as a temporary measure made necessary by war was to become more and more obviously a permanent fixture of US policy.

The case of *Indochina* should also be mentioned in reference to President Truman's 27 June speech, not only because of its relevance to one of our case studies but also because it further illustrates our theme concerning the regional implications of the American decision to intervene in Korea. Secretary Acheson had declared on 8 May 1950 that:

The United States Government, convinced that neither national independence nor democratic evolution exist in any area dominated by Soviet imperialism, considers the situation to be such as to warrant its according economic aid and military equipment to the associated states of Indochina and to France in order to assist them in restoring stability and permitting the states to pursue their peaceful and democratic development.

In the same statement ordering the Seventh Fleet 'to prevent any attack on Formosa' or 'against the mainland', Truman 'directed acceleration in the furnishing of military assistance to the forces of France and the Associated States in Indochina and the despatch of a military mission to provide close working relations with those forces'.[39]

Thus in all three spheres of Sino-American interaction in the 1950's, statements made by President Truman in the short time between 25 and 27 June 1950 were to have a crucial effect. In the short term, the Chinese Communists would be deterred from implementing their plans to invade Taiwan.[1] From the first crisis sequence relating to the Communist attack and the collective response, a combination of crisis dynamics and American initiatives were to set the stage for that 'entirely new war' which would destroy the chances for even a limited victory by the United Nations command (UNC) within Korea itself.

The 28 June response of Chou En-lai to Truman's statement of the previous day was unusually swift and unequivocal, revealing PRC surprise and anger at both the abrupt change in US operational policy and the extent of the new American commitment. First, Chou condemned the US decision and attempted to shift the blame for aggression from Stalin to Truman:

All that Truman's statement does is openly expose his premeditated plan and put it into practice. In fact, the attack by the puppet Korean government of Syngman Rhee on the Korean Democratic People's Republic at the instigation of the US Government was a premeditated move by the United States to invade Taiwan, Korea, Viet-Nam and the Philippines.

Then he reasserted China's over-riding interest in occupying Taiwan:

All the people of our country will certainly fight to the end single-mindedly to liberate Taiwan from the grasp of the American aggressors. The Chinese people, who defeated Japanese imperialism and Chiang Kai-shek, the hireling of American imperialism, will surely be victorious in driving off the American aggressors and in recovering Taiwan and all other territories belonging to China.[41]

Thus Peking charged not only that the Korean War was caused by an attack from Seoul backed by Washington, but also that this presumed attack was the result of a premeditated conspiracy encompassing a large part of the area bordering China's southern flank. In so doing, it subscribed to a black-and-white image

---

[1] Ironically, Ambassador Rankin complained to the State Department that the post-neutralisation commitment was inadequate. He wrote from the ROC capital that 'there is no evidence here of any tangible progress on our part subsequent to June 27th in preparing to ward off an assault on the island', citing the absence of critical military supplies (such as ammunition) for ROC forces and the lack of any 'comprehensive plan of action' for either the Seventh Fleet or the 13th Air Force on Taiwan.[40]

of recent history which made as little allowance for past American withdrawal of forces and hesitation about intervening again (including the current American rationale for neutralisation) as the US Administration seemed to do about Sino-Soviet differences concerning their order of priorities as between Taiwan and Korea. It remained for the two Korean crisis sequences, analysed in the next chapter – the first following US intervention and the second after PRC intervention – to bear the fruit of these historical distortions and mutual misconceptions.

Hence the stage was set for a Korean crisis which the Chinese had not instigated and whose consequences neither they nor the Americans were to desire. The occurrence of the conflict and the regional dimensions which it so swiftly assumed could only begin to be understood on the basis of their historical background and political context, both internal and international: the purpose of the present chapter. The ramifications of the Korean crises would, in turn, have an effect of the most fundamental importance on the character and scope of Sino-American crises during the remainder of the decade. The succeeding chapters will continue to show how conflict in an apparently secondary area would serve as the genesis for the course of the ensuing relationship between Washington and Peking.

3: Sino-American crises over Korea

The net military effect of the dramatic events occurring at the end of June 1950 was that MacArthur's forces were able to preserve a southern bridgehead against the North Korean onslaught. As early as 29 June – after his surprise over the Administration's decision to defend South Korea [1] – MacArthur conceived of the brilliantly successful amphibious landing at Inchon, behind the enemy lines, which would take place on 15 September. The painstaking but favourable reversal of Allied fortunes that summer, climaxing in this (in David Rees's words) 'impossible victory', was to be the military counterpart of the political internationalising operation undertaken by Truman and Acheson.

A series of United Nations Command advances and North Korean retreats was to have a crucial political impact: they would gradually become translated into a pattern of escalating UNC commitments and objectives. Instead of fighting a war to resist Communist aggression, MacArthur and his political superiors would prepare to fight until Korea could be reunified under 'democratic' control.

June: America intervenes

In June, of course, intervention, escalation and protracted war were unforeseen by Washington and Peking. Each phase in their involvement was conceived in strictly limited terms of time and place, based on interpretations of past historical experience.

The initial American intervention, seen as a response to an overt act of aggression, was developed after hasty analysis and little reflection. As Glenn Paige points out, 'There is no evidence that (the US leaders) considered any other alternative for meeting the crisis facing them, including that of doing nothing.' [2] US perceptions of the dangers associated with the crisis ranged from the fear that the attack might be the beginning of World War III (shared by Ambassador Dulles and General Ridgway) [3] to the belief that the Chinese Communists had already launched their invasion of Formosa (shared by Assistant Secretary of State Hickerson) to widespread surprise that the attack occurred when and where it did (shared by Secretary of State Acheson and Secretary of Defense Johnson).[4] The measures taken by President Truman were in an important sense a compromise response to the more or less panicky perceptions in the Executive Branch. As a whole, they were based on the President's view that appeasement of Communist aggression would lead to the same disastrous results as had the appeasement of German, Italian and Japanese aggression prior to World War II.[5] The US reaction was clearly intended to reinforce the US drive to contain the Communist menace and to bolster the 'Free World's' collective security system – an extension of the Truman Doctrine to the Far East. Secretary Acheson, in later testimony before the Senate Armed Services and Foreign Relations Committees, offered the following rationale as a justification for those momentous decisions:

This was a test which would decide whether our collective security system would survive or would crumble. It would determine whether other nations would be intimidated by this show of force.

The decision to meet force with force in Korea was essential. It was the unanimous view of the political and military advisers of the President that this was the right thing to do. This decision had the full support of the American people because it accorded with the principles by which Americans live.[6]

In addition, it appeared that the decision-makers were concerned with the political consequences of a failure to react. In the wake of the 'loss of China' to Chinese Communists in 1949, a firm response was deemed essential in 1950, not only because it was psychologically essential [a] but also because the crisis ac-

---

[a] Joseph de Rivera argues that there was a widespread failure 'to imagine what the loss of Korea would *mean*. When Korea was attacked the United States rushed to its defence – not because of its strategic interest (which was low) nor because of its terrain (which was disadvantageous), but because not to have done so would have destroyed the idea of collective security, encouraged Soviet aggression elsewhere, and damaged American prestige. But these non-strategic factors had been given weight neither in the Defense Department's recommendation to withdraw troops nor in the State Department's lack of formal commitment to defend Korea. Nor were these factors considered by the planners in the Soviet Union. The government of neither nation anticipated what the invasion would *mean* to the United States.'[7] I would accept that the non-strategic dimension was by and large ignored, but would also argue that the strategic dimension was of great importance, although perceived differently over time.

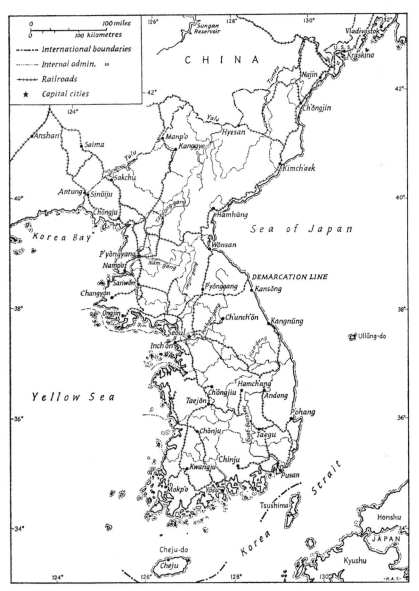

Fig. 4. The Korean peninsula

centuated the primary strategic importance of the Korean peninsula.

There are two important points to remember in examining the
character of US decision-making regarding Korea. The first is
that there was virtually no prior contingency planning for coping
with a fundamental military challenge to the Syngman Rhee
regime. From the beginning, when the United States objected
to the Government of the 'People's Republic of Korea' as being
vulnerable to Communism, until 1950 when Dean Acheson defined the so-called US 'defense perimeter' in the Far East, it was
quite clear that American policy was limited to the strengthening of the conservative regime of Syngman Rhee. Only the crisis
itself would transform the US Administration's view of Korea
from an area of peripheral interest to 'an area of great importance', in Dean Acheson's retrospective account, 'to the security
of American-occupied Japan'.[8]

Secondly, American success in remaining one step ahead of
the Security Council was crucial for establishing American leadership of the UN Command (UNC). The reason continued to be
a combination of momentum and processed information, readily
available from Washington and amply reinforced by UNCK
and ROK reports from Seoul. The 27 June Resolution of the
Security Council serves as the most obvious case in point, for
it can easily be interpreted as partly an *ex post facto* justification
of the steps already taken by the US Government.[b] It recommended 'that the Members of the United Nations furnish such
assistance to the Republic of Korea as may be necessary to repel
the (North Korean) armed attack and to restore international
peace and security in the area',[10] within the meaning of Articles
41 and 42 of the UN Charter, articles which call for interruption
of economic and diplomatic relations with the aggressor and for
military enforcement measures to restore the peace.

This resolution, fraught as it was with ambiguity, was to be
exploited both immediately and in the long term as a justification
for further measures to escalate the conflict. 27 June 1950 was to
the Korean War what 7 August 1964, the Tonkin Gulf Resolution, was to become to the Vietnam War – a date of good inten-

[b] Acheson admits that 'some American action, said to be in support of the
resolution of June 27th, was in fact ordered, and possibly taken, prior to
the resolution', and he adds that 'If Malik [the Soviet delegate] returned to
the Security Council, we would have to carry on under the existing one
[of 25 June, declaring a 'breach of the peace' and calling for a cessation of
hostilities]. If he did not return, it would pass without opposition.'[9]

tions but dangerous consequences. From the outset, it could be seen that 'to repel the armed attack' implied driving North Korean forces up to the 38th Parallel but not beyond, whereas 'to restore international peace and security' could be, and eventually would be, interpreted as a mandate to eliminate the aggressor's military strength and to destroy the bases of aggression within the DPRK; 'the area' came to be interpreted as all of the Korean peninsula up to the Yalu – and if MacArthur had had his way, Manchuria would have been the inevitable target of an ever-widening security perimeter. These events were going to take place in the face of a 29 June statement of Secretary Acheson to the American Newspaper Guild – which should rival his 12 January speech in notoriety – that US action would be 'solely for the purpose of restoring the Republic of Korea to its status prior to the invasion from the north, and of re-establishing the peace broken by that aggression'.[11]

Escalation of the crisis

The 27 June Resolution was only one phase of a concerted response, one which the United States was responsible for initiating as well as for internationalising. Within two weeks of the Resolution, naval and air forces from Britain, Australia and New Zealand had already joined those of the United States in the war theatre. As early as 29 June, US ships and planes were authorised to strike military targets north of the 38th Parallel, and Army units were committed to South Korea – in spite of Presidential assurances to the contrary two days previously.[12] Washington had extended its commitment, not only by engaging ground forces but also by permitting operations throughout the peninsula – with the significant proviso that MacArthur's forces were to 'stay well clear of the frontiers of Manchuria and the Soviet Union'.[13] It is unfortunate that this proviso would hold the greatest force when the risk of Chinese intervention was minimal, and the least force during the period of greatest danger.

On 30 June, General MacArthur, reporting that the South Korean army was completely disorganised and in confused retreat, recommended that an American combat regiment be committed to the Pusan Perimeter as the nucleus for two further divisions to be committed from Japan 'for early offensive action in accordance with his mission of clearing South Korea of North Korean forces'.[14] Truman endorsed his commander's suggestion the same morning and even went beyond it by further authorising a naval blockade of the North Korean coast and by then granting MacArthur 'full authority to use the troops under his command'.[15]

That this series of US initiatives added up to unilateral escalation is clear. As Acheson put it, 'A doctrine that later became fashionable with Presidents, called "keeping all options open" (apparently by avoiding decisions) did not appeal to Harry S Truman.'[16] The United States had engineered a concerted response ranging from dramatic economic assistance to the Philippines and to Indochina, to commitment of sea and land forces to the Korea-China theatre. It had succeeded in effectively internationalising this response under the UN aegis, thereby providing a legal framework for future acts to prevail over Communist aggression while retaining US leadership over the collective security venture. Internally, General MacArthur had established his prerogative of military initiative, secure in the knowledge that the chain of command through the Joint Chiefs of Staff and the Department of Defense to the White House would confirm his decisions. The joint stance of the United States and the United Nations had resolved into an uncompromising posture, one which would result in a like response from North Korea's allies, and particularly China.

June–August: the PRC responds to escalation [17]

Through mid-September, the Chinese leaders would act very cautiously indeed, confining themselves to abandonment of their plans to liberate Taiwan in June, to mobilisation of forces and resources, to expression of general support for North Korea, and eventually to explicit threats of intervention.

In June, the PLA had to suspend plans to launch an invasion of the off-shore islands and then Taiwan. By the 15th, they had completed their preparations to invade, having built up their coastal forces from 40 000 to about 156 000.[18] The crucial question for Taipei and Washington was whether a PRC attack to the south would be co-ordinated with the DPRK attack in the northeast. Taipei established an emergency, round-the-clock invasion alert; Washington unilaterally announced its plans to neutralise the Straits area; Peking was left with no option but to accept the superiority of opposing forces for the time being, although it might previously have hoped that a rapid North

Korean advance could blunt an effective US response to a PLA invasion of Taiwan.[19]

The Council of the Central People's Government recognised this in its meeting of 28 June, although with very poor grace. Chou En-lai denounced America's 'armed aggression against the territory of China' and 'blatant violation of the United Nations Charter', which was one more step in the 'secret plans of American imperialism to seize all of Asia'. But the most action-oriented part of his statement contained no threat of immediate action; rather, Chou had to content himself with a Last Judgment vision of ultimate US collapse, in which 'the oppressed peoples of the East will incinerate the criminal American imperialist warmakers in the angry fires of the great struggle for national independence'. At the same meeting, Chairman Mao took a relatively philosophical stand: 'The affairs of Asia should be handled by Asians, and not by Americans. American aggression cannot but evoke widespread determined resistance on the part of Asian peoples . . . Imperialism has a bold front but is empty within because it does not have the support of the peoples.' [20]

In July, the increased likelihood that the UNC would be able to hold the Pusan Perimeter against North Korean threats paralleled increased cautiousness in Chinese Communist commentaries on the Korean conflict. Towards the end of the month *Jen-min Jih-pao* (*People's Daily*) warned its readers that the allied build-up 'doubtless increases the difficulties facing the Korean people',[21] and *Shih-chieh Chih-shih* (*World Culture*) later advanced the opinion that 'A prolonged war of attrition will naturally increase the difficulties of the Korean people but it will increase the difficulties of the American imperialists much more' [22] – both clear indicators of China's resignation to the possibility of a protracted and arduous conflict in Korea. Whereas Peking reacted swiftly and articulately against the inter-position of American forces in the Taiwan Straits, it responded more slowly and circumspectly to the events in Korea. This asymmetry in the PRC's response probably revealed (a) China's uncertainty about the future course of the Korean crisis, (b) its concentration on the status of its Taiwan campaign, allowing Moscow and Pyongyang to worry about Korea, and possibly (c) its frustration with an outcome which sacrificed its priority of Taiwan for Russia's priority of Korea.

In August, Peking restricted its declarations to statements of moral support and solidarity with Pyongyang. The PLA Commander-in-Chief, Chu Teh, indicated on Red Army Day that 'We, the Chinese people, feel that the people of Korea are struggling for justice. We should extend *moral* support to them and persistently oppose the American aggression in Korea' (author's emphasis).[23] This moderate verbal backing was reinforced at the highest level by Mao himself on 14 August, the fifth anniversary of Korean liberation from Japan, and in Chou En-lai's simultaneous greetings to Kim Il-sung.[24] A week would elapse before a direct Chinese message to the UN and still another before any real threat would emerge.

July to October: the US dominates the collective response

As the Security Council began to consider alternative systems of command and control through which it could channel resources and execute decisions, the United States maintained a decisive voice. In July, Secretary-General Trygve Lie failed to establish an international 'Committee on Co-ordination of Assistance for Korea' to promote continuing UN participation in, and supervision of, the military security action.[25] Although both England and France favoured this proposal, the United States felt that it might be too cumbersome a limitation on local military decision-making, whereupon a substitute Anglo-French draft resolution placing the unified command under a United States commander was passed on 7 July.

Therefore, no provision whatsoever was made for any continuing UN supervision of the military action in Korea. When President Truman appointed General MacArthur to the UN Command on 8 July, it was as if the President of the United States were simply assigning to one of his generals one more mission, without disturbing the line of command. MacArthur remained Commander-in-Chief, Far East (CINCFE), Commanding General, US Army, Far East, and Supreme Commander Allied Powers in Japan. Indeed, the General's vision seemed to be limited only by his constitutional subordination to Truman as Commander-in-Chief.[26] Any reports prepared by MacArthur on the military situation in Korea were reviewed and initially accepted by his superiors in Washington and then presented by the US representative to the Security Council.

It is clear from the above description that there was in fact no 'system' of command and control. The United States had succeeded in monopolising the day-to-day decision-making by accepting responsibility for the UN Command. In cybernetic terms, the US had taken control of the output from the June decisions and could influence its direction and intensity, and by and large dictate what feedback (if any) would reach the original decision-makers in the Security Council. In effect, the US had the best of both worlds: it had succeeded in spearheading a collective response to the North Korean aggression with all of the legitimacy of the United Nations Charter behind it (aided by the fortuitous absence of the boycotting Russians from the Security Council), while removing the UN Command from direct UN control. The effect was to be negative, neutralising possible alternative options for an early, peaceful settlement.

The rise and fall of diplomatic alternatives

As in the case of the Vietnam War later, there was no dearth of such attempted initiatives. At the end of June, the Yugoslav representative proposed a cease-fire during which the DPRK would be invited to send a representative to the Security Council; [27] his proposal failed. The United Nations Commission on Korea, in one of its first acts after the 25 June attack, pressed unsuccessfully for mediation in order to achieve a cease-fire and initiate North–South discussions which could lead to reunification.[28] In spite of the Soviet interest they appeared to elicit, Yugoslav, Indian and even British proposals all foundered on US opposition to any compromises attained under duress. For example, Washington informed London on 10 July that it desired to liquidate Korean aggression 'without concessions that would whet Communist appetites and bring on other aggressions elsewhere', refusing to accept a 'forced trade' of Formosa for Korea or even PRC representation at the UN under what Truman and Acheson regarded as the 'duress and blackmail then being employed'.[29]

The initiatives toward conflict resolution were not restricted to these specific proposals. For those who cared to seek them out, subtle signs remained that the Communist position was still flexible. One possible sign was the return of USSR Ambassador Malik in August, in the presence of the Republic of China's delegatee, T. F. Tsiang – a reversal of position which made Malik an object of ridicule by Western delegates. Malik might well have been instructed to opt for an innovative approach when, on

4 August, he expanded on previous Indian proposals by calling for 'an end to hostilities' of the 'internal civil war' and a withdrawal of 'all foreign troops' after an all-Korean conference in which the PRC would be restricted to nominal, ad hoc representation and in which a representative from Chiang Kai-shek would also presumably participate.[c]

It is difficult to believe that Peking enthusiastically approved of these Russian moves, which represented partly a desertion of and partly a rebuff to their Chinese allies: it was more than two weeks before Chou En-lai cabled the PRC's endorsement of the Malik proposals to the UN, underscoring for the first time Peking's vital interest in a Korean settlement. On the one hand, Moscow had suspended its protest against Chinese Nationalist representation at the UN, and on the other, it had restricted Peking's role in a proposed conference of prime importance to the PRC. Moreover, Ambassador Malik's 4 August proposal was a striking contrast, possibly tactical but nonetheless real, to the dogmatic Communist formula of the DPRK as the sole legitimate representative of the Korean people.

In retrospect, it was an error for the Western powers to have already closed all peaceful options for the near future, for in so doing they might have lost the chance to engage a still-flexible opponent, the Soviet Union, in productive dialogue leading to a peaceful compromise. Under conditions of escalation, however, it had become extremely difficult to explore such alternatives with an open mind. Both the momentum of the military operation in Korea and the pressures for firm diplomatic back-stopping in the United Nations and Allied capitals were characteristic of the increasing system dominance of the crisis interactions between the antagonists. The time for mutual flexibility and receptivity to compromise had not arrived.

The MacArthur connection

At the same time that possible diplomatic options were being foreclosed in New York, new provocations – for both the Chinese and the Americans — were originating from Tokyo. From his

---

[c] The lifting of the Berlin blockade in 1949 was preceded by similar Russian hints interspersed in an apparently uncompromising posture. Informal discussions between Ambassadors Jessup and Malik at the UN had ferreted out this shift in Soviet policy;[30] in 1950, by contrast, Ambassador Austin felt no need to engage in such sophisticated Kremlinology.

headquarters in that city, General MacArthur was doing his best to strengthen the US strategic commitment not only to Korea but to Nationalist China. At the end of July, the Joint Chiefs of Staff (JCS) recommended a survey of Formosa's defences, on the assumption that the Administration had upgraded that island's strategic importance, and on 1 August, MacArthur flew to Formosa without consulting Washington. (The previous time he had asked to go to Taipei, in the aftermath of the neutralisation order, he had been refused permission.) Chiang Kai-shek had no difficulty in securing MacArthur's promise of 'effective military co-ordination between the Chinese and American forces' followed up promptly by the arrival of three squadrons of jet fighters in Taiwan.[31] Unbelievably, no one in Washington admitted to knowing anything about the General's movements, and the President was forced to reiterate the limits of US policy regarding Formosa, both by cable and by his personal emissary, Averell Harriman.[32] Yet by contrast with the mild governmental crisis which MacArthur's unauthorised movements were provoking in Washington, the Chinese response was relatively moderate, in line with its cautious approach to US actions in Korea and Taiwan in July and August. Instead of exploiting MacArthur's trip as new evidence of America's aggressive intentions, the mainland press first suppressed the news of his visit to Taipei and then, in delayed commentaries, protested 'American aggression and invasion of Taiwan', without claiming any increased US threat to the PRC.[33]

In spite of MacArthur's assurances to Harriman that 'he was a good soldier and knew how to obey orders', he continued to press for a more militant strategy vis-à-vis the Communists. On 25 August, he sent a message to the annual convention of the Veterans of Foreign Wars, in which he declared that 'it is the pattern of Oriental psychology to respect and follow aggressive, resolute and dynamic leadership – to quickly turn on a leadership characterised by timidity or vacillation', and reasserted at length the strategic importance of Formosa to the United States, attacking the 'threadbare argument by those who advocate appeasement and defeatism in the Pacific that if we defend Formosa we alienate continental Asia'.[34]

By now, the National Security Council and in particular the President were sufficiently aroused by this divergence from official policy to successfully insist that MacArthur withdraw his message, but they failed to seize the opportunity to dismiss the

General then and there, much to the President's later regret. And even though Secretary Acheson and the President attempted to correct the false impression created by their viceroy in the Far East, it is nevertheless true that the latter's pronouncements remained on the record, often only partially qualified either because of the sympathies of Secetary Johnson and General Bradley or because of well-meaning attempts to disguise intra-governmental friction. Thus both America's friends and enemies – and particularly Peking, which had little capacity or desire for differentiating between US pronouncements – were left with the solid evidence that the General was still in charge in Tokyo, that Taipei was still the beneficiary of US protection, and that the Administration had done nothing effective to mitigate a further escalation of the Far Eastern conflict.

With the deepening Chinese Communist commitment to North Korea, especially after August, came worsening prospects for a negotiated settlement. Yet even in August, Peking had made its anxieties clear, from Chou En-lai's cable to Lake Success on 20 August to the significantly more extreme article of 26 August in *Shih-chieh Chih-shih*. The article noted that the US invasion of Korea 'seriously threatens the security of China' and that 'It is impossible to solve the Korean problem without the participation of its closest neighbour, China . . . North Korea's enemy is our enemy. North Korea's defence is our defence.' [35] These declarations may well have helped to reinforce the US Administration's determination to keep the conflict 'limited' to the Korean peninsula, although this determination was directed more to keeping the Soviet Union out of the conflict than to appeasing the PRC, which was considered to be the Russian bear's paw.[d] More important than these declarations, however, were the apparent transgressions of Chinese air space in violation of standing JCS directives. According to Chinese charges, US aircraft crossed the Yalu on the 27th and attacked both the Talitzu rail terminal and the Antung airfield; on the 29th, American pilots were alleged to have fired on Chinese fishing boats in the Yalu River.[37] The following day, US authorities conceded a possible 'mistake' and offered to compensate Peking for any proven damage, and

---

[d] Robert Lovett, then Deputy Secretary of Defense, claims that the Administration was fully briefed on Chinese threats by Bohlen and Kennan – both better known for their knowledge of Russia than of China.[36] If this is the case, the communication gap between Washington and Peking was even wider, and the threats even more susceptible to distortion, than I have argued here.

two days before, the Pentagon reiterated the limits on US forces by directing that they 'shall exercise particular caution not to violate the Soviet or Chinese territory or territorial waters'.[38]

The PRC's response both to the pronouncements of MacArthur and to the infringement of their territorial limits was uninhibited internally, but cautious externally. Anti-American propaganda reached a peak from 27 August to 7 September – in clear psychological preparation of the Chinese populace for direct conflict with the United States.

This paralleled the PRC's now direct concern with the course of events in Korea, as the North Korean forces confronted rapidly increasing Allied resistance. Nevertheless, official denunciations of the new threats perceived by PRC leaders were relatively moderate in tone. Whereas US moves in the Taiwan area were officially labelled 'an act of open aggression' in Chou En-lai's cable of 6 July, Chou called the most recent developments 'a serious criminal action encroaching upon China's sovereignty', significantly omitting to indicate how the Chinese might eventually respond.[39]

In view of the new Chinese interest in Korean developments, it is tragically ironic that Ambassador Austin did not search for openings in Ambassador Malik's position. Rather, he chose to assert that the Soviet delegate, as President of the Security Council in August, had

made every effort to stop our work and keep us from our business [and was responsible for] doing this on the time of the Security Council and on the time of those poor boys over there who are under fire while we monkey and twist the rules and the Charter of the United Nations solely for the purpose of preventing progress toward peace.[40]

That room for political initiatives had disappeared at least for the time being was amply demonstrated by the Security Council's paralysis in the month of August. Even the US Resolution of 31 July, condemning the DPRK for its defiance of the UN and calling upon all states to cause North Korea to cease this defiance, was not voted upon until 6 September and then vetoed by the USSR. Jacob Malik failed to get the item of a possible peaceful settlement on the Council's agenda. With the United Nations bogged down by procedural disputes, the time was clearly one in which political power would only come out of the barrel of a gun. It was during that time that General MacArthur was able to break the North Korean tide and establish a secure line, running north along the Naktong River and east from Taegu, which came to be known as the Pusan Perimeter.

September–October: further escalation

After a daring amphibious landing at Inchon on 15 September, the UN Command was able to interdict the Communist Cholivan-Seoul supply line and thereby cause a collapse of the North Korean front. Within a couple of weeks, MacArthur's troops had reached the 38th Parallel. The 'armed attack' had been 'repelled' and the terms of the 27 June Resolution, as interpreted in their most limited sense, were fulfilled. But the war itself was no longer limited: the military momentum had overcome political restraint more than two months before.

As American public opinion thrilled to MacArthur's swift thrust northward, the possibility of crossing the 38th Parallel became a probability. Public pressure combined with newly devised strategic and political arguments proved irresistible to the Truman Administration. It was likely that Syngman Rhee would order ROK forces north of the Parallel regardless of UN action.[41] From the military point of view, complete defeat of the North Korean forces would not be possible until all of the DPRK had been occupied; moreover, such complete victory could demonstrably justify the sacrifices already suffered. Even more important, from the political viewpoint, was the impulse to construe the 27 June Resolution as broadly as possible in order to 'restore international peace and security' in the entire peninsula, if not as General MacArthur would have it – in an area of contention ranging from Manchuria in the North to Japan and Taiwan in the south, ranging over the China, Japan and Yellow Seas and the Formosa and Korea Straits. What was perceived as necessary, essentially, was escalation which could reunify Korea and eliminate the source of aggression. This assessment had a revolutionary effect on American foreign policy commitments. From excluding specified non-Comunist states (as in Secretary Acheson's National Press Club speech), the policy was to take a new road leading in the long term to Secretary Dulles' obsession with the creation of a globalised, pro-Western security system.

The escalation of the Korean conflict was to entrench this overall movement in foreign policy. Any inhibition as to the sanctity of the 38th Parallel, which had originated as a temporary line of demarcation, seemed eliminated by the original North Korean crossing. The argument against crossing the 38th Parallel should have centred both on the wisdom of relying on a policy of occupation to eliminate aggression and on a careful reassessment of the likelihood of Soviet or Communist Chinese intervention. Except for George Kennan's and Paul Nitze's ineffectual opposition to crossing the Parallel, what debate there was seemed restricted to (1) a preoccupation with the balance of forces immediately at hand and (2) a downgrading of the enemy's potential for escalating their own commitment and accepting enormous sacrifices to preserve their vital interests.[42]

Different and more varied considerations might have come into greater play, had the Security Council or (in the contingency of a veto) an allied consultative committee been at the centre of decision-making. For instance, Prime Minister Nehru took seriously the reports of Indian Ambassador K. M. Panikkar from Peking that the PRC would probably intervene to protect its own state interests against the threat of an unpredictable and powerful UN Commander, particularly if the latter's forces crossed the 38th Parallel. But Delhi was unable to convince Washington of the gravity of the warning; Truman and his associates interpreted it as perfunctory rhetoric.

Too many cards were stacked on the side of pressing the advantage; to use General Ridgway's metaphor, 'MacArthur was in the full flush of the hounds chasing the hares there – and that's all there was to it: pursue them to the [Sino-Korean] border, cast aside all cautions, and press forward'.[43]

The Joint Chiefs of Staff therefore approved MacArthur's plan to cross the Parallel, for which he had been pressing since the end of August, but which gained even greater authority after his Inchon victory. On 27 September, the JCS cabled the General that 'Your military objective is the destruction of the North Korean Armed Forces' and authorised him to conduct military operations . . . north of the 38th Parallel in Korea, provided that at the time of such operations there has been no entry into North Korea by major Soviet or Chinese Communist Forces, no announcement of intended entry, nor a threat to counter your operations militarily in North Korea'. Significantly, the directive explicitly forbade any crossing of the Sino-Korean or Soviet-Korean borders or even any non-Korean presence in the northernmost provinces of Korea.[44] The JCS thereby displayed some sensitivity to the manner in which Moscow or Peking might perceive and react to an Allied drive toward the Yalu, as opposed to a crossing of the 38th Parallel, a sensitivity which their field commander unfortunately did not share. Their instructions for the contingency of Sino-Soviet intervention were far less precise, however, amounting to an ambiguous injunction for caution in the face of 'major Soviet units', continuation of operations as long as Russian and Chinese warnings did not sound too serious, and consultation with Washington. A 'for your eyes only' telegram from Secretary Marshall added to this ambiguity by stressing that 'We want you to feel unhampered tactically and strategically to proceed north of the 38th Parallel', and MacArthur gratefully replied that 'Unless and until the enemy capitulates, I regard all Korea as open for our military operations.' [45] The net effect of these messages was a clear command not to indulge in maximum provocation but an ambiguous authorisation to proceed cautiously if the Commander (who was much too optmistic in the first place) felt that there were grounds for doing so.

Further reinforcement from the General Assembly

The initiative remained in American hands. The General Assembly referred the Korean question to its First (Political and Security) Committee, which followed precedent established by the Security Council in late June by refusing to invite a North Korean representative and welcoming the participation of the ROK in its deliberations. The First Committee debate was distinctly pro-American in flavour and results. Having accepted the US Government's view that the 27 June Resolution had given MacArthur ample authority to cross the 38th Parallel, the tacit understanding seemed to be *ab initio* that only means designed to strengthen that particular interpretation of the resolution would be appropriate. A western draft resolution thereupon became a means of placing the United Nations *imprimatur* on future military actions.

As passed on 7 October by a vote of 47-5-7, the new Resolution provided, *inter alia,* that:

(a) All appropriate steps be taken to ensure conditions of stability *throughout* Korea;
(b) All constituent acts be taken; including the holding of elections, under the auspices of the United Nations, for the establishment of a *unified, independent and democratic government* in the sovereign state of Korea; [e]

---

[e] Author's emphasis. The phrasing represented a return to pre-1947 UN terminology. On 30 September, Ambassador Austin had argued not only

and, after noting that all 'sections and representative bodies' of both North and South Korea would be invited to co-operate with the UN in restoring peace, holding elections, and establishing a unified government, the Resolution resolved that a UN Commission for the Unification and Rehabilitation of Korea (UNCURK) should succeed the UNCK and fulfil the steps described above.[47]

This extraordinary document was to have profound consequences for the escalation of the Korean War. It played on the initial successes of the Unified Command over the summer months, victories that were highly contingent on the continued non-intervention of North Korea's allies. It also represented an attempt to internationalise control over General MacArthur and the UN Command. A favourable military situation had inspired an atmosphere of political optimism, which had in turn generated a further step upward on the escalation ladder, by authorising a vague programme of 'all appropriate steps' and 'all constituent acts', taken without consultation of Pyongang and Peking and through the instrument of a Commission run entirely by Western-oriented powers.

Chinese warnings

In accepting the case for forcible Korean reunification, the Western bloc disregarded PRC attempts to make clear how seriously it viewed the prospect of a non-Communist neighbour next to Manchuria. On 25 September, the PLA Acting Chief of Staff, General Nieh Jung-chen, told Ambassador Panikkar that China would not 'sit back with folded hands and let the Americans come up to the [Chinese] border'.[48] And on the 30th, Chou En-lai told the Council of the Central People's Government that in spite of the Chinese people's desire for peace, 'in order to defend peace, they never have been and never will be afraid to oppose aggressive war. The Chinese people absolutely will not tolerate foreign aggression, nor will they supinely tolerate seeing their neighbours being savagely invaded by the imperialists.' [49]

Chou's speech was publicised in *Jen-min Jih-pao, Shih-chieh Chih-shih* and *Hsüeh Hsi (Study)*, all three of which gave the

that 'The aggressor's forces should not be permitted to have refuge behind an imaginary line' (the 38th Parallel) but that 'the artificial barrier which divides North and South Korea has no basis for existence either in land or in reason'.[46]

warning special prominence after the UNC advanced into DPRK territory in early October. The Command's crossing of the 38th Parallel represented both a failure of Peking's careful attempts to deter such a move and a clear test of Chou's definition of such a move as a *casus belli*.

On the whole, it emerges fairly clearly that Western insensitivity and UNC over-optimism were mainly responsible for the failure of Peking's strategy of deterrence. The Chinese, after all, had skilfully orchestrated both indirect and relatively direct signals, to which they gave substance by nearly doubling their troops in Manchuria, from 180 000 in the summer to more than 320 000 in September.[50] This skill in handling an acute crisis situation is at first glance surprising at such an early stage in the life of the PRC but is less so in the context of the decades of CCP administrative and strategic experience. By contrast, American crisis handling appears less sophisticated in the Korean conflict: Washington continued to minimise or ignore the significance of Peking's threats, to press ahead vigorously in the UN while giving full operational control to MacArthur's Command

True to form, General MacArthur took the political acts at Lake Success to their logical extreme and, the day after the 7 October Resolution, issued an ultimatum to the North Korean Commander: unless the enemy would lay down its arms, cease hostilities, and 'co-operate fully with the United Nations in establishing a unified democratic government of Korea' the Unified Command would at once proceed to take such military action as may be necessary to enforce the decrees of the United Nations'.[51] MacArthur did this in spite of the fact that the General Assembly lacked the power to legislate and the authority to execute decrees. There was no DPRK response to this demand for unconditional surrender, but on 10 October, a PRC Foreign Ministry spokesman – by now a voice crying in the wilderness – declared that 'The Chinese people cannot stand by idly with regard to such a serious situation created by the invasion of Korea by the U.S. and its accomplice countries and to the dangerous trend toward extending the war. The American war of invasion in Korea has been a serious menace to the security of China from its very start.'[52]

Continued US unresponsiveness

The Chinese, then, were continuing the attempts that they had begun in late summer to deter the Americans from expanding the Korean conflict. Not until mid-October, however, did Washington show much sign of taking these threats seriously or indeed of being fully aware of their existence. For instance, Secretary Acheson told a press conference on 4 October that 'there was reason to believe that Communist China would not send troops into North Korea',[53] although he never revealed what that reason might have been. Official resistance to such threats was no doubt increased by the failure of the Russians to intervene or to create incidents elsewhere (as will be seen, a simultaneous European crisis was one nightmarish possibility very much on the minds of American leaders). It was easy for the State Department to ignore repeated protests by Chou En-lai against alleged UNC violations of PRC air space and bombings of Chinese territory.[54] While an increasingly powerful source of external constraint would be the Allied, particularly the British, participants in the UN Command, Chinese threats and protests were to remain insignificant until the point of intervention, and the neutralists' warning and protests remained doomed to impotence. In Joseph de Rivera's assessment, US 'cognitive imbalance created by the Chinese threats was deftly reduced by a series of ingenious devices',[55] including American downgrading of direct and indirect PRC threats as well as capabilities.

As if to confirm this state of affairs, General MacArthur proceeded to 'mop up' North Korea's forces, by countermanding on 24 October the Joint Chiefs' 27 September directive keeping UN forces away from the Korean border. To a timorous JCS request for his reasons – 'as your action is of some concern here' (!) – MacArthur replied that it was a 'matter of military necessity' to reinforce weak ROK forces in the northernmost provinces (it did not occur to him to leave this territory unoccupied) and emphasised that he was operating within the limits established both by his September instructions and in his October conference with the President.[56] To the President's statement on the 26th that only Korean troops would approach the Yalu, the General publicly responded on the 27th that 'the mission of the U.N. force is to clear Korea'.[57]

Yet another independent initiative from the field, therefore, eliminated the all-important buffer area created by an allegedly over-cautious headquarters. The latter could have established a stronger crisis threshold, but failed to; their Commander could have interpreted their somewhat ambiguous directives more conservatively, but decided to take advantage of the ambiguity by pressing forward with his own strategy. The one barrier between Chinese warnings and Chinese action dissolved, as the deployment of UN forces gave increasing substance to Chinese fears of enemy forces on the Sino-Korean border, if not in Manchuria itself.

The one crisis threshold that by and large prevailed was the sanctuary status of Manchuria itself. Chinese observers undoubtedly believed that their intervention had guaranteed their territorial security, but it is nonetheless true that UNC forces could have engaged in massive attacks on Chinese or Russian territory but refrained from doing so – even though the prohibition against air strikes was less absolute in practice. This precarious maintenance of the prohibition against attacking Manchuria met with a great deal of military criticism. Admiral Radford felt, for instance, that 'The big question in the Korean War that really wrecked us was the decision not to cross the Yalu and destroy the logistic base of the Chinese intervention. That would have stopped the Chinese cold.'[58] He made no mention, however, of the possible effects such an action might have had on Moscow or, for that matter, on the UN allies. General Ridgway criticised this military consensus on equally cogent grounds: 'Would (the American people) have approved our attacking on into Manchuria? On into the heart of the great mainland of Asia, a bottomless pit in which all the armies of the free world could be drawn and be ground to bits and destroyed? I doubt it.'[59]

On 5 November, MacArthur was forced to admit in a special report to the Security Council that 'the United Nations forces are presently in hostile contact with Chinese Communist military units deployed for action against the forces of the Unified Command'.[60] While the Chinese intervened because their attention was captured by the actions of MacArthur rather than the declarations of Truman and Acheson, the Administration had based its decisions on MacArthur's prediction that the PRC would not intervene;[f] the General predicted and acted as he did because

---

[f] According to the Vice Secretary-General of the Democratic League, who defected in 1956, several top PLA generals opposed PRC intervention into the Korean War, even as late as early October.[61] If this was in fact the case, US decision-makers quite possibly missed an opportunity to exploit internal differences in the PRC leadership, just as Moscow and Peking might have done more to exploit the differences on the wisdom of further escalation among US decision-makers. This all makes for interesting theoretical speculation, but the reality of the narrowing of perceptions during crisis makes it very difficult for decision-makers to maintain a subtle diplomatic, let alone strategic, stance.

he expected continued freedom of action, up to and including the bombing of PLA lines even in China, making it impossible for Peking to intervene even if it wanted to.

China intervenes

For the United States, the logic of intervention and escalation and the dictates of prestige had built up to the point where the momentum created by past policy had begun to make total victory an ultimate *sine qua non* of American policy. This same momentum had gradually brought an end to Chinese inertia, as the elimination of the territorial gap between American and Chinese forces triggered PRC intervention. No longer could Peking view the Korean theatre as an area of peripheral interest and concentrate, as it had in the spring, on an invasion of the off-shore islands and then Formosa and the Pescadores as part of the over-all campaign to reunify China under Communist rule. The events which so drastically altered the priorities of Chinese strategic policy in 1950 were (1) the initial successes of North Korean forces which, under Soviet tutelage, proved to be much stronger than Peking might have anticipated; (2) the counter-thrust by the UN Command accompanied by MacArthur's threats against the buffer of the northernmost DPRK provinces, the Yalu hydroelectric dams and even against Manchurian territory; and (3) the American movement of the Seventh Fleet into the Taiwan Straits, which, along with the threat against Manchuria, seemed to represent a direct threat to the territorial integrity and security of the PRC. All these factors, in the historical account of 'Chinese People's Volunteers' (CPV) Commander Yang Yung, 'seriously threatened China's security'.[62]

A more specific exposition of the reasons for Chinese intervention appeared in the second issue of *Shih-shih Shou-ts'e* (*Current Events*) on 5 November, in an injunction to 'Hate the United States for She Is the Deadly Enemy of the Chinese People.' The article pointed out that 'Since the US started the war of aggression against Korea, she openly occupied our territory Taiwan', and that the 'U.S. invasion in Korea is expanding every day. . . The path pursued by the U.S. now is the old path pursued by Japan; Japan, too, invaded Korea and Taiwan first, and then from Korea invaded Manchuria, then North China, and then all of China'.[63] These two points were supported by the claim that both the US and Canadian governments had supplied several hundred planes and tanks to Taipei since January and by a list of accelerating US invasions of Chinese waters and airspace which became familiar reading to the Chinese from then on.[64] From the Chinese point of view, the US record was further blackened by its rearmament of Japan, building up military bases in the Pacific, and espionage and commando operations in co-operation with the Kuomintang on mainland China itself. 'This series of American aggressive and provocative actions proves that the U.S. has already determined to intensify the aggression.' [65]

It was MacArthur's successes which gave the Chinese leaders the most immediate cause for concern. They saw a distressing relationship between MacArthur's arrogant over-confidence and the inefficacy of their own warnings in the face of it.[g] As MacArthur combined a promise to have the 'boys home by Christmas' with an over-ambitious and, in the event, disastrously counterproductive thrust toward the Yalu – aggravated by his repeated (albeit largely declaratory) threats to the Manchurian heartland – it was indeed difficult to see how the Chinese could afford *not* to intervene. Chinese intervention became inevitable, if only for the sake of maintaining a buffer between its primary opponent and itself – although likely also as a response to requests for help from Moscow and Pyongyang. Ironically, this did not seem inevitable to Washington. On 1 October, James Reston described Administration reactions to Chinese warnings transmitted through New Delhi as follows: 'In spite of the Republican Party's conviction that the Chinese Communists always do the Kremlin's bidding, the chances are that Mao Tse-tung will hesitate to commit suicide'.[67] It was not difficult for Truman to accept the optimistic appraisal which MacArthur provided him at Wake Island on the 15th:

Had they interfered in the first or second months it would have been decisive. We are no longer fearful of their intervention. We no longer stand hat in hand. The Chinese have 300,000 men in Manchuria. Of

---

[g] In November, the Chinese press published articles 'on the black record of this mercenary of Wall Street', in which he was characterised as a 'general of modern American style, reckless and swashbuckling, on the fringe of mania and preparing to jump right after Forrestal and, withal, a poor soldier', and concluding that 'His record in the Pacific so far has been that of a man more skilled in running than in military arts – a veritable paper tiger, a war-mongering killer of civilians, a dangerous lunatic.' [66] In spite of themselves, the Chinese commentators seem to conclude that 'dangerous lunatics' are more to be feared than reasonable commanders, and certainly more so than 'paper tigers'.

these, probably not more than 100 to 125,000 are distributed along the Yalu River. Only 50,000 to 60,000 could be gotten across the Yalu River. They have no Air Force. Now that we have bases for our Air Force in Korea, if the Chinese tried to get down to Pyongyang there would be the greatest slaughter.[68]

Four days later, UN forces entered Pyongyang, and the National Security Council came to the conclusion that PRC intervention was unlikely.[69] They were soon proved wrong.[h]

According to Whiting's statistics, between mid-October and 1 November, 'from 180,000 to 228,000 crack Fourth Field Army troops crossed into North Korea', of which more than two-thirds had been in Manchuria since July.[71] This assessment is confirmed by a memorandum on 'Chinese Communist Participation in Military Operations in Korea' in the Dulles Papers, which states that the first known Chinese Communist unit to enter Korea from Manchuria was one regiment (the 370th) of the 124th Division of the 42nd Army which crossed the Yalu at Manpoju on 16 October 1950. Between then and the 20th elements of the 39th and 40th Armies crossed the river and moved into the mountains in the south.'[72] During the first half of November, major elements of the First and Third Field Armies joined the Fourth Field Army in Korea; the number of troops increased to between 200 000 and 300 000 men, with the stakes increased to units from seven to nine CPV regular armies.[73]

As Chinese forces moved into Korea, the Chinese press launched the 'Resist America, Aid Korea' movement, which succeeded the 'Resist American Invasion of Taiwan and Korea' movement of the preceding summer. A key editorial appeared in the 28 October issue of *Shih-chieh Chih-shih,* which marked the transition from partial to total mobilisation but preceded the announcement of the 'volunteer' movement to aid the DPRK. Rather than phrasing its message in terms of international Communist solidarity, the journal opted for an appeal to the core value of security with an anti-imperialist veneer:

It is very clear now that American imperialism is following the beaten path of Japanese imperialism – the wishful thinking of annexing Korea, and then from there invading the North East and then North

---

[h] Major General Willoughby again thought in terms of likely Chinese intervention in mid-October,[70] but as in the previous spring, his fears and qualified predictions were ignored both by MacArthur and by the Joint Chiefs, probably because Willoughby's assessment was entirely at variance with official consensus – and wishful thinking.

China, East China, and finally the whole of Asia . . . Therefore we must be on the same front as the Korean people to oppose and to end the American imperialist aggression . . . Rise up in the struggle against the American imperialist aggressors, to aid our heroic Korean brethren, and to defend peace in the Far East! [74]

It immediately became clear to the UNC that this was no empty rhetoric, for between 26 and 31 October, the 7th Regiment, 6th ROK Division and II Corps and the 5th and 8th US Cavalry were attacked and either partially or totally destroyed by overwhelming Chinese Communist forces. General Walker was forced to pull back the over-all Eighth Army and dig in along the Ch'ongch'on River. A week later, however, the 26th Regiment, 3rd ROK Division and the 7th US Marine Regiment could claim a hard-won victory over the 124th PLA Division, forcing the Chinese to withdraw from the Chinhung-ni area.

Limiting the level of violence

As both sides were testing each other's strength, more by crude blows than by subtle reconnaissance, they were coming to recognise limits on their future operations. For the Chinese, these limits were defined by their naval and air inferiority and by their strategic experience from the Anti-Japanese Wars, which commended the superiority of men over weapons and validity of the formula,

> The enemy advances, we retreat;
> the enemy camps, we harass;
> the enemy tires, we attack;
> the enemy retreats, we pursue.[75]

For the Americans, the limits were defined not so much by their military power as by the success of the enemy's deterrence against further escalation after the PRC intervention. It was clear to the Joint Chiefs the long-term manpower requirements, particularly in Europe, would make it difficult to confront increasing Chinese Communist forces; [76] it also became clear that the alternative options of attacking the Manchurian sanctuary or of resorting to a nuclear threat had become too risky. Washington had to guarantee the security of Europe and Japan and to take account of the nuclear capacity of the Soviet Union.

There were those who advocated testing these operational limits. On 5 November, General MacArthur ordered General

George Stratemeyer to use his full air power to destroy all of the Yalu bridges and every installation, communication and civilian centre in North Korea, except for Rashin, Suiho Dam and other hydroelectric plants.[77] On instructions from the State and Defense Departments, the Joint Chiefs first postponed Stratemeyer's massive operation and then redefined it, rescinding their order against bombing within five miles of the Sino-Korean border and authorising MacArthur 'to go ahead with your planned bombing in Korea near the frontier including targets at Sinuiju and Korean end of Yalu bridges . . . The above does not authorise the bombing of any dams or power plants on the Yalu River.'[78] Dean Acheson cites the constraints of British pressure and UN Security Council opinion as important factors in securing the postponement of the 5 November order.[79] The JCS redefinition of MacArthur's order, eliminating any reference to a concerted scorched-earth policy and reducing the chances of direct attacks on PRC territory, was probably the result of Sino-Soviet deterrence and of developments in the field. The PLA had begun to be involved; Washington was concerned about how much further Peking would become committed: taking out the Yalu bridges would only be a temporary measure until the river froze for the winter. Moreover, MIG-15 fighters suddenly appeared along the Yalu in late October, six to nine of them engaging US aircraft on 1st November.[80] They communicated, more successfully than any words, PRC determination to interdict any US bombers straying over the Sino-Korean border; in the aftermath, the JCS was strong enough to resist military arguments for 'hot pursuit' of enemy aircraft.

For two weeks following the 26 October–7 November UNC-PLA engagements, no further Chinese Communists attacks were mounted. This was a period, rather, of consolidation of position on both sides, a lull in which political alternatives to continued sanguinary conflict could have been, but were not, explored by either side. Rather, both Chinese and American military commanders prepared for further battle, within the important limits established during the first engagements; the Chinese relied on Mao Tse-tung's strategy of '"luring the enemy in deep" precisely because it is the most effective military policy for a weak army strategically on the defensive to employ against a strong army',[81] and the Americans fell into the enemy's trap by refusing to adopt a continuous defensive position across the Pyongyang-Wonsan line.

By this stage in the conflict, leaders in Washington, aware as they had become of the dangers of prolonged Sino-American confrontation, had asserted a degree of control over the escalated crisis. This control would not preclude further fighting, but it would for the first time instate limits on the *scope* of that fighting. PRC intervention had ensured the beginning of a phase of declension for UNC involvement in the crisis, after which the control of both Washington and Lake Success over their field Command would increase and their political stance vis-à-vis the enemy would become more flexible. The degree of Allied control was not enough, however, to preclude General MacArthur's disastrous announcement of the launching of a 'general assault', designed to 'for all practical purposes end the war', on 24 November. This happened to be the very day of the arrival of the Chinese Communist delegation headed by General Wu Hsiu-ch'uan in New York, at the invitation of the UN Security Council.

MacArthur's announcement was in clear contrast to the previous, moderately hopeful political trends in the United States and in the United Nations. An 11 November PRC statement, while alleging that the US aggressor was a threat to Chinese security and asserting that the 'struggle against aggression will never cease', emphasised the need for peaceful settlement: 'In order to achieve a peaceful settlement of the Korean question, it is essential, above all, to withdraw all foreign troops from Korea. The Korean question can be solved only by the people of North and South Korea themselves; this is the only way in which the Korean problem can be solved peacefully.' [82] In reply, Ambassador Gross read President Truman's press conference statement made on 16 November – it will be noted *after* the wholesale CPV intervention. A long sentence held out a parallel ray of hope:

Speaking for the United States Government and people, I can give assurance that we are supporting and are acting within the limits of United Nations policy in Korea, and that we have never at any time entertained any intention to carry hostilities into China; so far as the United States is concerned, I wish to state unequivocally that because of our deep devotion to the cause of world peace, and our long-standing friendship for the people of China, we will take every honorable step in the Far East.[83]

Unfortunately, these political overtures were obviated first by General MacArthur's inauguration of the disastrous 'Home by Christmas' offensive, and then by the great Chinese counter-offensive of 26 November.

As General Wu expostulated in the United Nations, the counter-offensive of the so-called 'Chinese People's Volunteers'[1] was unfolding in Korea. This counter-offensive, following a month of cautious testing of enemy strength and determining of enemy weaknesses along a wide front, was not only the result of an intractable strategic situation in Korea – occasioned by MacArthur's determination to press northward to the Yalu and the great hydroelectric dams – but also of a favourable military opportunity, for a seventy-five mile gap had opened between General Almond's X Corps, which landed at Wonsan on the eastern front, and General Walker's Eighth Army on the western front. (This gap was intentional. General MacArthur first assumed that the Chinese could not field more than 60 000 troops against the UNC, which he felt he could handle easily; if they *did* produce more, 'he assumed that . . . the United States would unleash its full air power against them', according to General Ridgway.[84] Thus MacArthur had banked on the PRC's failure to intervene effectively in devising his now infamous Pincers Movement to entrap the North Koreans.)

Split in two parts, the UN Force was also atomised because of the mountainous terrain. As early as 31 October, Teng Ch'ao wrote in *World Culture* that 'The rugged mountains of North Korea are an ideal graveyard for the imperialist invaders', who have 'innumerable scattered military bases in the Pacific and Atlantic which they have to guard with their limited manpower'.[85] Moreover, despite the UN forces' superiority of numbers (1.5 to 1) and firepower, the Chinese were able to take advantage of the tactical situation and utilise their *local* superiority to overwhelm UN units. As Mao Tse-tung taught in his 1938 treatise *On Protracted War,* a temporary concentration of a

> big force under cover beforehand alongside the route which the enemy is sure to take, and while he is on the move, (can) advance suddenly to encircle and attack him before he knows what is happening, and thus quickly conclude the battle. If we fight well, we may destroy the entire enemy force or the greater part or some part of it, and even if we do not fight so well, we may still inflict heavy casualties.[86]

In Maoist terms, the CPV forces had moved from the strategic defensive to the strategic offensive; in any terms, the Chinese

---

[1] Peking possibly opted for labelling its PLA units 'volunteers' in order both to retain flexibility in its commitment to the DPRK and to try to reduce the chance of reprisals against its own territory.

counter-offensive had precipitated a full-scale UN Command retreat to the Sinanju-Hungnan line below Seoul.

Aftermath of China's intervention

The twin disasters of unexpected Chinese intervention and even
more unexpected collapse of the UNC lines were to arouse pressures in the United Nations as well as more specific demands, on
the part of America's allies, for greater reliance on political alternatives to the bankrupt military policies of MacArthur. The
first response of the Truman Administration was in the nature of
a prohibition: a key National Security Council meeting on 28
November rejected MacArthur's logical but extreme demand to
extend the conflict into Manchuria and even into China proper.[j]
Further escalation in this direction, the NSC felt, might prompt
Moscow to intervene – either in Korea or in Europe, where they
did not want to jeopardise plans to build up NATO strength.[88]

The NSC meeting represented a clear confirmation of the limited war strategy which had been taking hold, at long last, over
the previous month. The Pentagon further recommended continued refusal of Chinese Nationalist forces, not so much for
fear of provoking the PRC as for fear of forfeiting the more effective UK contribution. They also favoured increasing US military power but pointed out that no new divisions would be
ready for Korea until 1 March 1951. At any rate, it had become
clear to all, too late to make much difference, that 'We could not
defeat the Chinese in Korea because they could put in more men
than we could afford to commit there.'[89]

Operational caution was soon made discordant by a dose of
rhetroical combativeness which followed – perhaps intended to
discourage the enemy from pressing their offensive as well as
to deceive domestic militants about the change in strategic
course. On 29 November, Acheson spoke of Peking's intervention
as an 'act of brazen aggression . . . the second such act in five
months . . . This is not merely another phase of the Korean

[j] General MacArthur began to capitalise on this restraint as early as 1 December, when he told *US News and World Report* that respect of the
Manchurian sanctuary had put the UNC under an 'enormous handicap,
without precedent in military history'. Four days later, President Truman
prohibited 'direct communication on military or foreign policy with . . .
publicity media in the United States' by all military and diplomatic representatives, and he wrote later that 'I should have relieved (MacArthur)
then and there.'[87]

campaign. This is a fresh and unprovoked attack, even more immoral than the first.' [90] On 30 November, an extension of the US rhetorical counteroffensive came during the President's press conference, when Truman remarked that the US would 'take whatever steps are necessary to meet the military situation'.

Q.: Will that include the atomic bomb?
A.: That includes every weapon we have.
Q.: Mr. President, you said, 'Every weapon we have'. Does that mean that there is active consideration of the use of the atomic bomb?
A.: There has always been active consideration of its use.[91]

The qualms that this impulse to keep options terrifyingly open produced on US allies, and especially on Britain, were enough to send Prime Minister Attlee scurrying to Washington early in December to dissaude Truman from using the Bomb and to persuade both Truman and Acheson (who were already convinced) to relinquish all thought of 'liberating' North Korea.

It is more than likely that Truman's press conference statement amounted to an ill-considered, off-the-cuff threat. It may well have prepared the way for more effective use of atomic threats by the Eisenhower Administration, but use of the Bomb was an altogether unreal option at the time. This is so not only because of the five-year precedent of non-use following Hiroshima and Nagasaki, but also because Soviet nuclear capability was probably an adequate deterrent against such an attack. Thirdly, although the Chinese cannot have failed to remember that it was Truman who had ordered – and never regretted – the earlier bombings (of Asians, no less) which had brought an immediate end to the Pacific War, their ideological downgrading and sheer ignorance of the danger of nuclear weapons, in addition to their then-primitive economy and dispersal of population, made the Chinese Communists less vulnerable than their Soviet allies to nuclear threats. When Ambassador Panikkar attempted to impress on General Nieh the vulnerability of Manchurian industry to US attack, the latter laughed and responded that 'We have calculated all that . . . They may even drop atom bombs on us. What then? They will kill a few million people . . . After all, China lives on the farms. What can atom bombs do there?' [92]

Most likely, the credibility of the Soviet deterrent rather than Mao's view of nuclear weapons as paper tigers was the principal factor in UNC reasoning. This view is supported by the State and Defense Department briefings provided President Truman before Prime Minister Attlee's visit. Both Departments concurred in interpreting PRC intervention as a Sino-Soviet gambit, in which Moscow was prepared to risk even global war in supporting Peking. They anticipated Soviet intervention in the event of an attack on Manchuria, and suspected a global design in which Moscow schemed simultaneously for the disruption of NATO and the UNC, the erosion of the Western position in North- and Southeast Asia, and a general 'attack on the world position of the United States', in which 'Other aggressions in Asia and Europe could not be counted out.' [93] This was no doubt an exaggerated view of both Soviet power and Sino-Soviet solidarity, but the view did have the beneficial effect of further strengthening the crisis threshold by making a transgression of this threshold subject to a credible enemy threat. At the very least, exaggerated American perceptions this time limited rather than expanded the extent of US reactions after Chinese intervention, whereas they would become relatively bolder in the crises over the Taiwan Straits, where Peking would lack credible Russian support on the nuclear level.

Prime Minister Attlee's visit, then, made hardly any difference on US nuclear thinking. Nor was Attlee able to obtain an American promise to engage in joint decision-making on nuclear matters in the future. Furthermore, the course of the crisis rather than the Prime Minister's reasoning was responsible for Washington's abandoning its objective of uniting Korea by force: his view that 'withdrawal from Korea and Formosa and the Chinese seat in the United Nations for the Communists would not be too high a price' to pay for a cease-fire which would permit an extrication of the exposed Allied forces, was rejected outright by his less skittish allies. Where Attlee does seem to have had a constructive influence was in persuading Truman and Acheson to express their willingness to negotiate, although the latter maintained – correctly, as it turned out – that the Chinese thrust would have to be reversed and the military situation stabilised before talks could produce any real hope of an acceptable compromise – here again the decision-making waiting upon the action on the field. Thus, within a short period of time, US strategy abruptly shifted from aggressive MacArthur-dominated confrontation with the Chinese and North Koreans and forceful pursuit of total victory within a limited context, to a Washington-dominated attempt to stabilise the line of military confrontation and then negotiate from 'a position of strength'. The final communiqué of the Truman-Attlee talks captured the somewhat ambivalent character of this shift, averring that there would be 'no thought of appeasement or of rewarding aggression', while expressing continued readiness 'to seek an end to the hostilities by means of negotiation'.[94]

This rapid change of policy was to represent as much a phase of declension for the United States and its allies, as the decision to agree to negotiate an armistice would be for Moscow and Peking the following spring. It was the more important phase of declension for the course of the conflict as a whole, because for all practical purposes it constituted a revocation of means and ends inherent in the 7 October Resolution – namely, forceful reunification of Korea – and permitted a fresh combination of political and military resources toward the more realistic end of negotiated compromise based on the original war aim of defending South Korea. Trumbull Higgins, in *Korea and the Fall of MacArthur,* expressed the long-term significance of this critical phase: 'After a brief flirtation with the terrifying potentialities of a policy of liberation, a chastened, uncertain, but still stubborn Democratic Administration was returning to its true love – containment.'[95]

The extent to which the Administration's attitudes had shifted was shortly illustrated by its response to renewed pressures to expand the war. In December, General MacArthur again recommended using Chinese Nationalist troops in Korea, encouraging Nationalist attacks on the mainland, blockading the PRC coast and destroying Communist Chinese industrial capacity by bombing. If he was not permitted to widen the war and if he did not receive further reinforcements, he told the Joint Chiefs, he would have to withdraw to Pusan in order to evacuate Korea. This recommendation had no effect on US strategy, which then was fully committed to resisting further enemy advance, inflicting maximum damage on the foe, and evacuating if necessary to ensure the defence of Japan.[96]

The new political phase in the Korean conflict had obviously begun in the United States. It did not yet extend to the Chinese Communists, however, who were preparing to exploit their military advantage to gain a full victory over the United Nations forces, undertaking two major offensives in the first half of 1951. Their New Year's Eve offensive succeeded in re-capturing Seoul and in driving UNC forces to a line forty miles south of the South Korean capital. On 25 January, the UNC launched a counter-attack, which managed to expel the enemy from most of South Korea by April. On 22 April, the Communist forces began a fresh assault, which brought them across the 38th Parallel, but not to Seoul, before it ended on 19 May.

This five-month period of alternating advance and reverse in the field coincided with similarly alternating overtures and de-mands from the rival political centres. Overtures from the Gen-eral Assembly's Good Offices Committee in December met with Communist demands for what amounted to UN withdrawal from Korea, US withdrawal from Formosa, an end to Western rearma-ment, and recognition of the PRC.[97] The General Assembly ap-proved the Committee's January report and called for an im-mediate truce followed by political settlement and a great power conference to discuss Far Eastern problems, including PRC rep-resentation at the UN and the future of Formosa, but this over-ture met with a Chinese rebuff as the CPV's New Year's Eve offensive was nearing its peak. In a 17 January telegram, Chou En-lai charged that 'the purpose of arranging a cease-fire first is merely to give the United States troops a breathing space' and declined to talk peace until UN troops left Korea and US forces gave up protecting Taiwan.[98] As their offensive realised maximum gains, having met with increasing resistance, the Chinese Com-munists offered, through the Indian delegate at the UN, to ac-cept a cease-fire as soon as a seven-nation Far Eastern peace conference convened and a 'definite affirmation of the legitimate status of the People's Republic of China in the UN' was as-sured.[99]

On 24 January, the day before the 'Ridgway offensive' was initiated, Prime Minister Nehru said that he was 'convinced' that Peking was 'eager to have negotiations', but Indian efforts again met with stiff US resistance – 'you can't shoot your way into the UN' was Ambassador Austin's helpful comment – and insistence on condemnation of the Communists for their aggressive be-haviour. Washington's political rigidity, which began as a product of the unacceptable loss of Seoul, was further encouraged by the relative success of the Ridgway offensive and the interven-tion of the UN's Additional Measures Committee. The most en-during symbol of this period was the General Assembly's brand-ing Communist China an aggressor by a vote of 44-7-9 on 30 January, in spite of Indian warnings that such a step would seriously antagonise Peking and hence reduce the chances for a peaceful settlement of the conflict.

The so-called 'Kansas line' which the Ridgway offensive established near the 38th Parallel by 9 April permitted Washington to feel more confident about undertaking cease-fire talks while providing maximum security to South Korea. The failure of the April–May Communist offensive to disturb this line, first in the West and then in the East, was due to the success of General Van Fleet's Eighth Army counter-offensive – which inflicted an estimated 200 000 enemy casualties, yielded 17 000 prisoners of war (a record number), and confirmed the stabilised military situation. With the approval of the Joint Chiefs of Staff in May, General Ridgway[k] did not attempt to advance beyond the Kansas line – in clear contrast to the MacArthur strategy of the previous autumn. Similarly, the Communists had begun to recognise the fact that the Korean crisis had reached a declension point for them as much as it had for the United Nations in December and January. Thus the alternation of advances and reverses, overtures and demands had become sufficiently stabilised and the declension points for both sides (as well as for the conflict itself) sufficiently co-ordinated, to permit successful diplomatic overtures to take place. The second protracted crisis phase of the Korean conflict was coming to a close.

On 23 June, Soviet Ambassador Malik proposed that 'as a first step discussions should be started between the belligerents for a cease-fire and an armistice providing for the mutual withdrawal of forces from the 38th Parallel'.[100] Gone were the Chinese Communist conditions of January: Peking confirmed this tacit concession by endorsing Malik's proposals in *Jen-min Jih-pao* on the 25th. Between 30 June and 3 July, the military commanders of both sides arranged for armistice talks, which began in Kaesong on 10 July.

Conclusion

The importance of the Korean War for both China and the United States cannot be underestimated. As a limited war, it demonstrated to both sides the possibility of restricting conflict

[k] General Matthew Ridgway succeeded General Walker as Commander of the Eighth Army, after the latter's fatal car accident on 23 December 1950. He then succeeded to General MacArthur's Command after the latter's relief for insubordination on 10 April – MacArthur had appealed to House Majority Leader Martin for the use of ROC forces in Korea, over the head of the hitherto intimidated but henceforth outraged President – and General James Van Fleet assumed command of the Eighth Army.

in terms of area (the Korean peninsula), weapons (well below the nuclear threshold) and even commitment – maintaining the fictions of international commitment (the UN Command) on the one side and of volunteer commitment (the Chinese People's Volunteers) on the other. Over its entire course, the conflict forced Washington and then Peking to experience the painful consequences of vain attempts to destroy the perceived aggressor rather than to accept a compromise with him.

No subsequent Sino-American crisis exhibited the structure of direct engagement, of which the second crisis sequence (following PRC intervention) is a unique case. The process of escalation due to sequential and unilateral (rather than responsive and bilateral) initiatives, typical of the Korean crises, revealed the lack of effective communication between Washington and Peking. Neither side succeeded in effectively communicating either threats or reassurances; both sides were forced to rely on, and accept the limitations of, the course of the conflict itself.

Communications problems were aggravated by the nature of the channels, the variations between targets and audiences and the differences in frames of reference. Peking had to rely mainly on Moscow for outgoing initiatives to the UN and incoming information from the West, although neither its interests nor its perceptions necessarily converged with those of the Russians at all times. Washington received much of its information about PRC intentions through New Delhi, which it was inclined to distrust as a biased party whose communications could not be taken at face value.[1]

To the distortion of information engendered by the channels must be added the confusion of signals resulting from varying targets and audiences. At the UN, the Russians had to impress the Americans on behalf of their allies and to reassure the Chinese that they were serving their best interests; the Chinese leaders had to mobilise their population without jeopardising their sense of security, while alternating between flexible and bellicose external stances; the US Administration had to orchestrate threats and reassurances, satisfying domestic and allied critics while impressing its antagonists. No wonder, then, that statements aimed essentially at one target – for instance, US attempts to rally allied support in September 1950 by emphasising

[1] According to President Truman, 'Mr. Panikkar had in the past played the game of the Chinese Communists fairly regularly, so that his statement could not be taken as that of an impartial observer.' 101

PRC hostility, were mistaken by another audience – for instance, the Peking leadership, which could easily conclude by October that its diplomatic flexibility had become counter-productive. Finally, the different frames of reference presented formidable interpretive problems when Peking and Washington came to analyse the information which survived, in often unrecognisable form, the channeling and targeting obstacles. A totalitarian system steeped in its Sino-centric past can be expected to have difficulty in coming to terms with an apparent chaos of Western contradictory statements and postures,[m] just as a democratic system reaching the height of its global rôle might well fail to recognise the value-laden consequences of a fresh invasion of a traditionally Sinic political and cultural area.

In the final analysis, then, neither side could hope to depend on a resolution of the conflict by means of effective diplomatic communications; both sides were gradually beholden to the strategic communication that evolved in and around Korea itself. As long as it maintained a forward momentum through its successes in maintaining the Pusan perimeter and then sweeping the North Koreans back towards the Yalu, the United Nations Command was restricted neither by Sino-Soviet threats nor by the earnest recommendations of US allies and the half-hearted directives of the Joint Chiefs of Staff. Only after CPV intervention and the débâcle of the 'Home by Christmas' campaign did recommendations and directives have a real effect: the course of the crisis had brought the Americans to their phase of declension, which in turn upgraded the inputs from Washington and downgraded those from Tokyo – to the extent that the President would finally relieve the General of his command.

Similarly, the escalation of CPV commitment, and therefore the escalation of the second crisis sequence, did not become restricted until the UNC counter-offensives of spring 1951 enforced a stabilisation of the conflict along the Kansas line. As Washington adopted a more flexible diplomatic stance, Peking became less flexible and cautious; as Peking's successes enabled it to consider possible compromises, Washington became more rigid and more disposed to demand international sanctions

[m] This is well illustrated by the rule of thumb offered by *People's China* in mid-November 1950: 'In plain fact, it has been repeatedly proved, in Korea, in Taiwan and elsewhere, that whenever the Americans say one thing, this can be taken as complete evidence that they mean to do the opposite.' [102]

against the PRC. Only strategic stalemate – the ultimate convergence of originally sequential declension phases – could ensure the relatively effective communication that diplomatic impasse had denied, leading to armistice talks but not soon to a cease-fire, let alone a resolution of the conflict itself.

The structure and process emerging from the preceding analysis of the Korean crises established highly important precedents for succeeding Sino-American crises. As will be seen, these precedents would make it possible for Washington and Peking to engage in more effective and sophisticated strategic communication in the course of the Indochina and Taiwan Straits crises. Initiatives would become more responsive and bilateral, and crisis behaviour more concerted: no longer would the declarations of either side be almost automatically incredible if not actually ignored; the actions of each side would stimulate responses which would have far less of the distorted and exaggerated quality characteristic of those in the Korean crises. Moreover, escalation, declension and de-escalation would be mutually shared by the US and the PRC, and the development of the Sino-American crisis system would not be subjected to the same extent of asymmetry experienced in 1950–1. Instead of direct conflict, caused by ineffective communication and sequential ecalation, Washington and Peking could begin to participate in and sometimes manipulate crises indirectly, occasionally approaching but never reaching intimate engagement in conflict. By widening or narrowing the gap between their strategic positions, Chinese and Americans would learn to engage in crisis behaviour without incurring the excessive risks of the intra-war model of Korea.

This case study of the first year of the Korean War also shows that Sino-American crises are readily susceptible to analysis within a framework of international and domestic climates. These climates placed the conflict well within the realm of the possible at the beginning of the 1950s, but it was the sequence of the crises within the war itself which made its concrete course both probable and comprehensible. To put it another way, once having determined the potential range of Sino-American weather in the Cold War 'climate', it was then necessary to identify and explain the day-to-day fluctuations in the level of tension, or to complete the analogy, the barometric variations of the crisis interactions.

Further theoretical issues in this and the other case studies – in addition to the interplay between context and crisis – have been (1) the relationship between the processes of escalation and declension, (2) the role of ambiguity in crisis situations, such as the effect which the January 1950 declarations by the US Administration had on Sino-Soviet behaviour, or the effect which the Security Council resolutions in June had on the leeway for Allied operations, and (3) the influence of third-party patrons and clients on the evolution of a crisis, such as the complex role of the Soviet Union in supporting the DPRK and acting as surrogate for its allies in the UN or the relatively simpler attempts of Seoul and Taipei (or for that matter, MacArthur's semi-autonomous Command) to commit the West further to their own causes.

Historically, the Korean War established spheres of Sino-American commitment in a country which had long suffered foreign domination. Instead of becoming a channel for further aggression as in the past, however, Korea became one further barrier in the stalemate of the Cold War. Neither China nor America seemed to have consciously directed their policies toward this end: far more concerned with the security of Manchuria and Japan, each side was drawn by the Korean crisis into the peninsula, which it then accepted as essential to its own security, as a buffer between the enemy and its own territory or 'defence perimeter'. The Americans, furthermore, felt committed to other nearby areas, including Indochina and the Taiwan Straits. It became natural for Washington and Peking to enshrine their new positions into matters of all-embracing principle, both moral and power political. For instance, a high State Department official wrote in 1970 that:

Almost from the beginning of my experience with the Far East I held the view (as I do today) that the United States as a great power, facing on both the Pacific and Atlantic Oceans, has a valid interest in insuring that the coastal or off-shore areas on the far sides of both oceans should not, for reasons of our secure survival as a nation, be dominated by a hostile totalitarian military power. Turning to the Pacific, it has seemed clear that with our limited population we could never expect to dominate or control the mainland of Asia with its countless millions of people. This led me (as I know it did Foster Dulles) to the conclusion that our interests in the Pacific area would be best served by a strong Japan under a friendly government and positions from which we could exert our sea and naval power,

consisting of an 'island chain and peninsular positions running from the Aleutians through Japan, Korea, Guam, Taiwan, the Philippines, and through Southeast Asia (and particularly Malaysia) to Australia and New Zealand'.[103] Peking and Washington would proceed to give substance to principle in the ensuing crises over Indochina and the Taiwan Straits.

Part Two: The elaboration of confrontation

4: Transition from Korea to Indochina

The American transition

If the first concern of the Eisenhower Administration was to resolve the war in Korea as quickly as possible, surely the second was to avoid being caught in another Korea, in another protracted war with the inordinate sacrifices of deeply engaged land forces. This concern had been one of the main themes of the Republican presidential campaign in 1952, expressed most succinctly when Eisenhower told an Illinois audience in October that 'if there must be war' in Asia, 'let it be Asians against Asians, with our support on the side of freedom'.[a][1] As will be seen, the President would prove predictably reluctant to commit forces to Indochina in 1954.

Alongside – and yet contrasting with – this emotive appeal to the pacifist and isolationist strands in the American political personality, the Republicans promised, first, 'liberation', to free 'captive' nations from Communist rule and, second, 'massive retaliation', to deter aggression by threatening to counter it with massive, retaliatory bombing. These declarations appealed to the militants of the nation. Conservatives would also appreciate the accompanying emphasis on fiscal retrenchment – made possible because massive retaliation would be cheaper than maintaining conventional forces in a state of readiness.

Thus in May 1952 Dulles urged as part of his proposed 'Policy of Boldness' what he called 'roll-back', a measure designed to replace the 'defeatist' containment doctrine of yesteryear.[2] At the same time, Dulles defined his concept of effective deterrence: 'The only effective way to stop prospective aggressors is to convince them in advance that if they commit aggression, they will be subjected to retaliatory blows so costly that their aggression will not be a profitable operation.'[3] Eisenhower also attacked 'mere containment' and spoke for a programme which 'must in-

---

[a] President Eisenhower was unwittingly echoing the words if not the spirit of Chairman Mao's earlier statement, quoted on p. 45, that 'the affairs of Asia should be handled by Asians, and not by Americans'.

clude as one of its peaceful aims the restoration of the captive nations'.[4] This paradoxical platform – promising both standstill deterrence (indistinguishable from 'mere containment') and roll-back (implying a territorially expanded Free World) – was nevertheless extremely popular in 1952, striking responsive chords among various Taftite elements of the Party.

The platform was translated into a programme of action soon after the Republican victory in November. On board the *Helena* in December, Eisenhower warmed to his old *bête noire* Admiral Radford, whose views on strategy were in many ways a fortissimo version of the Dullesian outlook. As David Rees points out, 'The Admiral had all the right political as well as military ingredients, for whereas Bradley [the previous JCS Chairman] represented containment, Western Europe and limited war, Radford antithetically personified atomic retaliation, Asia, sea-air power and thus the much advertised new dynamic approach of the upcoming Administration.'[5] It was also on board the *Helena* that Eisenhower and Dulles agreed on the essence of the creed of massive retaliation as described in the Pittsburgh speech; on alighting in New York on 14 December, following a personal visit to the Korean theatre, Eisenhower asserted that henceforth the enemy would be impressed 'only by deeds – executed under circumstances of our own choosing'.[b][6] The great irony of this statement was that the enemy was intended to be – and in fact would be – impressed by *threats* rather than deeds in crises impinging upon the central balance of power. This was to be particularly the case with regard to the threat to expand wars beyond thieir original boundaries and to escalate them to the nuclear level.

An immediate confirmation that Republican strategy would consist essentially of a combination of rhetorical militance and operational caution – coinciding substantially with Mao's injunction to 'despise the enemy strategically but respect him tactically' – could be seen in terms of the Korean conflict. Despite General MacArthur's pressure on President-elect Eisenhower – who had served under the former in the War Department and the Philippines in the 1930s – to bomb mainland China or even resort to nuclear attack in the PRC did not withdraw from Korea, Eisenhower decided to accept the crisis threshold established by his

b It is interesting that Dulles' 'massive retaliation' speech of January 1954 should have aroused such controversy when virtually the same creed was expressed in May and December 1952.

predecessor and not to engage in 'offending the whole world, the free world, or breaking faith' by crossing the Yalu.[7] Along-side the President's operational caution, however, his Secretary of State engaged in rhetorical militance. Thus during his visit to New Delhi in late May 1953, Dulles told Nehru that if the Korean 'fighting had to be resumed', the US 'would go all-out to win and would restrict neither its effort nor its weapons'.[8] (Dulles appeared unaware of the irony that while Nehru failed to make Chinese threats credible to Washington in 1950 and 1951, he was being asked to relay American threats to Peking in 1953.)

Associated with this more aggressive posture was the development of the 'New Look' strategy, which would affect American crisis behaviour in three important ways. First the impetus of fiscal restraint, reinforced by an inflexible Treasury Secretary, resulted in the notion that a 'great equation' between restricted military expenditure and economic prosperity would result in enhanced national security. Second, and related to the first, the 'crisis year' approach to strategic planning was replaced by that of the 'long haul'. This shift – from employing a hypothetical 'year of maximum peril' as a stimulus for maintaining high military manpower levels, to relying, in the long term, on a broader industrial-technological base for emergencies [9] – was used to justify demobilisation and reductions in the defence budget. The main danger was that this 'new' concept would in effect result in the old condition of military unreadiness, resulting in massive crisis-bred build-up, which proved so dangerous from 1945 to 1952.

Third, a Radfordian emphasis on sea-air-nuclear power – in which the role of the Air Force in US strategy was expanded at the expense of the Army – permitted economies, but it also suggested a more indiscriminate response or no response at all to local, often ambiguous moves by the other side. This emphasis provided the rationale for Eisenhower's announcement on 26 December 1953 of a gradual withdrawal of American soldiers from Korea and of the commitment of 'highly mobile naval, air, and amphibious units' which was held rather dubiously to oppose any future aggression in the Far East 'with even greater effect than heretofore'.[10]

Both the 'great equation' and the Radfordian emphasis contributed to Dulles' over-all view of effective deterrence through massive retaliation, expressed most notably in his 12 January 1954 speech to the Council on Foreign Relations in New York.

Here he stated that 'local defence' was being 'reinforced by the further deterrent of massive retaliatory power'. The basic decision' taken by the National Security Council was 'to depend primarily upon a great capacity to retaliate, instantly, by means and at places of our choosing . . . This permits of a selection of military means instead of a multiplication of means.' This was 'the modern way of getting maximum protection at a bearable cost' against 'a political aggressor, who is glutted with manpower': [11] what many have called the doctrine of a 'bigger bang for the buck'.

With respect to Korea and Indochina, Republican strategic thinking relied heavily on the threat of massive retaliation as an effective deterrent against Peking. There was a willingness, indeed an eagerness, at the highest levels to attribute the successful conclusion of an early Korean armistice agreement (signed at Panmunjom on 27 July 1953) to the credibility of the threats to broaden the war to include Manchuria and even (by clear implication) to resort to the atomic bomb. The utility of making a threat of not necessarily limited escalation – in the context of far more restricted escalation in real terms – would be rated sufficiently high for Dulles to repeat it with respect to Indochina – which the Administration rather glibly assumed would be the next target of an aggressive China after being frustrated in Taiwan and Korea.[c] In the apposite setting of the American Legion Convention at St. Louis, Dulles warned on 2 September 1953 that: 'There is the risk that, as in Korea, Red China might send its own army into Indo-China. The Communist Chinese regime should realise that such a second aggression could not occur without grave consequences which might not be confined to Indo-China.' [13] Secretary Dulles reiterated this warning at the end of the year as well, when he told his press conference on 29 December that US reaction to aggression 'would not necessarily be confined to the particular theatre chosen by the Communists for their operations'.[14]

Going hand-in-hand with President Eisenhower's warning to a

---

[c] Issuing such threats was believed not only to strengthen the French posture in Indochina but also to reassure right-wing Republicans that the Administration was not about to 'sell out' in Asia. Those like Senators Jenner, Knowland and Taft, who denounced the Panmunjom armistice because they felt (as Hanson Baldwin put it) that 'Korea was the right war in the right place at the right time [to contradict Bradley's gloomy assessment] if we are to stop the spread of Asiatic Communism',[12] would not and did not take kindly to half a loaf in Indochina.

Governors' Conference in Seattle, on 4 August, that the subversion of Indochina would be regarded as an act 'of a most terrible significance', Dulles' statement appeared to take the US commitment to Indochina even further, by implying that a Korea-style intervention on the part of the PRC would result in American counter-measures against China itself. These threats may well have been intended to serve as a protective umbrella for increases in US aid to France and the Associated States, which General J. W. O'Daniel's military mission to Indochina recommended in mid-1953: on 30 September, the US pledged 385 million dollars in addition to the 400 million dollars already set aside for Indochina.[d] But the threats would also be – as they were meant to be – taken seriously in and of themselves, even if they had no immediate applicability.[16] A top secret 'Talking Paper' for Secretary Dulles' use in the NATO ministerial meeting in the midst of the Indochina crisis in April 1954 would assert that 'we and our Allies must be free to use atomic weapons against appropriate elements of the enemy's military power where it is to our military advantage to do so. We must be enabled to strike an aggressor where it hurts.' Writing in pencil in the margins, Dulles emphasised that 'this by no means involves excluding the use of atomic power', for (no doubt bearing in mind the Korean experience) 'if an aggressor is allowed in advance to limit his losses by gaining for his most valued assets a sanctuary status, then aggression would be encouraged. An aggressor glutted with manpower and occupying a central position would always be able to calculate on gaining from each local aggression more than he would lose.'[17] In the context of the Indochina crisis, as we shall see, Dulles would read 'Communist China' for 'aggressor' and 'Indochina' for 'local aggression'. In spite of giving quite a fright to some NATO allies, however, he would soon discover the limits of nuclear brinkmanship. The strategy might have served a positive function as a deterrent against direct Sino-Soviet confrontation of American power, although that had already become relatively unlikely in the aftermath of the Korean crises. Having ensured that Sino-American crises would be handled indirectly and below the nuclear thresh-

[d] This investment was consistent with Dulles' view, expressed in a speech broadcast nationwide the previous July, that confronting Communism in Indochina 'will save us from having to spend much more money to protect our vital interests in the Pacific'.[15] Others would come to question how attractive a bargain large-scale US aid for Indochina has represented.

old, the strategy then had a negligible effect on the actual course of each crisis, either in Indochina or in the Taiwan Straits.

Limits on American crisis control

The Administration's statements, and the rationale on which they were based, exaggerated the degree of American control over the dynamics of the Korea and Indochina crises. There was very little place in the self-centred vision of Dulles and his colleagues for recognition of the de-escalatory effect of 'outside' factors – such as the resource requirements of the Chinese economy or the death of Stalin (on 5 March 1953) or the final, cathartic and devastating battle of Pork Chop Hill (16 April to 11 July), to mention examples from the domestic and international settings as well as from the final stage of the Korean conflict.

A curious irony arising out of the events of the spring of 1953 was the Administration's allegedly 'more than rhetorical' decision [18] to 'unleash' Chiang Kai-shek. In his State of the Union message on 2 February, Eisenhower announced that he was 'issuing instructions that the Seventh Fleet no longer be employed to shield Communist China' from Nationalist attacks. The President insisted that the order did not imply aggressive intent, 'but we certainly have no obligation to protect a nation fighting us in Korea'.[19]

This 'de-neutralisation' order was duly interpreted in Washington as a further incentive for the Chinese Communists to come to terms, unless they were willing to risk being subjected to attacks against the mainland from Taiwan.[20] The problem, however, was that this threat (such as it was) had an ambiguous effect: on the one hand, it increased the pressure for a negotiated settlement, but on the other, it appeared to open the door for a renewed Communist attack on the Nationalists, and it certainly invited a final jockeying for position before the truce. If the Chinese Nationalists were a greater menace to mainland security, the outcome might have been different. Instead, the Republican orchestration of threats, from the *Helena* to the State of the Union message, was to lead to the final, and most deadly, spring Communist offensive of the war, and in July, a Chinese Nationalist attempt to wrest Tungshan Island from the Communists would end in complete failure.[21] In the end, Taipei would be forced to conclude that any large-scale operational attempt to reassert control over the mainland entailed excessive losses, but even as early as 1953, its US ally was beginning to retreat from the ambitious declaratory policy of the spring. Whereas Washington's representative, General Chase, initially gave Taipei a go-ahead signal, he was subsequently ordered by Admiral Radford to 'hold your horses.' (Radford disapproved of the original decision to 'unleash' Chiang because the Administration was not prepared to give concrete support to an ROC attempt to invade; he recalled in an interview that 'We had quite a time slowing them down after this apparent go-ahead signal.') [22]

As with Korea, so also in the Indochina crisis, there would be a tendency to exaggerate American influence on the outcome. The official warnings delivered in August and September 1953 – which accompanied American fears that the PRC would take advantage of the Korean truce to step up aid to the Viet Minh – were probably as superfluous as increased US aid to the French Unionists was ineffective: the indigenous insurgents would be successful, on their own, in combatting the forces of France and its Associated States in Indochina, and would have resisted Chinese interference; also, the PRC was unlikely to cross the Sino-Vietnamese border in force except in response to a threat similar to the one represented by the UNC drive from the Ch'ongch'on to the Yalu. As we shall see shortly, the orchestration of threats in the spring of 1954 was to have far more effect on the development of the Indochina crisis than on Chinese crisis behaviour *per se*. In a sense, what was to be an acute crisis for Washington would be more of a diplomatic and strategic challenge for Peking.

The problem of ambiguous threats

A further consideration with regard to the credibility and effect of warnings and threats [e] is the role of *ambiguity* – more prevalent during the Eisenhower than during the Truman years – in communications with the opponent. In the case of messages – occurring in the form of public statements, press releases and 'leaks' (inspired or otherwise) – there is a built-in confusion aggravated by the intentional exercise of ambiguity. For example,

[e] There are two relevant distinctions between these and other terms: (1) a 'credible threat' is not necessarily 'effective', in that it may not succeed in deterring a response deemed essential by the opponent; and (2) a *warning* signal may reveal the fact that there are interests at stake which may be defended or pursued, whereas a *threat* goes further in transmitting to the enemy an intention to take action in certain contingencies.

Eisenhower's statement, at his first Presidential press conference, that he was not then considering blockading or embargoing the PRC, was in direct opposition to Dulles' statement the following day (17 February 1953) that the Administration was canvassing a 'whole series of pressures of varying kinds which could be adopted' to prevent Chinese Communist trade with the West, including blockade and embargo. In the case of Roosevelt and Hull, there could not have been any doubt that the President's word was final; in the Eisenhower Administration, on the other hand, observers were confronted with the disconcerting image of a *troika,* in which Eisenhower, Dulles and Radford could be seen pursuing divergent policies at the same time. It is true that Dulles would be at pains to reassure Eden, during the Indochina crisis, that 'he was inclined to criticise' some of Radford's more extreme remarks, and that at any rate 'Only the President and himself could express their Government's opinion.' [23] Even assuming that Chou and his colleagues did not take Radford seriously, they were still to be confronted with a Janus-like US foreign policy, with Eisenhower generally the conciliatory and Dulles almost always the hostile face. To a lesser extent, this had been the case in Korea where MacArthur and Acheson often released contradictory signals at the same time.

Exercise of ambiguity, then, can result in increased confusion over intentions; it can also serve to increase the likelihood of potential miscalculation on the part of the opponent. On the other hand, an ambiguous posture can make commitments appear to extend further than they actually do: 'bluff' is particularly useful where the stakes are not too high and where resources cannot be stretched to the extent desired. The stakes increase, however, during an international crisis, and national commitments often tend to expand to the limits of the 'bluff' in order to avoid damaging blows to their credibility. (A key example of this phenomenon will be seen in the 1958 Taiwan Straits crisis.)

The Chinese transition

The Chinese position in 1953–4 differed from the American in many ways. As we have seen, the US strategic 'transition' consisted first of an ideological commitment to seize the initiative and, second, of a retreat from the complications inherent in that commitment, combined with grudging acceptance of the limits imposed by crises on the wielding of initiative. In general, the

Chinese case could be said to consist of a return from the un-familiar engagement of mechanised forces on foreign soil to the re-deployment of troop concentrations on native soil, particularly in the coastal and southwest provinces.

The Korean War taught the Chinese military planners at least three lessons. First, they would continue to benefit from a built-in advantage in being able to select one or two single areas of concentration, unlike the Americans whose globalised commitments forced an uneven allocation of increasingly scarce manpower in separate theatres at the same time. This advantage was a function of diverse factors: the stabilisation of the Korean front after the July 1953 armistice, the securing of the Sino-Soviet border (at least for the time being) as a result of the February 1950 Sino-Soviet treaty of friendship and alliance, and the relative safety of the Sino-Vietnamese frontier due to the tacit acceptance of the sanctuary status of Kwangsi and Yunnan provinces by Paris and Washington. (The latter remained conditional on continued PRC non-intervention on the side of the Viet Minh, which at any rate was in a position far superior to that of Pyongyang in 1950.)

Second, the Chinese had demonstrated their ability to withstand American power in a conventional war – a far more demanding test for the People's Liberation Army than that which had been offered by Chiang Kai-shek's forces in the last year of the second civil war – and to fight technically superior forces to a stalemate, in spite of terrible casualties.[24] In delivering his 'Report on the Work of Resisting U.S. Aggression and Aiding Korea' to a September 1953 meeting of the Central People's Government Council, General P'eng Teh-huai declared that 'the war against aggression was won' despite 'conditions in which our military equipment could not compare with that of the enemy'.[25] He might have added that the limits of action (before a large-scale reprisal against Chinese territory might ensue, possibly on the nuclear level) had been correctly assessed – permitting Peking to draw conclusions about the applicability of US nuclear threats in the future.

Third and more negatively, the Chinese Communists were confronted with the economic cost of large-scale conventional war, including the maintenance of approximately 700 000 troops in Korea [26] – a cost which was only partially offset by the accelerated domestic mobilisation which wartime conditions obtained. This mobilisation – in the form of confiscation of whatever private enterprise remained, withholding of wages, intensive bond and voluntary contribution drives, and implementation of the 'Three-Anti' and 'Five-Anti' campaigns ᶠ – was to yield an estimated $1250 million to help finance the war effort and to take emergency measures to arrest inflation and restore production. Soviet aid – though very limited – had to be diverted in large part to military uses, including (to Peking's dismay) the purchase on credit of Russian weapons supplied to the PLA. As a result, the task of long-range planning and development would have to wait officially until 1953 and operationally until 1955.[27]

This costly experience, when juxtaposed with the good fortune of the Viet Minh successes in 1953–4, was to be an important reason for Peking's restricted part in the war 'to annihilate the French colonialists, the American interventionists and the Vietnamese traitors.'[28] As Ho Chi Minh put it in July 1950, 'The united strength of the peoples of Viet Nam, Pathet Lao and Khmer will suffice to wipe out the French colonialists and U.S. interventionists. As the U.S. imperialists have been defeated in China so will they be defeated in Viet Nam. We will meet many difficulties, but we are sure to win in the end.'[29] On the one hand, the aid provided by the PRC would include arms shipments in meaningful proportions as well as, in 1953–4, a limited number of military advisers. This aid was to be instrumental in inflicting severe defeats on the French in the border area, during the Viet Minh's 'Operation Le Hong Phong I', leading to Viet Minh control of northern sectors comprising the Cao Bang–Dong Khe–That Ke triangle by mid-October 1950.[30] After the Korean War, the increase in Chinese aid – especially in heavy artillery – would enable General Giap, the Viet Minh commander, to mount a successful final offensive, culminating in the siege and fall of Dienbienphu (7 May 1954), perhaps earlier than would have been possible otherwise. This coup in timing in a conflict whose eventual *dénouement* promised to favour the Viet Minh at any rate would help to ensure the failure of the *Plan Navarre* – named for its proponent, General Henri Navarre, the French Commander-in-Chief – which called for an increase in the size of French Union and native forces by 150 000 men with an increase

---

ᶠ The 'Three-Anti' campaign attacked the corruption, waste and bureaucratism of officials. The 'Five-Anti' campaign reached farther down, accusing the petty bourgeoisie of tax evasion, bribery, fraud, embezzlement of state assets, and theft of economic secrets.

in American support as well, and which projected French victory through a dramatic offensive in 1954–5.

On the other hand, the major part of China's resources would be reserved for the task of economic construction at home, under the provisions of the first Five-Year Plan inaugurated in 1953. It would be possible for Peking to rely on the Viet Minh to be the main force in the war against the French Unionists, and to remain satisfied with increasing its contributions whenever US aid threatened to restore the military advantage to the French. There would simply be no need, then, for another Korea-style intervention. Nevertheless, as we shall see in the next chapter, Americans would persist in viewing Chinese aid as the crucial factor in the Indochina equation – most notably, perhaps, in the case of Dulles' alarmist testimony before the House Foreign Affairs Committee on 5 April 1954, which was to culminate in a charge that a Chinese Communist general was directing operations from Viet Minh headquarters.[g][31]

The more modest role played by the PRC would be set, therefore, within a somewhat revised strategic vision which had evolved during and after the Korean War. This shift becomes apparent if we recall, by way of contrast, Liu Shao-ch'i's militant WFTU speech of 23 November 1949, in which he had proclaimed China's proletarian internationalist duty to support the 'entirely righteous' 'war of national liberation' to 'complete victory'.[32] In much the same way, John Foster Dulles, in May 1952, did 'venture to be dogmatic' in asserting that 'Policies that do not defend freedom in Asia are fatally defective' and in declaring, 'We must move promptly to get out of the present morass' of 'containment and stalemate'.[33]

Thus, like the Americans, Chinese decision-makers were finding themselves forced to recognise limits on their freedom of action. As we shall see, each side would develop doctrines to rationalise its relationship with the other: the Chinese would come to make a distinction between their obligations in wars against outright 'aggression' (like Korea) and in wars of 'national liberation' (like Indochina); the Americans would move from roll-back and liberation to a gradual elaboration of deterrent strategy and an increased manipulation of risk, under the frightening label of 'brinkmanship'. And yet neither side would succeed in controlling the emerging crisis system. In the case of

[g] See p. 106.

Indochina and the Taiwan Straits as had been the case in Korea, Washington and Peking would be forced to come to terms with their interdependence, accentuated at times of crisis escalation. This they would manage to do more successfully and with better grace as the decade grew older.

5: Indochina 1954: crisis by proxy

USA up to 1954

Two major political divisions affected American crisis behaviour in the spring of 1954: first, a division between unilateral interventionists and non-interventionists in the Executive Branch, and second, a division between the same unilateralists and a generally cautious Legislative Branch. The first division had its immediate origins in the September 1953 decision to finance and advise the implementation of the Navarre Plan. As the Viet Minh consolidated its control over the countryside and began to seriously threaten the garrison at Dienbienphu, 'Operation Vulture', the contingency plan for US intervention, was increasingly advocated by Admiral Radford and his French counterpart, General Paul Ély. It was the French request to put Operation Vulture into effect – requiring an American air strike against the Viet Minh – that precipitated concerted domestic opposition to unilateral US intervention, spearheaded within the Government by General Ridgway, the Army Chief of Staff.

The second division, between the Executive and Legislative Branches, had its roots in Congressional discontent over Truman's exercise of executive initiative during the Korean crises, and in Eisenhower's subsequent promise to consult Congressional leaders over any similar actions in the future. Meetings between Dulles and these leaders made it quite plain that American intervention would be acceptable only in concert with its other allies, including Great Britain, and probably only after a declaration of war.

These two political divisions would eventually be resolved by the President himself in favour of the anti-interventionists. His decision would be based largely on the military sense in their assertions: he tended to agree both that an air attack would have a negative impact – endangering the French side and probably leading to an increased demand for ground forces – and also that the French position at Dienbienphu was, at any rate, hopeless. He also judged, given Congressional and public opinion, that American action without allied support would be politically and diplomatically unacceptable.[1]

An ideological division appeared as well in Government thinking, between anti-colonialism and anti-communism. This helps to explain the schizophrenic nature of American policy, which had supported the Viet Minh before 1946 – primarily because Roosevelt had favoured national self-determination for Indochina – but whose enthusiasm for the Viet Minh had cooled in the late 1940s. President Truman's neutrality had given way to outright opposition after Soviet recognition of the Ho Chi Minh government on 30 January 1950 – so much so that Secretary Acheson asserted in a 1 February press statement that Moscow's action 'should remove any illusions as to the "nationalist" nature of Ho Chi Minh's aims and reveals Ho in his true colours as the mortal enemy of native independence in Indochina'.[2] Soviet recognition of Ho's government was followed on 7 February by American recognition of Bao Dai's. As Dulles put it that year,

The stage is thus set for a test of influence. The chances for the success of a non-Communist government would have been improved if the French had moved more rapidly to grant real independence. As it is, there is a civil war in which we have, for better or worse, involved our prestige. Since that is so, we must help the government we back. Its defeat, coming after the reverses suffered by the National Government of China, would have further serious repercussions on the whole situation in Asia and the Pacific.[3]

Two years later, the outcome of the Three Power consultations in London and Paris would bear out his analysis: according to the June 1952 communiqué, France retained a 'primary role in Indochina' as did the US in Korea – forming part of the worldwide resistance to 'Communist attempts at conquest and subversion' – and US aid to national armies in Indochina would be increased within the limits of Congressional authority to do so.[4]

The crucial issue confronting this schizophrenic policy was the question of whether the United States ought to intervene militarily to forestall a collapse of the French garrison at Dienbienphu, which would seriously threaten, in turn, a collapse of the Franco-American 'mutual security' investment in Indochina: it was this issue, above all, which informed American crisis behaviour during the period of my case study. It is interesting to note that the policy debate during the crisis period – that is, late

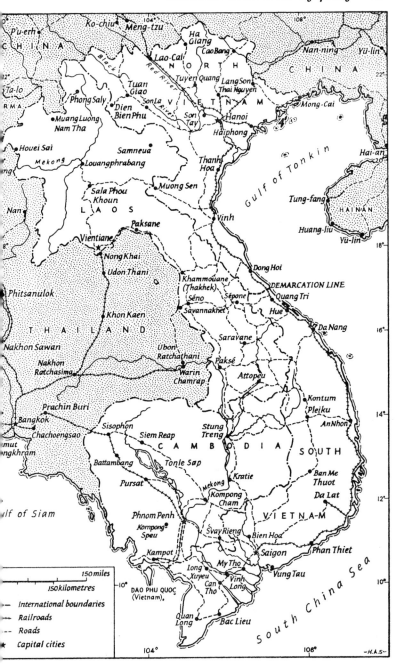

Fig. 5. Indochina

March to May 1954 – was no longer formulated very much in terms of anti-communism or anti-colonialism (both inherently negative commitments) but more in terms of the possibility of staging a successful intervention, avoiding Chinese response in kind and drawing upon Congressional and public support. This attempt to shift away from a negative style of policy formulation reflected the re-orientation from ideological debate to a calculated assessment of political-military costs and benefits in the cause of crisis management – an ambivalent development.

China, 1954

In contrast to American policy – divided over ends and means, strategy and tactics – Chinese policy was dominated by demands for political-economic consolidation. On the domestic political level, 1954 was the year of the promulgation of the PRC Constitution – which was to provide a Soviet-style legal basis for the Chinese state – by the National People's Congress convened in September. On the economic level, 1954 was the second year of the first Five-Year Plan, and a principal concern among Chinese planners was to keep up the pace set in 1953.

To this end, the fourth plenary session of the CCP Central Committee, held in February 1954 (the first since the days just before the Korean War), was to concentrate on the hardening of discipline among Party cadres and on the firm upholding of the 'general line' on socialist reconstruction. In terms of manpower requirements alone, reconstruction was to make Chinese military intervention in Indochina most unlikely: the sacrifices endured by the CPV in Korea, the relative sense of security on the southwest frontier, and the dilapidated state of communications in the area (the Yunnan railway was out of commission at the time) were additional arguments against overt, massive, Korea-style intervention by the PLA.

If the situation were to change dramatically, however, the threat of intervention could be resurrected. This would conceivably have been the case (1) if the level of military operations were to increase radically in the border areas, or (2) if the Vietnam People's Army (VPA) were in serious danger of collapse, or (3) if Chinese territory were directly attacked. In the meantime, the PRC was taking steps to consolidate its defences along the frontiers of its Southwest Military District, presumably to forestall any 'spill-over' from the Indochina conflict, as well as to thwart Chinese Nationalist attempts to infiltrate secret agents and commandos from Southeast Asia.[5]

In 1953–4, contingencies requiring PRC intervention proved to be hypothetical, but an incident during a far less fortunate year for the Viet Minh, 1950, is an example of the likely extent of the Chinese commitment. In August 1950 the French published a captured document, which they believed to be authentic, revealing a Sino-Vietnamese agreement that Peking would send volunteers to support the VPA in the event of a major French offensive in the border areas, but would withdraw after the termination of the offensive.[6] General de Lattre de Tassigny took this document seriously enough to refrain from asserting control over the Sino-Vietnamese border, which he could have done at a time of VPA defeat.

The search for a status quo acceptable in revolutionary terms and viable in pragmatic ones became the keynote of the Chinese foreign policy sphere. It will be seen that Peking was anxious to gain full acceptance as a significant member of the international community, to erode the Nationalists' international position as much as possible and to have China rank as a Great Power. Portraying China as a moderate nation would be the keynote of this period.

The Indochina crisis in its international context

The mid-1953 warnings (described in the last chapter) by Eisenhower and Dulles to Peking and Moscow, accompanied by considerable threats, did not prevent the conflict from becoming a full-scale and acute international crisis in the spring of 1954. A fundamental error made by the US Administration was to assume that if they wanted to (which they did not), Moscow or Peking could prevent a Viet Minh victory over French Union forces simply by withdrawing their aid and support. The conflict would be determined in Vietnam: unlike the Korean War where external factors were most important, this seven-year war was almost exclusively a contest between a united, nationalist front and French colonialists. The Indochinese Communist movement had roots dating back to the early years of the inter-war period and had captured the allegiance of other nationalist forces during its intermediate stage.[7]

More generally, the state of the Far East in 1954 can be viewed in terms of the conflict between Peking's assertion of political influence in Asia, on the one hand – derived from its test of strength in Korea, in the battlefield and over the conference table – and Washington's determination, on the other, to deny further concessions of any sort to Peking, primarily by extending the system of restrictions and restraints developed during the Korean War. China remained 'the central problem in the Far East' and was, in American eyes, 'a decisive factor in the future destinies of Korea, Japan, Formosa, Indochina, and Southeast Asia, not to mention India, Pakistan, and possibly countries even more remote'.[8] In the words of the then-Director of the State Department's Office of Chinese Affairs, Walter McConaughy, the American course for 1954 was 'calculated to limit the capability of the enemy for further aggression and to build up the strength of our friends'. A policy of 'pressure and diplomatic isolation', he argued, would 'at least slow the growth of the war-making potential of Communist China and retard the consolidation of its diplomatic position'.[9]

The regional confrontation of Chinese and American power was to have serious implications for the international setting as a whole. Before 1954, the international climate had appeared to some to be thawing in the aftermath of the Korean truce and the succession to Stalin. Most notably, Premier Malenkov was heading a 'New Course' in domestic policy, linked both to his sensing 'a certain relaxation in the international atmosphere' and to his rejection of the Leninist thesis of war as the inevitable by-product of capitalism. This rejection of inevitable conflict was no doubt the result of the increased Russian awareness of the dangers of nuclear war – Moscow announced a hydrogen device on 12 August 1953 – but it was also the function of a Russian sense of increased security, so much so that Malenkov declared on 8 August that he saw 'no objective basis for conflict' between the superpowers.[10]

Malenkov's optimism, however, was not shared as fully by Americans, Chinese, or even other Russians. In the USSR, a Central Committee faction led by Nikita Khrushchev was to press the Stalinist argument that Moscow should be prepared for nuclear world war, which, they felt, remained a possibility as long as Washington would continue with 'intensive preparations for a new war'.[11]

The Chinese gave modified approval to Malenkov's view, by conceding that the international situation had 'somewhat eased', but they asserted at the same time that Washington was 'unwilling to bring about a further easing of international tension'.[12] Moreover, the opinion expressed by *Jen-min Jih-pao* in mid-October 1953, that the United States 'has not abandoned its desperate attempt to turn Asia into the hotbed of a new world war',[13] remained the main theme in the Chinese outlook. In a 4 January leader, the same organ emphasised that 'wide and irreconcilable discrepancies exist between the peace gestures and the policy practised by the US ruling circles'.[14]

This view was confirmed for Chinese observers by Dulles' 12 January 1954 speech [a] which, with Eisenhower's State of the Union message and the American hydrogen bomb tests over the Marshall Islands on 1 and 26 March, would become the occasion for renewed anxiety that 'massive retaliation' was very much a live option in Indochina.

Limited escalation of the crisis

The net effect of these perceived threats from the United States was to be increased Chinese tactical caution but no change in policy direction. Basic Chinese self-assurance was the product of (1) a correct assessment of the low-risk positions inherent in the conduct of wars of national liberation, (2) an understatement of the potential effects of a nuclear exchange, and (3) the lessons drawn from the Korean crisis experience shared with the Americans.

Peking could and did rely on its secondary position in the Indochina conflict to protect it from US attack. It was far more difficult for Washington to act against Peking when it was so abundantly clear that indigenous forces were taking a primary role in Southeast Asia. Secondly, both the Maoist faith in the superiority of men over weapons and the PRC's reliance on the Soviet nuclear umbrella made the Chinese less vulnerable psychologically to US atomic threats. From 1951 through 1954, as Alice Hsieh notes: 'The United States was consistently described (by the Chinese Communists) as a military menace . . . But the sting was drawn, to some extent, by having the menace presented as largely a matter of blackmail, which was being rendered ineffective with the disintegration of the American atomic monopoly.' [15]

Two important and related lessons which the Korean conflict must have taught both sides were the importance of maintaining

a See pp. 81–2, 98.

a 'crisis threshold' and of engaging in crisis by proxy. In Korea, transgressions of successive buffer zones had eroded the threshold – physical and psychological – against rapid escalation and intervention. Subsequently, in Indochina, both China and the United States came to display a tacit understanding of the limitations of threat and control in conditions of crisis, and refrained from intervention by relying on their respective proxies. This understanding was expressed well in retrospect by Sherman Adams:

let's assume Korea never happened and you came along face to face with the Indochina dilemma. The French were faced with extermination and came to you and wanted money and major military support. Without the Korean experience we might have been inclined to become more involved. We might have been willing to shoulder some of the arms that we were not willing to commit without British and Free World co-operation in facing up to the loss of Indochina.[16]

And yet the series of American actions and declarations was, at the time, the occasion for a steady rise in international tension. On 12 January, Secretary Dulles articulated his Government's massive retaliation policy for the Council on Foreign Relations in New York and for the global audience beyond. While this declaration encouraged an adverse climate in East-West and more specifically Sino-American relations, it could not deter the Viet Minh from extending as well as strengthening their position in Indochina. Thus, they launched an invasion into northern Laos on 30 January, and by 11 February they had reached the outer defences of Luang Prabang. At the same time, both they and the French had begun to concentrate their forces in Dienbienphu and its surrounding hills, in preparation for a final *coup de grâce* against each other.

A striking characteristic of the Indochina crisis was its relative autonomy from great power machinations. In the case of Washington, Secretary Dulles' relatively militant posture was first blunted by an aura of official optimism and then neutralised by the President himself. On 9 February, Secretary of Defense Charles Wilson excluded the possibility of US intervention, either on the ground or in the air, because a French 'military victory' was viewed as 'both possible and probable'; even in late March he was reported to feel that Chinese intervention would neither call for increased US involvement nor significantly reduce the West's prospects for victory.[17] And on 18 February, Admiral

Radford and Acting Secretary of State Smith assured a House Foreign Affairs subcommittee that the French would succeed in preventing any Communist victory in Indochina.

The President, however, was far from convinced by these assessments. Both his private reading of the military situation in Indochina – based on his own combat experience and the strongly negative reports of General Ridgway – and his personal reluctance to let Indochina become a second Korea led Eisenhower to discourage direct US intervention. Thus on 10 February, he said that it would be a 'great tragedy' for the US to get involved and that he was doing all that he could to avoid involvement: 'No one could be more bitterly opposed to ever getting the United States involved in a hot war in that region than I am. Consequently, every move that I authorise is calculated, so far as humans can do it, to make certain that this does not happen.'[18] The resulting ambivalence in US posture – reflecting the division between interventionists and non-interventionists in Washington – was a severe irritant to Paris, which by 1954 had become almost entirely dependent on American support for its operations in Indochina. Privately, the French protested that American ambivalence was lowering their forces' morale and tempting the Chinese to intervene. The Viet Minh, no doubt, vastly preferred US hesitation to physical intervention, especially since the latter seemed a logical extension of the massive US aid programme already in existence.

The US posture, while lacking such an explicit objective, nevertheless had the effect of inducing a similar Chinese ambivalence. In terms of motivation, character and results, the approaches of Washington and Peking offered interesting parallels. Both were concerned to assure domestic reconstruction, psychological and material, in the aftermath of the Korean conflict. Both were ambivalent in their concrete relationship toward Indochina: while Peking did not reveal the 'hawk-dove' controversies which wracked Washington, its actions failed to match its rhetorical commitment to the cause of Indochina's liberation. Rather, Peking deferred accrediting an ambassador to the Democratic Republic of Viet Nam until September 1954, although the PRC and DRV had recognised each other in January 1950 and a DRV ambassador had been assigned to Peking from April 1951 onwards. Peking might well have been refraining from committing itself prematurely to Viet Minh fortunes; by contrast, the PRC and DPRK had exchanged recognition in October 1949, with a

North Korean ambassador in Peking by January and a Chinese ambassador in Pyongyang by August 1950 (although that delay seemed significant as well). Moreover, the Chinese rôle through the crisis was restricted to some aid for its Indochinese proxies – a commitment which did not begin to match the scale of US subsidies.[b]

Hence the limits of Chinese capabilities and commitments coincided with an uncharacteristic strength of American Presidential restraint; the combination succeeded in withstanding the test of crisis. This did not constitute concerted crisis management; it amounted, rather, to parallel crisis behaviour which resulted in crisis control.

As a whole, the immediate pre-crisis context of February 1954 strengthened this crisis threshold in spite of the adverse climate created by Secretary Dulles' pronouncements on massive retaliation, and the 15 February announcement of General Weyland, Air Force Commander in the Far East, that a dozen of his B-26 bombers and 250 of his airmen were being posted to two coastal bases in Indochina. At the same time, Moscow and Peking seized the occasion of the fourth anniversary of the Sino-Soviet alliance to reaffirm their mutual support and to denounce the actions of the 'US ruling circles against the people of China and Asia by supporting the dregs of mankind' (i.e., America's allies) 'to create tension and continue their aggressive war'.[20] And on 18 February, the Big Four Foreign Ministers, having met in Berlin, decided to convene a conference on Korea and Indochina, scheduled for 26 April at Geneva.[c] Communist China was invited to join the Big Four, in tacit confirmation both of its great power status and of the essential contribution it could make to an eventual settlement of the conflict. This invitation came in spite of everything the US State Department did to minimise its significance and emphasise America's continued non-recognition of Peking – steps that were probably taken as much to appease the Republican right wing as to maintain a self-righteous diplomatic posture: Secretary Dulles insisted on eliminating any reference to the PRC

[b] The aid that the Chinese did supply to their allies in Indochina was at least facilitated by their accelerated repairs or construction of roads in Yunnan: between 1950 and 1953, 1390 kilometres of highways were renovated and 1960 kilometres were built from scratch, making more than 5700 kilometres available to Sino-Vietnamese traffic.[19]

[c] Anthony Eden wrote that 'The only worthwhile result of the Berlin Conference was incidental; it called the Geneva Conference into being.'[21]

as one of the Big Five, although he reluctantly accepted Eden's view that Peking would be affected by and therefore had to be party to an Indochina settlement.[22] Walter McConaughy reassured the Women's National Republican Club on 3 March that: 'The Chinese Communist regime will be present (at the Geneva Conference) only because of its aggressor role, and it will be called upon to give an accounting for its aggression . . . Far from dealing with it as a Great Power, we do not even deal with it as a legitimate government.'[23]

It was understandable that the Chinese did just the opposite: for instance, Soong Ching-ling (Mme Sun Yat-sen) declared that 'For the first time in modern history we have taken up our responsibilities as one of the Great Powers, a position worthy of the Chinese People. When we speak, we speak not only for ourselves, but for all of Asia.'[24] If China was to speak for all of Asia, it was entirely possible that it would approach its rôle in Indochina not just from the point of view of its obligations to its Vietnamese comrades, but also in the much wider context of its Great Power responsibilities. Toward the end of March, Peking suggested how it viewed its rôle vis-à-vis Washington. The New China News Agency expressed the hope that 'an atmosphere conducive to the improvement of international relations will be created . . . with a view to enabling the Geneva Conference to achieve positive results'. 'But ruling circles in the United States, greatly fearing such a favourable atmosphere, have been trying to get the diametrically opposite. Since the Berlin Conference, they have not only not abandoned their activities for building a military crescent for aggression but rather intensified them.'[25]

The Berlin Conference tended, therefore, to strengthen the crisis threshold induced by the positive content of Sino-American ambivalence. On the one hand, the negative consequence of such ambivalence was uncertainty as to the strength of this crisis threshold as it was being tested by the increasingly acute crisis of late March/early April 1954. The tests were functions of both the intramural and the adversary aspects of the crisis. The intramural aspect consisted of increasing incentives for (1) the losing client to obtain the further involvement of its Great Power patrons and (2) the winning client to secure guarantees from its own patrons against such a contingency. The Associated States occupied the rôle of losing client vis-à-vis the French, as did the French vis-à-vis the Americans: whereas Bao Dai was only nominally independent from the authorities in Paris, the latter constantly had to compromise their desire for a free hand in Indochina with their need for American aid, which eroded their freedom of action. The Viet Minh, as the winning client, could be more or less satisfied with vague Sino-Soviet guarantees, but their reliance on aid and support from their patrons was to prove crucial in their accepting a compromise settlement in Geneva.

The adversary aspect of the crisis engaged the substance of Sino-American interactions in those two spring months. Like backers in a series of horseraces, leaders in Peking and Washington felt that their prestige was on the line, did what they could to assure the success of their entries, but concluded that they would not (even if they could, which was doubtful) intervene on the track, although each was less certain about the other. In the American case, the enormous scope of military aid inevitably entailed a concomitant investment of prestige. On 16 March, the Assemblée Nationale in Paris learned that the US was paying 78% (the State Department admitted to only 64%) of the cost of the Indochina war: in 1954, US aid would amount to $1.4 thousand million and the French would contribute just $394 million. On 23 March, following a visit by General Ély to Washington, Secretary Dulles confirmed that the US would give France as much equipment and supplies as would be required to defeat the Viet Minh. On the 27th, following a thirty thousand mile trip in the Far East, a Congressional mission led by Representative Walter Judd reported that 'For the free world to seek a truce is to engage in appeasement equivalent to an Indo-Chinese "Munich".' [26] And on the 28th, New China News Agency (NCNA) Commentator Kiang Nan concluded that US officials believe 'an armistice and peaceful settlement in Indo-China to be dangerous, and even fatal'.[27]

It is hardly surprising, then, that Dulles proceeded to justify his position in terms closely related to both prestige and ideology: a Viet Minh victory, he made clear in his important 29 March speech to the Overseas Press Club in New York, would lead to no less than Communist domination of all Southeast Asia and to a decisive blow against freedom. 'Under the conditions of today,' Secretary Dulles declared, 'the imposition on Southeast Asia of the political system of Communist Russia and its Chinese Communist ally, *by whatever means*, would be a grave threat to the whole Free World community and . . . should be met by *united action.'* [d] [28] This declaration lay at the heart of Administration intentions and of US behaviour for the course of the Indochina crisis. A Communist take-over 'by whatever means' – violent or non-violent – would meet with the same response, predicated on America's success in keeping the French committed and getting the British involved. The Chinese concluded gloomily that the speech represented a 'new step in the scheming of the United States to intervene in Indo-China', in which Secretary Dulles 'declares threateningly that war is what he wants'.[30] At no point, however, did Peking suggest that it was going to alter the character of its own commitment. Washington's position fell significantly short of an undertaking to intervene unilaterally, and it was far from certain that London would under-write an Allied involvement. The uncertainty as to the concrete character of the Western response, as opposed to the clarity of US objectives, was characteristic all along of Washington's indirect participation in the crisis. It was this fundamental uncertainty which undermined US efforts to erect a clear and firm deterrent according to Dulles' maxim that 'The chances of peace are usually bettered by letting a potential aggressor know in advance where his aggression will lead him.' [31]

The US Administration's difficulty was increased, furthermore, by its desire to deter not only direct PRC aggression – which was unlikely in the first place – but also PRC aid to its Vietnamese allies. Anthony Eden correctly drew this distinction, in *Full*

[d] Author's emphasis. This was one of the key sentences of the speech leaked to the press before its delivery. The entire text was communicated to Congressional leaders and the British and French Ambassadors, which is even further evidence of the speech's importance and of the Administration's careful stage-managing of its delivery. It was a speech which, according to a leader in the New York *Herald Tribune* (a newspaper very close to Administration thinking at the time), 'was said with deliberate intent to create certain effects, and what was left unsaid was neither less deliberate nor less meaningful'. The leader then offered the following interesting (if only for its uncritical quality) interpretation: 'The speech was evidently designed to exert a steadying influence on the situation in the Far East. Its first objective was to constrain, to stabilise, to keep manageable and calculable, forces which have been threatening to get out of hand. There are the forces in France which have seemed to want peace in Indo-China at any price. There are the forces in this country which have been ready to scuttle Geneva even before the conference begins. And most important, of course, there are the forces in Communist China which already have expanded participation in the war and which constantly hold out the menace of total involvement. To moderate all these, to hold the balance with the hope of achieving a tenable solution, was certainly Mr. Dulles' underlying aim.' [29]

Circle, between 'warning China that some specified further action will entail retaliation, which might be an effective deterrent, and calling upon her to desist from action in which she is already engaged. I cannot see what threat would be sufficiently potent to make China swallow so humiliating a rebuff as the abandonment of the Vietminh without any face-saving concession in return.'[32] While the temptation to interdict road links, as well as to blockade the China coast, continued to beckon in 1954 as it had in 1950, the fear of escalation up to and including Peking's invoking the Sino-Soviet treaty was sufficient to prevent any serious consideration of JCS contingency plans for such action.

Declension phase

It was the events occurring in Indochina itself which first brought the crisis to its peak and later assured its eventual de-escalation. The focal point of these events was the French stronghold of Dienbienphu, which both sides had come to accept as the arena for a decisive confrontation. Dienbienphu was ideal for the Viet Minh, whose hold of the surrounding mountains remained unshaken by vigorous French air strikes and whose encirclement of the beleaguered garrison was to prove to be France's undoing. The irredeemable local inferiority of the French and their allied forces was clear to all save the French themselves and the more myopic of their American supporters. It was only a matter of time before intensive Viet Minh attacks on the French garrison, launched on 31 March, would lead to decisive victory and the loss of France's élite troops in Indochina. This the Viet Minh underscored when they staged a massive attack, advanced to within a mile of the stronghold's centre and then withdrew to regroup – within three days of Dulles' New York speech. It was a testament to the courage and tenacity of General Christian de Castries and his men that they were able to hold out for eight weeks, and it was no mean feat for the forces of General Giap to press their siege in the face of constant air attacks.

Yet the time bought by General de Castries' forces failed both ironically and tragically to serve the interests of either local party in view of (1) the full extent of the French *débâcle,* military and psychological and (2) the inability of the Viet Minh to transform their hard-won victory into sizeable political gains. The eight weeks served only to permit a rise in Sino-American tension as the two nations jockeyed for political-military advantages prior to the Geneva Conference. China's political advantage became assured by the success of her Vietnamese allies, secured by the role promised her at the Berlin Conference, and protected by her Russian patrons.

America's position, to the contrary, was jeopardised by the military weakness of her proxies, and Secretary Dulles knew it. General Ély arrived in Washington on 20 March and claimed to have convinced both Radford and Eisenhower of the need for immediate US intervention on the side of the beleaguered French Unionist forces, especially after the success of Viet Minh surprise attacks the week before.[33] As early as 30 March, James Reston claimed in the New York *Times* to have it 'on the highest authority' that the Administration had made a 'fundamental policy decision' to 'block the Communist conquest of Southeast Asia' – even if the PRC did not intervene itself.[34] Dulles' suggestion that Ély have his request officially confirmed by the French Government was quickly followed, on 4 April, by a cable from Premier Laniel to President Eisenhower, simultaneously with a message from Ély to Radford, asking for American intervention. Eisenhower, Dulles and Radford met in the evening of 5 April, and the following day, the Secretary of State informed the astonished French Ambassador, Henri Bonnet, that Washington could not accede to Paris' request at that time.

This sequence of actions revealed several important points. First, Washington was sufficiently uncertain what course of action to take to mislead Paris about its intentions in early April. (An outraged Ély would later record this as an act of betrayal; at best it was a case of inept crisis handling.) Second, it rapidly emerged that Washington was not prepared to continue to subscribe automatically to a faltering French campaign in Indochina. But third, Secretary Dulles' refusal did not exclude alternative courses of action, particularly intensified threats to the enemy and preparations for 'united action' which would include British forces.

The Secretary's efforts to deter the Communists from pressing their advantage is epitomised in his restatement of the Administration's doctrine of massive retaliation in April. Robert Bowie, his Policy Planning Staff Director at the time, pointed out in an interview that 'in Dulles' mind it was quite essential to have some club in back of the decision-maker in order to be able to get any kind of respectable deal from the Chinese'.[35] On the other hand, Dulles came to recognise that Washington's willingness to use that club had to be made more credible to the enemy than he had managed to do in his 12 January speech. Hence he admitted that 'massive atomic and thermonuclear retaliation is not the kind of power which could most usefully be evoked under all circumstances'. Administration doctrine, the Secretary explained,

does not mean turning every local war into a world war. It does not mean that if there is a Communist attack somewhere in Asia, atom or hydrogen bombs will necessarily be dropped on the great industrial centers of China or Russia. It does mean that the free world must maintain the collective means and be willing to use them in the way which most effectively makes aggression too risky and expensive to be tempting.[36]

Dulles was therefore trying to bolster the credibility of US deterrence, which sorely needed greater effectiveness at a time of crisis. This he did by tailoring it more explicitly to the extent of enemy threat and challenge involved, building on the concept of selective (rather than indiscriminate) retaliation 'at places and times (of the free community's) own choosing' [37] which he had suggested but underplayed in January.

As the Administration's approach became more realistic, the limits on its scope for effective action became increasingly clear. When the Secretary met secretly with Congressional leaders on 3 April, the legislators were reported to be unanimous in pressing for a genuine coalition rather than favouring Radford's predilection for unilateral intervention from the aircraft carriers *Boxer* and *Essex*, patrolling nearby, and from Air Force bases in the Philippines.[38] Dulles pressed his case further when he warned the House Foreign Affairs Committee on the 5th that China was 'coming awfully close' to the kind of aggression which might result in US retaliation against China proper, as opposed to intervention in Indochina. What did this mean in concrete terms? In addition to his 29 March claim that 2000 Chinese soldiers were assisting the Viet Minh, Dulles specifically accused Peking of (1) providing General Giap with a number (probably no more than fifty) of technical advisers, headed by a General Li Chen-hou, (2) driving one thousand supply trucks, (3) installing and maintaining enemy communication systems, and (4) supplying weapons and ammunition to the Viet Minh.[39]

This is the only specific evidence which the Administration offered, publicly or semi-publicly, to corroborate its claim of PRC intervention in the crisis. Taking the information at face value, the most it reveals is a very strictly limited degree of PRC support for the Viet Minh, by no stretch of the imagination commensurate with the Franco-American support for the Associated States. Furthermore, not even French military sources in Hanoi were willing to corroborate Dulles' testimony – which the *Pentagon Papers* show to have originated in Paris – [40] and naturally Peking rejected his charges as slanderous lies, designed to 'deceive and hoodwink world public opinion, cover up the crime of active U.S. intervention in the Indo-China war and create a pretext for the United States to extend its intervention there'.[41] Chinese aid, while helpful, could not have been decisive; it did not need to be, since the Viet Minh took the full brunt of the conflict without any chance of collapse.

Nevertheless, it served the Administration's purposes to maintain the fiction of a significant Chinese, as well as Viet Minh, thrust. In making his statements to the Congressional leaders, Secretary Dulles was not so concerned about deterring the Chinese menace, although he did not mind making Peking more paranoid still about his possible reliance on the doctrine of massive retaliation. He was probably aware that the Viet Minh were the prime adversary, but he found it neither necessary nor advantageous to make a distinction between local proxies and great power patrons. What he and his associates really desired was for the 'Free World' to deny further gains to any 'Communist' opponent to win the 'test of influence' about which he had written four years earlier. Richard Rovere, in his 'letter from Washington' on 8 April, argued that 'it is patent that in [Dulles'] mind it is not the action or inaction of the Chinese Communists that really matters but the success of Communist armies of any national or ethnic composition'.[42] Dulles was far more concerned to rally America's allies, and especially a reluctant Britain, to his plan for safeguarding 'Free World' security through concerted intervention in Indochina. He was also trying to persuade the doubters in his own Administration that the enemy threat justified the course that he had begun to advocate at such a late stage. On the one side, there were those like General Ridgway who argued against any intervention on the grounds that it would entail ground involvement for which the US lacked the troops and should not run the risks of further escalation. On the other side, there were those like Admiral Radford who favoured short-term operations on the side of the French and whose views did little to persuade London to be more encouraging in its immediate response. Dulles favoured a middle course between these two camps, which would permit intervention on the basis of a coalition while ensuring regional collective security in the long haul. He professed to favour this course even if it entailed PRC intervention, in which case he would be prepared to advocate destroying Chinese staging bases with US air power [43] – a declaratory posture which would warm the heart of any good anti-Communist militant without running much risk of being translated into action.

In this compromise of sorts – which by no means precluded radical measures as long as they were undertaken in the context of allied action – Dulles was reasonably successful, for on 4 April Eisenhower accepted the Dulles-Radford recommendation for united action by Britain, France, the US and 'friendly' Asian nations

to oppose the Communist forces on the ground in Indochina just as the U.N. stepped in against the North Korean aggression in 1950. There was, of course, the clear risk that Peking would send its armies openly into Indochina as it had done in Korea, staging them out of bases in south China.

Dulles recommended that the dangers be faced, and that if the Chinese Communists intervened openly, their staging bases be destroyed by U.S. airpower. President Eisenhower concurred.[44]

The President then wrote to Prime Minister Churchill that 'the situation in Southeast Asia requires us urgently to take serious and far-reaching decisions' to establish, specifically, a 'new, *ad hoc* grouping or coalition composed of nations which have a vital concern in the checking of Communist expansion in area'.[45] Eisenhower later recorded, probably with considerable relief, that 'the British had little enthusiasm for joining us in taking a firm position and it seemed clear that Congress would not act favourably unless I could give assurances that the British would be by our side'.[46] In spite of its commitments in Malaya, London failed to be impressed either by dire Franco-American descriptions of the train of events in Indochina, or by Washington's recourse to geopolitical metaphor, contained in Eisenhower's classic statement of the domino theory on 7 April: 'You have a row of dominoes set up, and you knock over the first one, and what will happen to the last one is the certainty that it will go over very quickly. So you have a beginning of a disintegration that will have the most profound influence.' [47]

Neither the Secretary's 5 April 'United Action' speech nor his 10–15 April trip to London and Paris resulted in any immediate resolve to intervene on the side of the French. Dulles had been bound by his Congressional supporters to proceed only with Anglo-French support,[e] and Prime Minister Churchill carefully limited himself to an undertaking to examine the possibility of 'collective defence' in Asia and the Pacific in the long term. On 18 April, the British Ambassador in Washington, Roger Makin, declined to participate in a working party for united action, scheduled to meet on the 20th – thereby finally driving home to Dulles the impossibility of effective intervention prior to the Geneva Conference and inflicting the first major frustration on the Secretary of State.[f]

The second important limitation on US intervention, in addition to Allied reluctance to become deeply involved in the spring of 1954, was the Administration's growing realisation of the practical difficulties of intervening in the Indochina conflict. This realisation crystallised in General Ridgway's April report to the President, based on an Army survey of the logistic problems of the Indochina theatre, which was intended to dispel official ignorance about the cost in 'blood and money and national effort'.[53] No longer did officials who were relatively uninformed about military matters (including Nixon and Robertson) hold

---

[e] The specific terms set by the 3 April meeting were (1) US intervention only as part of a Eurasian coalition; (2) French agreement to accelerate their independence programme for the Associated States; and (3) a guarantee from Paris to keep its forces in Indochina after Washington intervened. Eisenhower stated that 'my judgment entirely co-incided with theirs'.[48]

[f] Secretary Dulles told his sister just after Makin's telephone call that ' "I would not have believed it. Eden has reversed himself and gone back on our agreement." This was one of the few occasions when I knew him to express quick and vehement indignation.'[49] The Anglo-American communiqué of 13 April read, 'We are ready to take part, with other countries concerned, in an examination of establishing a collective defence.'[50] Whereas Dulles believed this to be a short-term commitment, Eden felt it meant a long-term process.[51]

Louis Halle comments that Churchill's refusal to engage in joint action with the Americans, confirmed in Parliament on 27 April, enabled Dulles 'to give the impression that the failure to carry out the threat of American intervention at Dien Bien Phu was due entirely to British timidity and betrayal. Although a clear majority in Congress and among the American people, with the Korean War to sober them, were certainly opposed to such intervention, Dulles was now able not only to preserve but to enhance his image as the strong man of anti-Communism – deserted at a crucial hour by those who should have been marching at his side.'[52] Halle is no doubt correct in highlighting this Machiavellian ability of Secretary Dulles to make his own failure appear to be the failure of others, but it is just as important to recognise the readiness, however reluctant, of both Administration and Congress to intervene in the right circumstances.

sway nor did the Radford group of air-naval advocates prevail. Rather, the lessons of Korea, 'that air and naval power alone cannot win a war and that inadequate ground forces cannot win one either', were powerfully expressed by Ridgway, who later recalled that

It was incredible to me that we had forgotten that bitter lesson [of Korea] so soon that we were on the verge of making the same tragic error.

That error, thank God, was not repeated. As soon as the full report was in, I lost no time in having it passed up the chain of command. It reached President Eisenhower. To a man of his military experience its implications were immediately clear. The idea of intervening was abandoned, and it is my belief that the analysis which the Army made and presented to higher authority played a considerable, perhaps a decisive, part in persuading our government not to embark on that tragic adventure.[54]

Presented with hard military logic, and given a lack of immediate Allied response, the Administration was left with the difficult choice of either conceding to the antagonist at least a short-term advantage in the forthcoming Geneva Conference or of making one last effort to intervene unilaterally. On 16 April, Vice President Nixon informed the American Society of Newspaper Editors that the US might send troops into Indochina if the only alternative were Communist domination. He opined (in a speech which was supposed to be off the record) that 'France is tired of the war, as we were tired of Korea' and that 'the Vietnamese lack the ability to conduct a war by themselves or govern themselves'. The dangers were great, and American power might well have to meet them: 'If the French withdraw, Indochina would become Communist dominated within a month. The United States as leader of the Free World cannot afford further retreat in Asia. It is hoped that the United States will not have to send troops there, but if this Government cannot avoid it, the Administration must face up to the situation and dispatch forces.'[55] It is still not clear whether Nixon floated this trial balloon on his own initiative – entirely possible, given his ties with interventionist officials and Congressmen – or whether he had the secret blessing of Dulles and even of the President. The latter seems improbable in the light of available records; in response to the suggestion at the 5 April Congressional hearing that his 29 March speech did not exclude unilateral US action, Secretary Dulles responded that

'The threat is a grave threat to many countries and our judgment is that it should be recognised as such by them and I would hesitate to ask for action by the United States alone.'[56] But it is not impossible, given Dulles' dread of diplomatic humiliation, Eisenhower's personal weakness in the face of his forceful Secretary of State, and their mutual sensitivity to the right wing.

The Chinese were spared the need to face the concrete consequences of these American initiatives. While the drive for 'united action' became bogged down in enlightened British procrastination, the mention of unilateral intervention resulted in such opposition from Congress and the press that Dulles termed the Vice President's statement 'hypothetical' and characterised any use of US troops as 'unlikely', as early as 19 April. This qualification was certainly a rapid deflation of the interventionists' trial balloon; it could well have been an indirect rebuke to Nixon for poaching in hostile territory, if Dulles or Eisenhower had disapproved of, or even remained unalerted about, the impending initiative.

On the same day that Dulles made his comment, Nixon, 'greatly disturbed about some of the reactions' to his speech, offered the clarification that 'While he did not anticipate that the French would quit in Indochina, he thought that the United States would have to replace them if necessary to prevent a Communist conquest of Southeast Asia.' In Cincinnati the following day, he offered the further thought that 'The aim of the United States is to hold Indochina without war involving the United States, if we can. We have learned that if you are weak and indecisive, you invite war. You don't keep the Communists out of an area by telling them you won't do anything about it.'[57] The Vice President managed, therefore, to endorse Dulles' view that, given the lack of British support, the contingency of US intervention remained largely hypothetical, while maintaining his pressure to preserve a militant posture vis-à-vis the Communist adversaries. The latter were sufficiently impressed to denounce his 'adventurist policy' as a 'grave menace to peace and security in the Far East and Southeast Asia', in the words of the *Jen-min Jih-pao* commentator, adding that 'Nixon came out, immediately after Dulles, to bring greater pressure to bear upon Britain and France, with the sole aim of torpedoing the Geneva Conference. And he did it more crudely than Dulles.'[58] Nixon was fulfilling his natural rôle fairly credibly, therefore, as the uncompromising face of the Administration, whose rhetoric far exceeded in volume any effective operational measures to come to the aid of the French.

The possibility of intervention in Indochina had significantly decreased with the official statements and clarifications of mid-April, though Peking still did not, or pretended it did not, recognise this fact.[59] Paris was also reluctant to recognise this fact. As the situation of the Dienbienphu garrison deteriorated, French pressures for outside help increased concomitantly, coming to a head during the NATO ministerial meeting in Paris which immediately preceded the Geneva Conference. By then, the Viet Minh besiegers had increased their forces by one quarter to 40 000, and the French had unbelievably doubled theirs to 12 000, in spite of the enemy's complete encirclement of their base and its seizure of half their airstrip. And yet to French pleas for US air strikes against the Viet Minh, Secretary Dulles responded on 24 April that US air attacks could not rescue a garrison which was already doomed, according to American intelligence, and that anyway, without UK co-operation, Congress would not grant the President the powers which the Administration deemed a prerequisite for intervention.[60]

Nevertheless, the net effect of US pronouncements was to keep America's antagonists uncertain about US intentions while the fate of Dienbienphu, its (in the end) 16 000 defenders, and indirectly the French presence in Indochina, was being decided. The PRC's past experience with the disconcerting division between Truman and Acheson at the centre and MacArthur in the field had led it to almost automatically discount Administration rhetoric and read the worst into UNC operations; little in either the declarations or the behaviour of the Republican Administration led China to hope for a more positive outcome in the present crisis.[61]

Indeed, Washington's signals seemed to be even further complicated by the emotional, even irrational, impetus of some American officials to translate their anti-communist ideology into action regardless of cost and risk. One such official was Assistant Secretary of State Walter Robertson 'whose approach to these questions', in Eden's view (ironic if taken in the context of the 1956 Suez Crisis), 'is so emotional as to be impervious to argument or indeed to facts', and who continued to support US intervention in spite of the bleakest intelligence estimates of French prospects in Indochina.[62] Another good example was General

Nathan Twining, then the Air Force Chief of Staff (and JCS Chairman during the second Taiwan Straits crisis) who declared in retrospect:

I still think it would have been a good idea . . . to take three small tactical A-bombs – it's a fairly isolated area, Dien Bien Phu – no great towns around there, only Communists and their supplies. You could take all day to drop a bomb, make sure you put it in the right place. No opposition. And clean those Commies out of there and the band could play the Marseillaise and the French would come marching out of Dien Bien Phu in fine shape. And those Commies would say, 'Well those guys may do this again to us. We'd better be careful.' [63]

Given the degree of doubt that even Americans entertained about the eventual outcome of the intra- and inter-governmental debates in March and April, and that the Chinese continued to entertain through May, the ambiguous signalling of Eisenhower, Nixon and Dulles could only have further distorted Peking's fears of irresponsible American action. These fears were not assuaged by the Administration's well-known reluctance to be painted with the same brush of unfavourable compromise for which they had so successfully blamed the Democrats when they accepted the Korean armistice.

The Administration did not hesitate to capitalise on its reputation for unreliability of action. Even as late as 31 May – more than three weeks after the surrender of the garrison at Dienbienphu on 7 May – the French and American delegations were still ready to spread rumours that Washington might send three army divisions to Indochina if no satisfactory agreement were reached at Geneva, in spite of clear public and Congressional opposition to US intervention.[g] Bidault defended this ploy as 'distant thunder which might help the conference' when he described it to Eden.[65]

Even if the Chinese delegation was not that disconcerted by Washington's 'distant thunder', it still had to take account of further developments in the field, and of the potential for crisis-generated escalation inherent in these developments. American help in clearing the road from Tourane to the sea and in giving cover to French airbases was perhaps tangential in character. According to Dulles' later account, Washington tried to transmit a more direct warning signal by dispatching two aircraft carriers, the *Boxer* and the *Philippine Sea*, to the South China Sea,

[g] Polls revealed no more than five Congressmen categorically in favour of US intervention; up to 85% of the public opposed US involvement.[64]

in the vicinity of both China and Indochina. (Presumably the *Essex* was still in the area.) Their planes armed with tactical nuclear weapons, the carriers might have deterred any all-out effort by the Communists prior to the Geneva Conference, as Dulles later suggested. Rather in the tradition of gunboat diplomacy, he argued that 'It was a modern version of the classic show of force, designed both to deter any Red Chinese attack on Vietnam and to provide weapons for instant retaliation if it should prove necessary.' [66] Probably a more accurate interpretation, however, is that this move could not, and did not, credibly deter a major Communist victory over Dienbienphu, but as part of the other US actions in April it helped to add to Bidault's thunder. As far as can be seen, Peking continued to feel unimpelled to intervene to any greater extent than it had in the past. *Jen-min Jih-pao* confined itself to the rather sarcastic reaction that the dispatch of the carriers made it 'clear that the American adventurist intrigues have reached highly boisterous proportions',[67] but if Chinese decision-makers felt any greater qualms about the significance of these new enemy moves, they did not share them with the outside world. The trouble with the Franco-American thunder in late April was its unsuitability for the situation at hand: it did not prevent likely events from happening, nor did it particularly impress great power patrons who were coming to appreciate the limits confronting any attempt to control the crisis from the outside.

The most that Washington could claim for its elaborate signals was that they served as timely reminders, to both sides, of the virtues of restraint in the face of an increasingly self-controlling crisis. They were designed – as was Dulles' studied boycott of the Conference (in which he ostentatiously avoided any contact with Chou En-lai) – to make the Communist delegations more amenable to compromise. Instead of settling for a 'temporary' demarcation line along the 14th Parallel, as the Communists were demanding, or even along the 16th Parallel, as the French were preparing to accept, Molotov and Chou conceded the 17th Parallel in return for a US promise, given by Under Secretary of State Walter Bedell Smith on 21 July, to 'refrain from the threat or use of force' to upset the Accords. While no one succeeded in persuading Washington to accede to the Accords themselves, Moscow and Peking remained satisfied with obtaining tacit US acceptance of a compromise in Indochina – in effect, a recognition of the consequences of the Indochina crisis rather than of the legitimacy of the Geneva Conference, that is, of strategic interactions which Washington could not avoid, rather than of diplomatic parleys which US officials felt free to condemn.

Even though the extent of their proxy's military success reduced Peking's need to bargain with the West, Chou En-lai and his colleagues were attuned to the benefits of taking a more moderate line in a conference where prestige meant more than real estate, especially when that real estate might increase the power of their traditional Vietnamese enemy. The Chinese and Soviets could hope (1) to capitalise on the intramural crisis between Washington, on the one hand, and London and Paris, on the other, (2) to reveal by contrast the uncompromising nature of the American position, without provoking a US challenge to their nuclear guarantee, and (3) to impress the non-aligned states meeting at Colombo. It should be noted that this moderate stance was possible in the first place because of the superior Communist position on the battlefield. It might have been motivated, at least to a small extent, by a desire to make it easy for the Western parties to back down; it would certainly be in the interests of Molotov and Chou to make it as difficult as possible for Dulles to activate his 'united action' project by securing allied consent and participation.

The main problem for Chinese – and also Russian – diplomats, as a result of this position, was not to impress the non-aligned and socialist states of the world – this was achieved for China by the very nature of its diplomatic posture. The task was rather to impress the virtues of tactical compromise on the Communists' recalcitrant Viet Minh allies, who probably felt that the extent of their control over Vietnamese territory and the psychological defeat of the French at Dienbienphu warranted far more than the area north of the seventeenth parallel – one degree north of the post-war division between British and Chinese occupation zones – however temporary this division might be made to appear.

Could they have foreseen the consequences of agreeing to a two-year lull, the Viet Minh no doubt would have refused to abandon their fight to the finish; Peking and Moscow would have been forced to engage in the risky enterprise (as the latter saw it) of deterring Washington from broadening and intensifying the conflict. As it happened, however, there was enough apparent recklessness and well-hidden duplicity in the American approach to extract the (allegedly) short-term compromise, inherent in the Geneva Accords, from the other side. Perhaps unaware of

precisely which tactics worked and which did not, but nevertheless successful in the end, Dulles was able to exact concessions
through orchestrating direct and indirect threats with tangential
actions (including aid and logistic support) which carried in and
of themselves enough warning of further escalation.[68]

Aftermath of the Conference [h]

After Geneva, Dulles' abortive plan of 'united action' was to be
re-routed into the formation of the Southeast Asia Treaty Organisation (SEATO), just as the French rejection of the European Defence Community was to devolve into the Western
European Union as a means of incorporating West Germany into
the Atlantic Alliance. These initiatives in the West found responses
in the East: Communist opposition to the strengthening of NATO
and the creation of SEATO was followed by the negotiation of
the Warsaw Pact and the ascendancy of Khrushchev over Malenkov. Khrushchev's visit to Peking in September–October 1954,
accompanied by Bulganin (who became Premier in 1955),
Mikoyan, and Schvernik, suggests that the Chinese approved of
his ascendancy: Khrushchev's military thinking at the time certainly came much closer to Peking's point of view than had Malenkov's. A joint declaration issued on 12 October 1954, in the
context of increasing tension in the Taiwan Straits area, reiterated support for the 1950 Treaty and announced complete agreement on the international situation.

Despite these elements of 'freeze' in Cold War atmospherics,
it is possible to detect elements of 'thaw' as well. The co-operation between the co-chairmen of the Geneva Conference, Eden
and Molotov (who shared Malenkov's attitude), indicated a mutual readiness to limit the damage inflicted by Indochina, and by
the responses of the militants to Indochina, on possibilities for
détente. Geneva 1954 can be seen in this context as the beginning
of the road to the East-West summit held in the same city from
18 to 23 July 1955. In addition, Peking began to lay the ground-
work for a direct channel of communication with Washington.
The detention of seventy Chinese students and twenty-six American prisoners (from the Korean War) served as a bargaining
counter in the talks begun by U. Alexis Johnson and Wang Ping-
nan at Geneva on 5 June 1954. These contacts, actively encour-

[h] The negotiations at Geneva, Bandung or Warsaw will be considered only
inasmuch as they affect the tone of Sino-American crisis interactions.

aged by Nehru, U Nu and others, formed the origins of the Sino-American ambassadorial talks which would begin, also at Geneva, in August 1955.

For Sino-American relations, the essence of 1954 was that Chinese Communist power and prestige had increased in the Far East at the expense of the United States. As a result of Chinese intervention, North Korea and 'liberated' Tibet could be counted as gains for the East; thanks partly to Chinese and Russian support, so could North Vietnam. That Pyongyang was able to play Moscow against Peking and that Hanoi was learning how, that Lhasa could still retain a certain degree of autonomy, and that neither Korea nor Vietnam were reunified under Communist rule – all these appeared to be minor detractions from the over-all Chinese success, which Mao Tse-tung, Chou En-lai, and the newly appointed Minister of Defence, P'eng Teh-huai, could presumably hope to remedy in time. Indeed, it was not necessarily to the advantage of the PRC to have overly strong and united southern neighbours which might have challenged Chinese influence over Asian Communist movements or embarrassed China's overtures to Burma and India. Moreover, the potential irredentism of Pyongyang and Hanoi could serve to distract American attention from Chinese initiatives elsewhere.

Finally, it should be recalled that this regional alignment took place during – and was made possible by – a period of stabilisation of the super-power relationship. The main factor here was the strengthening of the nuclear stalemate, as a result of the Soviet possession of the hydrogen bomb and development of intercontinental bombers – a situation recognised by Soviet, US and even Chinese commentators.[69] While Soviet-US 'pax atomica' decisively undermined the credibility of first-strike threats by any power and strengthened the tacit agreement to keep wars limited, it also served to give more leeway to strategies of local insurgency and indirect aggression. Although Sino-American crisis relations in the latter part of the 1950s would operate within this framework of nuclear stalemate, sub-nuclear confrontation would persist over the thorny Taiwan problem.

Conclusion

With the Final Declaration of the Geneva Conference, on 21 July 1954,[70] both China and the United States could consider that one more sphere of the crisis relationship had become defined. The Declaration noted 'the clauses in the (Geneva Conference's) agreement on the cessation of hostilities in Vietnam prohibiting the introduction into Vietnam of foreign troops and military personnel as well as of all kinds of arms and munitions'. The succeeding history of the Indochina conflict was to make clear that the Geneva Accords would be more often violated than respected, beginning with the failure to hold general elections and reunify the country by 1956. The expectation that Vietnam would become unified under DRV authority was to be frustrated, and conflict would again become the lot of the peoples of Indochina.

In the context of Sino-American crises in the 1950s, however, Peking and Washington had made progress in their developing strategic relationship. They had learned how to avoid direct confrontation, while manipulating the risks of entering such a confrontation. They had become more sophisticated in their reliance on proxies – as contrasted with their virtual replacement of their proxies in Korea. They had come to recognise the limits on their influence over the course of a crisis, beyond which penalties would exceed any conceivable benefits. As a result, they were able to respect crisis thresholds, even in an arena which had no explicit geopolitical conventions to compare with the 38th Parallel or the Yalu. These thresholds served them well, effectively containing the escalation and facilitating the declension of the Indochina crisis.

Against all of these positive developments in Sino-American crisis interactions, the negative features seem to be of secondary importance. It can be argued, for instance, that US crisis handling would surely have led to a wider conflict were it not for the cautious, consistent and rational behaviour of the Chinese and the determined stonewalling of the British. To be sure, Dullesian rhetoric made Washington appear to be far too heavy-handed, but then again there were enough democratic constraints, Congressional and Presidential, to limit American risk-taking. Moreover, the appearance (as opposed to the reality) of a degree of irrationality seemed to yield greater gains for the West than the more reasonable counsels of London and the more 'regionalist' demands of New Delhi might have produced. It is only when one broadens the criteria of Sino-American crisis handling to take account of the more fundamental questions of war and peace in Indochina, and of the justice of manipulating the calamities of that strife-torn region for great power purposes, that the negative factors assume overriding importance.

But in the more limited context of Sino-American interactions, decision-makers in Washington and Peking could conclude, at least provisionally, that their commitments in both Northeast and Southeast Asia had become adequately defined. They could then return full circle to the crucial issue of the two Chinas, which had been deferred but far from forgotten since the leashing and then unleashing of Chiang Kai-shek at the start of the decade.

6: First Taiwan Straits crisis, 1954–1955

The resolve of America and China had been tested in two of the three major spheres of East-West confrontation around China's southern periphery. The remaining sphere was the Taiwan Straits, where the overriding issue remained the survival and legitimacy of both Chinas. Two necessary preconditions and one sufficient condition would bring this area to a state of acute crisis. First, the actors (Peking and Washington) would concentrate resources on a test of power in the area; second, the existence of a state of flux in the international setting (at least on a regional level) would induce such a test in order to more clearly define and stabilise the power balance; and third, the lack of a clear-cut resolution of this latter test would set in motion a crisis sequence which would serve as an alternative Sino-American confrontation short of all-out war.

Crisis context

Capability and will. The first precondition was the capability and will (two essential components of 'power') of Peking and Washington to engage in a more direct test of strength than was the case in Indochina.

With regard to China's capability, one must return to the paramount dilemma of poverty, which always acted as a built-in limitation on the scope of operational policy. The resources at the disposal of Chinese Communist strategists had been seriously taxed by the Korean War, further limited by assistance to the Viet Minh, and were being further claimed by the pressing demands of economic development accompanying the implementation of the first Five-Year Plan. On the other hand, the ideological doctrine that politics takes precedence over economics, combined with the ability to mobilise manpower on an enormous scale (in spite of the unfavourable ratio of population

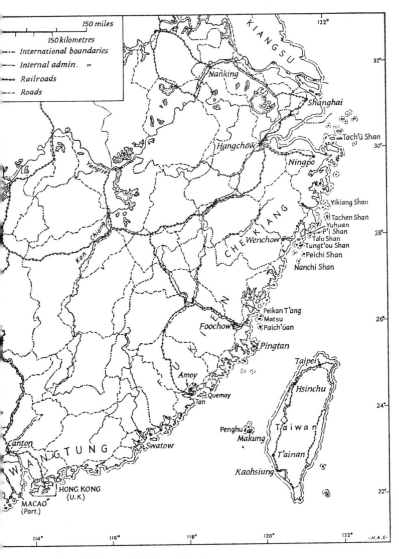

Fig. 6. East China and Taiwan Straits

to food supply) and the willingness, through totalitarian methods, to emphasise long-term economic growth over short-term consumer demands, have all given Peking greater freedom of manoeuvre than, say, Delhi or Djakarta.

In the American case, the inherent economic limits were obviously not as severe. Nevertheless, a combination of extensive and expensive global commitments and determined budget-cutting – enforced by the Treasury and manifest in New Look cutbacks in the level of 'peacetime' armed forces – imposed limitations which were very real. Moreover, recent experience in the form of economic recession in 1953–4 had shown that not even determined balancing of the national accounts could ensure a continuation of wartime prosperity.

These limitations, resulting from contradictions of a different order from those of the Chinese scene, had no small influence on American troop cutbacks in Korea, refusal as yet to commit land forces to Indochina, and reluctance to become committed to massive aid ventures such as a Marshall Plan for the Far East, which diplomats like Chester Bowles had long been urging. For Sino-American crisis interactions after 1954, the question became one of how US sea-air-nuclear power would counterbalance Chinese land power.

With regard to will, Peking, as a result of the Geneva Conference, could look forward to increasing influence on the Asian mainland and plan for a test on its maritime flank. This was in line with Mao Tse-tung's strategy of striking 'in only one main direction at a time', articulated in his *Strategic Problems of China's Revolutionary War* (1936):

In 1933 the exponents of military equalitarianism put forward the theory of 'striking with two fists' and splitting the main force of the Red Army in two, to seek victories simultaneously in two strategic directions. As a result, one fist remained idle while the other was tired out with fighting, and we failed to win the greatest victory possible at the time. In my opinion, when we face a powerful enemy, we should employ our army, whether we have ten thousand, a million, or ten million troops, in only one main direction at a time, not two.[1]

The Chinese attitude towards the Taiwan Straits can be interpreted, therefore, in terms of a strategic impulse as well as in terms of its desire to press its foreign policy successes, achieved in Geneva, in the face of what it considered to be minimum opposition.

Before 1955, the US commitment to Taipei, though obvious,

was not well defined, whereas an objective as essential to Peking as the reunification of China could be expected to remain a central concern. Given sufficient will, the Chinese felt they would be able to occupy off-shore islands still held by the Nationalists – near to the mainland and far from Taiwan – without incurring US intervention. Beyond these islands, however, the likelihood of a direct test between Peking and Washington increased. This was true partly because there was no intermediate buffer – no proxy – such as Indochina, to make an indirect Sino-American compromise possible, but mainly because Taiwan was deemed an essential component of the American defence system in the Pacific. In Foster Dulles' words,

In unfriendly hands Formosa would seriously dislocate the existing, even if unstable, balance of forces upon which the peace of the Pacific depends.

It would create a break in the island chain of the Western Pacific that constitutes for the United States and other free nations the geographical backbone of their security structure in that ocean.[2]

In the case of Taiwan (Formosa) and the Penghu Islands (the Pescadores) about 100 miles off the Fukien coast of mainland China,[a] Washington would have either to rescue or to desert Chiang Kai-shek, and it was clear that it would do the former. In this case, it could not afford to repeat the luxury of indecision that it had shared with Saigon in refusing to sign the Geneva Accords while accepting the division of Vietnam.

Washington's Far Eastern policy in the mid-1950s was based in part on a perception of implacable Chinese hostility toward the United States. In a speech delivered at Los Angeles on 11 June 1954, John Foster Dulles described the Chinese nation as a 'mainland with many hundreds of millions of people under a despotic rule that is fanatically hostile to us and demonstrably aggressive and treacherous'.[3] American strategy was therefore directed toward building an 'island and peninsular screen' consisting of an alliance network of anti-communist states. Dulles considered these positions to be not only a shield to protect US power on the Western Pacific but also a sword to deter Chinese

[a] Taipei is 165 miles from Foochow; the shortest distance from Fukien to Taiwan (Pingtan to Hsinchu) is 88 miles. Makung (on the Penghus) is 100 miles from Amoy. By contrast, the contested off-shore islands would be within a twelve-mile territorial limit, which Peking would attempt to enforce during the 1958 crisis.

Communist attacks. In contrast to the Maoist preference for 'one main direction at a time', he subscribed to a

> broad strategy which underlies our desire to maintain at least a potential of three fronts against the Chinese Communists if they should commit open aggression – the one in Korea, the one in Formosa, and the one in Indochina – and the fact that we have those three fronts is far more protective of everybody than if, for example, we concentrated an effort on any one of those three fronts.[4]

Washington's attitude and will to defend the Straits area also consisted of a mixture of ideological and domestic political considerations, somewhat analogous to those prevailing in the Chinese attitude. The Administration was not prepared ideologically to accept the combination of (1) another victory for the international communist spectre, (2) a surrender of the bases essential to the re-establishment of the Free China of its dreams, and (3) the permanence of Communist rule which that surrender would imply all in one blow. Nor was it prepared politically to confront the 'Asia Firsters' led by Senator Knowland (nicknamed the 'Senator from Formosa') and Congressman Judd with news of the surrender of Quemoy and Matsu. On the other hand, the Administration would continue to reject extremist proposals ranging from all-out blockade to pre-emptive strike.

The Administration position was to be paradoxically strengthened as a result of the mid-term elections of November 1954. When the Democrats achieved control of the 84th Congress – never again to lose control in that Branch, after short-lived Republican rule in the 80th and 83rd Congresses – the effect of this victory was the reverse of what might have been expected: it would increase the resolve of the Republican executive to stand firm and draw the issue in such tight 'we-they' terms (the perceived threat from Peking would permit it to do this) that most of the opposition party would unquestioningly join the patriotic bandwagon, at least during Congressional roll-calls at the height of the crisis. This outcome diverged to a certain extent from the Chinese analysis and, by implication, the Chinese expectations. To the Tientsin *Ta Kung Pao*, for instance, the election results demonstrated popular opposition to war, economic depression and fascism, which were seen as the consequences of the Eisenhower Administration's foreign and domestic policies.[5]

It was the opposition-dominated 84th Congress which would come to adopt the joint Formosa Resolution – authorising the use of American armed forces for the defence of Formosa, the Pescadores, and related positions (i.e., the off-shore islands if so defined by the President) – on 25 and 28 January 1955, with only three 'nays' in each chamber. Similarly, the Senate would ratify the Mutual Defense Treaty with Nationalist China on 9 February by a bipartisan vote of 65 to 6.

The same bipartisan consensus under stress would serve the Administration well in resisting the militant pressures of the Republican Asia Firsters in spite of Chinese provocation. On 23 November 1954, for example, PRC tribunals would sentence eleven US airmen and two civilian employees of the US Army to long prison terms for espionage. On 27 November, following strong protests from the Eisenhower Administration, lame-duck Majority Leader Knowland would call for naval blockade of the PRC 'until these Americans are released'.[6] Two days later, Secretary Dulles – in a show of independence due partly to fears for the safety of the American captives and partly to the reduced electoral prestige of the Congressional wing of the Republican party – was to tell a Chicago audience that blockade would be an act of war; the imprisonment was 'a challenge to us . . . to find ways, consistent with peace, to sustain international rights and justice'. On December, however, he was to say that naval blockade was 'certainly a possibility' if peaceful means to obtain the release of the Americans were to fail.[7] The Administration was to be divided between a desire to secure the release of its airmen, who had in effect become Chinese hostages, and an impulse to retaliate against Peking for what it regarded as a long list of unjustified provocations. In the context of the ensuing strengthening of its alignment with Taipei, it is difficult not to agree with the leader which appeared in *The Straits Times* in late November: 'Peking could not have chosen a more certain means of hardening the American attitude, of worsening delicate relations, or of rendering futile the efforts of others to ease the tensions.'[8]

The Administration's domestic 'success' with regard to the mutual security treaty, the Formosa Resolution, and (partly) the issue of American prisoners would serve to compensate for restrictions on its freedom of manoeuvre which were built into its internal constitutional order and into its external alliance structure. The way would be left open for an extension of the somewhat Byzantine (Macmillan uses the word 'devious') diplomacy of Dullesian containment, expressed in terms of strengthened American resolve over the Taiwan Straits in the spring of 1955.

The solution for Peking, in the face of this increasing US resolve, would have been to defer the 'liberation' of Taiwan and the Penghus and to be satisfied with occupying the off-shore islands; if the two island groups had been clearly de-coupled, in terms of security as well as of geography, it would have been much more difficult for Dulles to argue that intervention was in the national interest of the United States. It is interesting, in this respect, that Mao had told Edgar Snow in 1936 that the CCP would enthusiastically support the independence of both Korea and Taiwan from China and Japan.[9] However, in 1943, the same Cairo Declaration which had promised Korea its independence promised Taiwan to China; since then, both Nationalists and Communists agreed that Taiwan was an integral part of China. From 1949, both resisted the notion of 'two Chinas', which became increasingly attractive (at least unofficially) to Europeans in the 1950s, Americans in the 1960s, and even the Russians – not only as a stop-gap measure but as a solution to the problem of recognition and UN membership of the PRC. In this respect, Quemoy and Matsu served as useful symbols, to both Taipei and Peking, of the indivisibility of China and of their claims to each other's territory which they were determined to 'liberate' peacefully if possible, forcefully if necessary. In late 1954, an NCNA commentary drew attention to the possibility of de-coupling the off-shore islands from Taiwan and the Penghus, only to reject it as an Anglo-American ploy 'to preserve the strength of the traitor Chiang Kai-shek's forces to avoid their complete annihilation by the Chinese People's Liberation Army' and an attempt by 'the U.S. aggressive clique' to 'hoodwink world public opinion by arranging for the traitorous Chiang Kai-shek group to "quit" the coastal islands'.[10]

American officials might have been much happier if the islands had never existed in the first place, or alternatively if they had sunk into the China Sea. *Faute de mieux,* however, Washington would slide into a commitment to protect Chiang's forces not only in Formosa and the Pescadores, but in Quemoy and Matsu as well. For an explanation of this extraordinary extension of the US sea-air-nuclear umbrella, one must turn to the first Taiwan Straits crisis itself, bearing in mind that prior to December 1954 – when the crisis would reach its peak – Washington had successfully resisted Chinese Nationalist pressure to conclude a formal mutual defence treaty to counter the 1950 Sino-Soviet treaty. Dulles would be able to exact a *quid pro quo* in granting the treaty to Taipei, however: he would obtain Foreign Minister Yeh's assurance that any 'use of force' against the mainland 'will be a matter of joint agreement' [11] – thereby officially re-leashing Chiang Kai-shek for the first time in the new Administration.[b]

The global balance in flux. The first precondition to a Taiwan Straits crisis was the capability and will of the actors to engage in a test of strength there. The second precondition was the existence of a state of flux in the international setting – at least on the immediate, regional level. In the last chapter, it was observed that 1954 was a year which contained elements of 'thaw' as well as elements of 'freeze'; attempts to stabilise the superpower relationship entailed difficult regional readjustments in relative power (just as the readjusted regional power would affect the development of Soviet-American relations).

The alliance-building activities of the United States and China could be said, then, to have a long-term stabilising effect, but in the short term they served to increase tension in the area. As Dulles was busily occupied in cementing SEATO (infelicitously labelling it an 'Asiatic Monroe Doctrine'), Chou En-lai seemed to genuinely fear that the alliance would entrench American hegemony at the expense of China. In a major foreign affairs report delivered on 11 August, he charged that Dulles' next step would be to form a northeast Asian counterpart, consisting of Japan, Nationalist China, South Korea, and the United States [13] – in spite of objections, especially on the part of Seoul, to any Japanese participation in a regional security pact.[14] Chou's fear was shared by Wu Chuan, writing in *Jen-min Jih-pao*: 'the American war group aims to link up these two military blocs [in southeast and northeast Asia] and form a hostile encirclement of China, tie the

[b] It is perhaps best, at this point, to put Chou En-lai on record as contradicting my interpretation of the American position prior to the winter of 1954–5. On 8 December 1954, Chou asserted that 'The United States Government, refusing to reconcile itself to the defeat of its imperialist policy in China, occupied Taiwan by armed force in June 1950 at the time it launched its war of aggression in Korea, and has been shielding the traitorous Chiang Kai-shek clique and directing it in its uninterrupted war of harassment and destruction . . . Now that . . . it is no longer possible, with the Korean War ended, to use that war as a pretext for the continued occupation of Taiwan, it has come out openly to manufacture this United States–Chiang Kai-shek "Mutual Security Treaty" for the outright seizure of China's territory of Taiwan and the Penghu islands.' [12] At the time that this statement was made, the Dulles-Yeh correspondence was still secret. See p. 142.

Asian countries together with the Syngman Rhee clique and Chiang Kai-shek gangsters as tools for U.S. aggression against China'.[15] This charge was not unfounded: Secretary Dulles had acknowledged in his 3 August news conference, that both a northeast Asian security pact and bilateral security treaty with the ROC were in the 'thought' stage.[16] More indirectly, Chou's claims were based on US preparations for such agreements in the spring and early summer of 1954 – particularly on General Van Fleet's tour of the Far East (as Eisenhower's special envoy) in May, in which such agreements had been reported to be favourably considered. From Taiwan, Reuters reported discussions of both bilateral and regional arrangements, both for the immediate goal of containing the further spread of communism in Asia and for the 'ultimate goal of mainland liberation'.[17] On 9 July, *Jen-min Jih-pao* produced a leader about the General's mission:

Van Fleet's conspiratorial provocations show that the U.S. ruling clique is completely defying the course of events in the world situation. It is incorrigibly hanging on to its adventurist policy though this is meeting with failure everywhere. The Chinese people and all peace-loving governments and peoples of the world have the strength to put a stop to the adventurist activities of the United States, and to prevent it from concluding a 'Bilateral Treaty of Mutual Security', to end the U.S. intrigues for rigging up military blocs . . . and to bring about a further easing of tension in Asia and the whole world, and it is imperative that they do so.[18]

This leader suggests a division between Peking's desire to maintain the flexible, conciliatory stance characteristic of its participation in Geneva and later Bandung and its impetus to make headway over the Taiwan question before Washington entered into bilateral and/or regional security pacts with Taipei. The contradiction between the 'Geneva stand' of Great Power rôle-playing and the 'Taiwan stand' of pursuing national interest would continue to beset Chinese foreign and strategic policy throughout the first Taiwan Straits crisis.

In his August report, Chou also accused Washington and Taipei of plotting to attack the PRC and declared that one of 'the tasks now before us' was 'to take determined action with regard to the liberation of Taiwan so as to safeguard China's sovereignty and territorial integrity'.[c]

---

[c] Harold Hinton points out that 'sovereignty and territorial integrity' could have been used 'in the hope of throwing upon the United States the onus

Taiwan is inviolable Chinese territory, its occupation by the United States absolutely cannot be tolerated, and it is equally intolerable to have Taiwan placed under United Nations trusteeship. The liberation of Taiwan is an exercise of China's sovereignty and China's internal affair; we will brook no foreign interference. Any treaties concluded between the United States Government and the Chiang Kai-shek gang entrenched in Taiwan are illegal and void. If any foreign aggressors dare to try to hinder the Chinese people from liberating Taiwan, if they dare to infringe upon our sovereignty and territorial integrity, if they dare to interfere in our internal affairs, they must take all the grave consequences of such acts of aggression upon themselves.[21]

This important declaration was to be the keynote of the Chinese political position on Taiwan from August 1954 to April 1955. Although the leader on the one hand, and Chou's accusation and declaration on the other, were couched in defensive terms, it was becoming clear that Peking was preparing to combine its threats with actions. On Army Day, Commander-in-Chief Chu Teh delivered an address which emphasised the PLA's duty to liberate Taiwan,[22] and throughout August, the mainland press published articles which (1) emphasised the justice of any Communist attempt to reunify China,[23] (2) exhorted the Chinese people to intensify their preparations to liberate Taiwan,[24] and (3) gave advance warnings, increasingly explicit and frequent, that the PRC seriously intended to achieve reunification. A Joint Declaration of All Democratic Parties and People's Organisations of the People's Republic of China Concerning the Liberation of Taiwan, widely publicised in late August and cited thereafter, stated that 'We solemnly proclaim to the whole world: Taiwan is China's territory. The Chinese people are determined to liberate Taiwan.'[25]

On 1st September, *People's China* published a lengthy article which was the most explicit statement of intent prior to PRC attack. It argued that

> The crimes and misdeeds of Chiang Kai-shek since he took refuge on Taiwan show beyond doubt that he is not only a quisling and a public enemy of the Chinese people, but also an inciter of trouble in Asia. To further ensure peace and order in this part of the world, the Chiang Kai-shek pirates must be eliminated and Taiwan must be returned to the fold of the Chinese People's Republic.

of violating its own principle of the Open Door by allegedly interfering in China's internal affairs'.[19] Even in Secretary of State John Hay's time, however, the principle was respected more in its breach than in its observance.[20]

It then concluded that 'The Chinese people, 600 million with one heart, will fight to accomplish this mission; and accomplish it they will.' [26]

On 3 September, the very day that the Manila Conference opened, Chinese artillery on the Fukien coast began to shell Quemoy. On 7 September, the Nationalists retaliated with air strikes against the mainland, losing three bombers that day over Amoy.[27] The first phase of the crisis had begun.

Hence the state of flux in the international political system, due in part to the American effort to create SEATO (and even conceivably a NEATO), affected both the timing of the probe and the will of the PRC to make that probe in the Taiwan Straits.

What was the background for the Chinese initiative in this particular area? In terms of the Straits themselves, the Nationalists continued to maintain a partially effective blockade from Shanghai to Canton, at a time of Communist foreign trade expansion and coastal development. The two Quemoys (sixty square miles of islands two miles off the port of Amoy), the nineteen Matsus (twelve square miles of islands ten miles off the port of Foochow – both opposite the Fukien coast), and the Tachens (equidistant from Taipei and Shanghai and opposite the Chekiang coast) played a useful part in maintaining the blockade. Furthermore, with American aid, Chiang's forces were occupying the off-shore islands in strength – for the first time in the decade. Following a grand tour of East Asia, Senator H. Alexander Smith, Chairman of the Foreign Relations Committee's sub-committee on the Far East, announced that ROC forces were 'growing in strength' and could be 'of very great importance' in any 'new crisis' with Communist China. 'At the very center of this problem' of peace in the Far East, he averred, 'is ultimately a free and independent China'.[28] Increasing Chinese Nationalist strength and American consciousness of its advantages appeared particularly ominous to Peking, at a time burdened with what Coral Bell has called Secretary Dulles' 'crashingly audible manoeuvres directed to setting up a military alliance in South-east Asia, the loud stage whispers with which he was conducting the quarrel with Britain and bargaining over conditions for military intervention with France' [29] – manoeuvres which kept up their pace through the Geneva Conference and into the summer preparations for SEATO. Dulles' efforts to strengthen the US commitment to the Asian rimlands, from Korea in the northeast to Vietnam in the southwest redounded to the benefit of Chiang

Kai-shek. As James Reston pointed out in April, in an article entitled 'Chiang's Stock Rises', 'the more deeply the United States becomes involved in the defense of that region, the more support (Chiang) can expect from Washington'.[30] The link between developments in Indochina and in the Taiwan Straits was reinforced by Seventh Fleet exercises off the mainland coast on 12 April. United Press International reported from the Formosan port of Kaohsiung that 'the U.S. military establishment sent some of its top authorities on amphibious warfare to Formosa to see just what Chiang Kai-shek might be able to do against the South China coast'.[31]

New China News Agency quickly reacted to this report, stating that 'These provocative acts of the U.S. ruling circles are obviously aimed at aggravating tension in Asia, wrecking the Geneva Conference and furthermore, carrying on their aggressive activities against New China . . . threatening peace and security in the Far East.' [32]

Peking's worries could only have increased with Korean President Rhee's bellicose 28 July speech before a joint session of the American Congress, calling for a joint Korean-Chinese-American assault on Communist China and, if necessary, on the USSR as well,[d] [33] and with Chinese Nationalist threats culminating in Premier O. K. Yui's reference to an invasion of the mainland in mid-August.[34]

This sequence of verbal probes on both sides served to aggravate each side's suspicions of the other's intentions, further distorting the conflict of interest in the Taiwan Straits area. I mentioned earlier the Communist Chinese identification of American with Japanese imperialism [e] and the fear that the imperialist forces were remaining deceptively quiet only in order to regroup later and attempt to forcibly regain Chinese territory. No doubt Peking continued to fear Japan's role in US strategy for the West Pacific; the pro-American Yoshida ministry in Tokyo, the American nuclear base in Okinawa, American control of the

[d] Peking appears to have taken this speech quite seriously, although for Washington it was an embarrassing reminder of deserted aspirations of rollback and liberation. Much of the impact of the speech was due, of course, to the forum in which it was delivered, but it should be recalled that Syngman Rhee had shown quite a knack for landing bombshells at sensitive points before – as when he jeopardised the Korean armistice agreement by releasing thousands of Communist prisoners of war or when he offered to send troops to Indochina after the Berlin Conference.

[e] See p. 10.

Ryukyus, and Peking's concern that the Japanese-American security treaty would be supplemented by a Tokyo-based NEATO could only heighten that fear. It is ironic that Peking's suspicion was shared in full measure by Washington: Dulles and his associates feared a PRC plot to regroup its armed forces and transfer them from the Indochina theatre to the Taiwan Straits at short notice.[35] Chinese troop withdrawals from Korea and non-interference in Indochina offered little consolation from this point of view: *reculer pour mieux sauter* was a spectre shared in both capitals. Nevertheless, the spring–summer international context, while troublesome, was not sufficient to provoke a direct PRC strike against Taiwan and the Penghus, even if that medium-term objective were militarily possible at the time – which it was not, in view of the overwhelming superiority of the Seventh Fleet over the primitive PLA Navy. I would argue that the context served another set of functions:

- as an occasion for the Chinese Communists to demonstrate their disapproval of the Manila Conference and a pretext for them to throw the Nationalist regime off-balance politically,

- as a stimulus for both sides to test the status of the off-shore islands, and

- as an incentive, together with the escalation in the autumn, for the Americans to strengthen their commitment to the Chinese Nationalists.

The first function was perhaps the most influential factor in Peking's timing, for bombardment of the off-shore islands was the most feasible means of indicating to what extent Peking disapproved of the Manila Pact which was about to be signed on 8 September. (One week later, Dulles told a nationwide audience over radio and television that 'This effort to intimidate the Manila conference was a total failure.') [36] Since the threat from the ROC was perceived as part and parcel of the over-all US-instigated menace from the south, such a demonstration had the added virtue of confronting the nearest, most provocative and yet most vulnerable 'imperialist' position at hand. It is true that the Nationalists had used the past five years to consolidate their control of Taiwan and to increase their strength, with American aid. Yet they had no explicit US guarantee of the security of the relatively safe Taiwan and the Penghus, not to mention the far more exposed off-shore islands which did not benefit from the physical interposition of the Seventh Fleet. Moreover, the Chinese Communists had concentrated more than 150 000 troops on the southern coast, facing less than half that number – Taipei had managed to squeeze into the Quemoys nearly 50 000, into the Matsus approximately 9000 and into the Tachens 15 000. These two-to-one odds boded ill for the islands' defenders, no matter how valorous and well entrenched, unless Washington would intervene on their side.

The second function was semi-autonomous in nature, in that continued Sino-American interactions, of the sort prevailing at the beginning of the year, would lead of themselves to a test in the Taiwan Straits. This should not obscure two important facts: that Chinese strategists expected such a test to be resolved in their favour, and that the Americans – absorbed with southeast Asian security dilemmas – failed to do enough to dampen these expectations in the spring and summer.

The Chinese Communists, in proceeding to act on their expectations of success, seem to have made two major tactical errors which are nevertheless understandable in the context of crisis. First, their July and August propaganda failed to distinguish between their designs on the off-shore (coastal) islands and those on Taiwan and the Penghus. *Jen-min Jih-pao*'s leader of July 24th was typical in this respect:

The Chinese people once more declare to the whole world that Taiwan is China's territory and they are determined to liberate it. They will never stop until their aim is achieved. The great Chinese people can never tolerate any encroachment on the territorial integrity and sovereignty of their country. Anyone bent on such encroachment will reap his due deserts.[37]

This distinction, admittedly, was difficult to make in view of the symbolic status of Quemoy and Matsu, which was reinforced under the stress of crisis conditions. The *raison d'être* of the Taipei regime was the recovery of the lost territory on the mainland; the forward position of these coastal islands represented a step in this life-purpose. For Peking to seize these islands, therefore, would mean not only the defeat of Chiang's élite forces but also a critical blow to the precarious psychological make-up of the Nationalist Republic. The off-shore islands symbolised the determination of both Taipei and Peking to rule over one China and reject the alternative of partition which had been forced on Germany, Korea, and Vietnam.

The Chinese Communist refusal to tone down the indivisibility of their designs on the Nationalists made it more difficult for Americans to resist the argument that the sooner a line was drawn in defence of Taipei, the better. The logical outcome of such a negative argument was a positive commitment (the third function) to the defence of the Republic of China. Most US officials felt that the total loss of Chiang's forces would be intolerable, for at least five reasons, however invalid these might seem in retrospect. First, their existence symbolised 'Freedom's' resistance to 'Communism' (both writ large). Second, Taiwan and the Penghus had become identified in American minds with the security of the West Pacific. Third, Chiang's forces in their forward position helped to tie down approximately half-a-million Communist troops. Fourth and fifth, the Nationalist hold on the allegiance of overseas Chinese in Southeast Asia and the Nationalist blockade of the south China coast tended to inhibit the effective expansion of PRC trade and contacts in *nanyang*, the 'south seas'.

The second PRC tactical error lay in the PLA's failure promptly to follow up its bombardment of Quemoy with a full-scale amphibious landing. PLA commanders may have judged that bombardment would weaken the island garrisons both militarily and psychologically, and make an eventual landing more feasible. If this was their judgment, they could not have failed to be influenced both by the failure of their forty-man landing force to reveal any significant Nationalist vulnerability in Quemoy in late August [38] (indeed, the ROC Air Force's retaliatory bombing in the following fortnight assumed proportions far in excess of the original probe) and by their recollections of major PLA losses in the attempt to invade Quemoy in 1949. PLA commanders may also have been held back by the desire of their superiors to limit themselves, on the one hand, to a demonstration of disapproval of US attempts to institutionalise collective security in the Far East, and, on the other, to a demonstration of intent to occupy the off-shore islands without incurring undue risks. All of these possibilities were compatible, furthermore, with the over-all PRC interest in probing anti-Communist positions whose guarantees remained ambiguous.

As if to test the relative efficacy of each, the PLA engaged in three different kinds of probes in September. Bombers which appeared over Tachen Shan in early September were repelled by ROC anti-aircraft fire. A preliminary PLA attempt in late September to land forces on Peikan T'ang island (one of the Matsu group) was beaten back by the island's defenders and counter-attacked by ROC bombers, which claimed to have sunk five motorised junks and damaged six others, out of a total fleet of forty to fifty.[39] And at the same time, sporadic gunfire was ex-changed between the Nationalist-held Quemoy and the Com-munist-held Amoy island groups, alternating with exchanges of surface-to-surface bombardments between islands and mainland coast.

Each probe was frustrated, but this did not discourage a build-up of PLA forces, on the coastal belt between Amoy and Hangchow, to a level of roughly 280 000 men by the end of September.[40]

Peking had clearly failed to foresee the full extent and implica-tions of Taipei's decision to resist and retaliate: the protracted test in artillery, air strikes and endurance developed into a process of escalating and expanding stakes – a process which made it well-nigh impossible for Washington *not* to intervene. What was surely intended as an exercise in risk-taking up to but not including American intervention was to lead irretrievably to outright American commitment and Communist Chinese loss of face. I refer primarily to what Thomas Schelling calls 'the more serious kind of "face" . . . consisting of other countries' beliefs . . . about how the country can be expected to behave. It relates not to a country's "worth" or "status" or even "honor", but to its reputation for action.'[41] The criterion of status may have been just as important in the thinking of Chinese leaders, however. On both counts, the outcome of this test must be considered the first major reverse for Peking's crisis handlers.

First, then, the test was defined in total unification, all-or-nothing, zero-sum terms [f] by Taipei and Peking, thereby inhibit-

[f] Excepted from this general conclusion is an anomolous range of islands be-tween the Tachen and Matsu groups. These comprised (1) Nanchi Shan, off Wenchow Bay, which the ROC did not occupy until August 1952 and which the Tachen Defence Command was preparing as a substitute for the Tachens as early as November 1954; (2) Peichi Shan, fifteen miles to the northeast, which Communist and Nationalist forces used successively as a staging point against Nanchi Shan, but which neither side bothered to occupy after 1952; and (3) Tungt'ou and Yuhuan Islands, respectively twenty-five and fifty miles to the north of Nanchi Shan, which served as advance command posts for the 7th PLA Group.[42] This range of islands is interesting because Washington never felt compelled to intervene over their fate and because Peking and Taipei tacitly accepted each other's stakes, with Peichi Shan as a no-man's-land between Communist positions

ing potential advocates of a middle course in Washington (and, for that matter, in Moscow). Next, the opportunity that effective *timing* might have provided Peking, in terms of minimising the chances of US intervention, was lost as a result of the indecisive September attack on Quemoy. The crisis thereupon shifted from the plane of Communist-Nationalist confrontation, with the Nationalists acting partly as US proxies, to that of crisis inter-actions primarily between the PRC and the USA.

Gradual escalation of the crisis

The lack of a clear-cut resolution of the September 1954 test in the Taiwan Straits resulted in unanticipated consequences. To start with, Taipei used the October breathing space which followed the PRC's initial probes to transform US concerns both with deterrence of further aggression and with construction of collective security systems into concrete political-military protec-tion of its exposed positions. This Taipei succeeded in doing by obtaining, first, substantial US operational commitment by the autumn of 1954 and, second, formal treaty commitments during the winter of 1954–5. On 17 August, President Eisenhower had told his press conference that he had issued instructions in early 1953 to defend Formosa, which 'merely reaffirmed orders that had been in force in that fleet since 1950. These orders are still in force. Therefore, I should assume what would happen is this: any invasion of Formosa would have to run over the Seventh Fleet.' [43] After a National Security Council conference at the Denver White House on 12 September, however, US strategy took a more active note than simply relying on the presence of the Seventh Fleet and remaining silent on the off-shore islands issue. On the one hand, when the State Department (with the prominent exception of Under Secretary Smith) and all of the Joint Chiefs save General Ridgway advised him to help the Nationalists to bomb the mainland, Eisenhower refused on the grounds that the risks were too high.[g][45] On the other

to the north and Nationalist positions to the south. In addition to revealing that Taipei had become resigned to the loss of the Tachens in November, the sparse accounts of these islands show how important contestation and investment of prestige during crisis can be for the future of off-shore islands with relatively little intrinsic value for their landlords.

[g] Eisenhower relates that he told Admiral Radford that 'We're not talking now about a limited, bush-fire war. We're talking about going to the threshold of World War III. If we attack China, we're not going to impose

hand, Eisenhower found it quite easy to approve Secretary Dulles' suggestion to ask the UN Security Council to institute a cease-fire in the Formosa Straits on the basis of the status quo, knowing full well that a Soviet veto would help to justify further Western steps to come to the aid of the ROC.[46]

In October, news of strengthening and consolidation both of US and ROC headquarters and of the 'Western Enterprises', a front for joint espionage activities by Washington and Taipei, were resulting in increasingly vocal protests from Peking.[47] It was becoming apparent to Communist decision-makers that their probes had not resulted in a green light from Washington; they faced instead an amber light, consisting of growing operational involvement by US advisers, supply vessels and aircraft, but still no formal commitment by the US Government to the defence of ROC territory.

In November, Peking produced further signals warning of its continued resolve to extract a more favourable outcome from the gradual escalation of the crisis. On the 1st, the PLA Air Force bombed both the upper and lower Tachens as well as Yikiang Shan (less than seven miles from the main Tachen group), and followed the bombings with artillery and gunboat attacks on Yikiang Shan, P'i Shan (both off the Chekiang coast), and the Paich'üan Islands (off the Fukien coast).[48] NCNA explained from the Chekiang Front that

Directed and protected by the aggressive junta in the U.S., the gang of Chiang traitors has been using these islands as an important base for plundering and seizing fishing boats and merchant ships on the seas, harassing the coastal areas of the mainland and menacing and undermining maritime shipping and the security of the people living along the coast.[49]

The Chinese Nationalists were able to hold firm, however, and even to counter-attack by sea and air against the Communist-held Hsienmen and Talu Islands off the Chekiang coast.[50]

limits on our military actions, as in Korea. Moreover, if we get into a general war, the logical enemy will be Russia, not China, and we'll have to strike there.' [44] It is hard to believe that Eisenhower articulated his thoughts quite so coherently at the time, but this superficially hawkish statement accurately reflects (1) his well-grounded fear of uncontrollable escalation, based in part on his position during the Indochina crisis; (2) his prejudice against gradual escalation, which gives the enemy the chance to adjust and respond effectively to modified circumstances; and (3) his operational compromise between these two conflicting attitudes, consisting of a rejection of massive-cum-selective retaliation in all but the most threatening contingencies.

In the face of successful resistance to its September and November attacks, the PLA continued its military build-up, delaying further intensive attacks until the following January. At the same time, US and ROC preparations to conclude a bilateral defence agreement were denounced in the strongest terms, which suggested that a treaty between Washington and Taipei would provoke a rapid escalation of the crisis. On 23 November, the Tientsin *Ta Kung Pao* declared that 'We stand strongly opposed to a U.S.–Chiang Kai-shek "mutual defence pact". If it is concluded in defiance of world-wide opposition, this blood-thirsty document will so far from preventing the Chinese people from liberating Taiwan, add to their righteous wrath.' [51]

The Americans and Nationalists remained undeterred by this rhetoric, however, and proceeded to capitalise on the lull in the crisis. On 2 December, Secretary Dulles and Foreign Minister Yeh signed a Mutual Defense Treaty whose scope was deliberately limited to Taiwan and the Penghus, unless both sides agreed to extend the treaty area. The preceding months of gradual crisis escalation were undoubtedly decisive in persuading Washington to commit itself to the extent of a guarantee of the two main islands held by the ROC, the islands of greatest strategic significance to the United States at the time. Whereas Taipei had proposed a security agreement as far back as December 1953, Washington had procrastinated until the stress of the Taiwan Straits crisis led it to view the advantages of a bilateral security pact in a new light. Peking's response to the signing of the Treaty was prompt: on the 3rd, the pact was labelled an instrument of US aggression, 'an outrageous act on the part of the United States Government to prevent the Chinese people from liberating their own territory Taiwan and the Penghu Islands'.[52] Two days later, *Jen-min Jih-pao* published a long leader denouncing the Treaty, insisting once again that 'Taiwan is China's territory', and asserting that the Chinese people love peace but

do not fear any sort of war threats and will not beg for peace by sacrificing their sacred territory.
The Chinese people's determination to liberate Taiwan is unalterable. The signing of the U.S.–Chiang Kai-shek 'mutual security treaty' is illegal and invalid and the American war clique must be responsible for all consequences that may arise from this illegal 'treaty'.[53]

It is noteworthy that the mainland press concentrated on denouncing the commitment to Taiwan and the Penghus, understating the possibility of Washington's extending its protection to the off-shore islands.[54] In so doing, Peking may well have been carefully preparing the way for seizing as many of the off-shore islands as possible, without surrendering its claims to the main islands, before the full extent of Washington's commitment would become defined.

According to Foreign Minister Yeh, Dulles 'revealed that he would have difficulty in having the treaty ratified if it included the off-shore islands'.[55] In the context of the subsequent Congressional debates in January and February, this seems unlikely, although there was an articulate minority which disapproved of the Administration's somewhat open-ended commitment. A more likely explanation is that the dangers of US involvement in conflict within sight of the mainland sufficiently exceeded the conceivable benefits – the maintenance of Kuomintang morale and the blockade of Amoy and Foochow, ports which could otherwise be employed for launching an invasion of Formosa – to forestall any cast-iron US guarantee of the off-shore islands. John Beal puts part of the thinking behind the ambiguous US commitment to the off-shore islands very well: because the islands were so vulnerable to Communist attack,

it was unwise to risk prestige by saying we would not permit them to be taken; furthermore, if we started naming 'related positions' specifically we would in effect be pledging American defense of every Nationalist-held pile of rocks off the China coast, or, by failing to name some, inferentially inviting the Chinese Communists to take them without opposition.[56]

He does not indicate clearly enough, however, the dilemma of US policy-makers, caught between a realisation of the advantages of having more than one hundred miles, rather than less than twenty miles, of buffer zone between Communist and Nationalist positions, on the one hand, and an understanding of the symbolic importance of the off-shore islands in maintaining morale, on the other. In short, while Quemoy and Matsu appeared more related to the insecurity of the mainland, in objective terms, than to the security of Formosa and the Pescadores, subjectively the ROC commitment to these off-shore islands was sufficiently intense to preclude any strong US pressure to evacuate them. As Eisenhower was to explain to Churchill in early February, US policy was influenced by the fact that the Chinese Nationalists 'are held together by a conviction that some day they will go back to the mainland'.

As a consequence, their attitude toward Quemoy and the Matsus, which they deem the stepping stones between the two hostile regions, is that the surrender of those islands would destroy the reason for the existence of the Nationalist forces on Formosa. This, then, would mean the almost immediate conversion of that asset into a deadly danger because the Communists would immediately take it over.[57]

The Administration opted instead for a policy designed to de-fuse the Taiwan Straits as a crisis area. The first step in this direction was to exact an ROC promise, on 10 December, to make any 'use of force . . . a matter of joint agreement, subject to action of an emergency character which is clearly an exercise of the inherent right of self-defense'.[58] This promise, contained in an exchange of letters between Dulles and Yeh, amounted to a Nationalist undertaking not to attack Communist territory, in return for a US guarantee of Formosa and the Pescadores. In another letter to Churchill, Eisenhower explicitly defined the limits which Washington had succeeded in placing on Taipei's freedom of action. Chiang agreed not to

conduct any offensive operations against the mainland either from Formosa *or from his coastal positions*, except in agreement with us. Thus we are in a position to preclude what you refer to as the use of these off-shore islands as 'bridgeheads for a Nationalist invasion of Communist China', or as a base for 'sporadic war against the mainland' or 'the invasion of the mainland of China'.[59]

American pressure seemed noteworthy, then, not for forcing the Nationalists to relinquish the main off-shore positions of Quemoy and Matsu – which all of the crisis actors had recognised as powerful symbols of Chinese reunification in the long (and in-definite) term – but for making Taipei recognise the impossi-bility of using them as short-term 'bridgeheads' in the face of both enemy and allied resistance.

Washington tended to consider its commitment as relatively modest, defensive and constructive in nature. To Peking, how-ever, these moves were very ominous indeed, in view of Dulles' apparent failure to rule out the use of force – while the Dulles-Yeh correspondence was kept secret for a month. Peking was more aware of American right-wing domestic pressures, US sponsorship of a pan-Asian anti-Communist collective security pact and US-ROC diplomatic collaboration. Chou En-lai himself declared on 8 December that the Mutual Defense Treaty 'can in no sense be called a defensive treaty; it is a treaty of naked ag-gression'.[60] Added to this, the 'continuous tactical training' of the

Seventh Fleet in mid-December was taken by Peking to be further confirmation of deliberate American provocation against
the PRC.[61]

Accelerated escalation of the crisis

In response to what they deemed to be US aggressive initiatives
in an area of primary interest to themselves, the Chinese stepped
up their denunciation on the declaratory level and intensified
their activity on the operational level, with the apparent aim of
securing maximum advantage while minimising the chances of
US intervention. In the same 8 December statement, Chou En-
lai warned the US that it would face 'grave consequences' if it
did not withdraw 'all its armed forces' from Taiwan: the PRC
was determined 'to liberate Taiwan and liquidate the traitorous
Chiang Kai-shek clique'. In addition, Peking secured a Soviet
declaration of 'full support' for its demands on 15 December,
and on Christmas Day the National Committee of the Chinese
People's Consultative Conference declared that 'the Chinese people will never rest until Taiwan is liberated' and that 'The attempt by the aggressive circles in the United States to occupy
Taiwan and extend aggression against China by means of their
treaty with Chiang Kai-shek can only strengthen the Chinese
people's determination to liberate Taiwan and put an end to the
Chiang Kai-shek traitor gang.' [62]

On the operational level, Peking continued to capitalise on the
thirteen American and other Allied prisoners from the Korean
War, still under its control. In effect, the prisoners served the
role of hostages, assuring a US reluctance to yield too far to
domestic and ROC pressures for more drastic action over the
Taiwan Straits. In line with this approach, the January 1955 mission of Secretary-General Hammarskjöld to Peking was restricted
to a joint communiqué with Chou En-lai, on 10 January, saying
that the 'talks have been useful and we hope to be able to continue the contact established in these meetings'.[63]

Peking drove home the contrived coincidence by co-ordinat-
ing negotiation with Washington and other Allied capitals,
through the good offices of Dag Hammarskjöld, with an intensification of its attacks on the off-shore islands. As the Communists
were accelerating their construction of jet airfields next to the
Straits, Chiang Kai-shek forecast war 'at any time'.[64] And on 10
January 1955, the ROC Defence Ministry announced that the

Tachen Islands were being subjected to the most intensive air attacks in the whole of the Civil War, in which an estimated one hundred PRC planes were engaged.[65] Three days later, NCNA Commentator Kiang Nan declared that 'Both the open understandings and secret assurances between the United States and the gang of Chiang Kai-shek traitors prove completely that the United States–Chiang Kai-shek treaty is a war treaty for aggression.' [66]

The pay-off of the new phase of PRC crisis strategy came in the following week. On 14 January, Washington leaked the Dulles-Yeh correspondence which had effectively re-leashed Taipei in December, and two days later, Hammarskjöld said that he planned to communicate the Nationalist pledge to Peking.[h][69] These moves served to signal provisional US restraint to the PRC even in the face of military attack on peripheral ROC positions. These signals were verified on the 18th, when four thousand PLA troops defeated one thousand Nationalist commandos, invading and occupying Yikiang Shan, eight miles north of the Tachens, without provoking US intervention.[70] The next day, over 200 PLA aircraft bombed the Tachens – provoking ROC bombing of coastal shipping but again no operational US response. In startling contrast to the hair-raising noises which poorly-controlled sources had emitted in the previous two years, Washington restricted itself to mild rhetoric for the time being: on the 19th, President Eisenhower shared with a news conference his pious hope that the UN would 'exercise its good offices' to obtain a cease-fire in the Straits.[71]

By mid-January, then, Peking had scored its first substantial success of the crisis by ensuring provisional American restraint, which in turn permitted it once again to concentrate its attention – and firepower – on the Nationalist enemy. The next logical steps would be the securing and extension of gains and the fur-

---

[h] Taipei ineffectually attempted to 'clarify' US and UN interpretations by emphasising that it would decide when to use force in self-defence, although it was only 'natural' for it to consult its American ally prior to doing so.[67] NCNA professed to discount the effectiveness of American 'releasing' of Chiang Kai-shek, citing Japanese reports that Washington secretly accepted Taipei's right to attack the mainland. Its conclusion that 'Western efforts to pretend that the United States–Chiang Kai-shek treaty is "defensive" have a hollow ring' [68] was contradicted, however, by the clear understanding between Dulles and Yeh that unilateral use of force was excluded for all practical purposes and by the operational – as opposed to the propaganda – response of the PRC.

ther testing of the limits of US tolerance for such alterations in political cartography.[72]

While it was superficially inconsistent with long-standing US policy to countenance any rewards for aggression, there were too many good, practical reasons for a mild policy of appeasement over the issue of the Tachens to stand in the way of ideological considerations. These reasons did not consist simply of the rationale that Chiang should so re-group and concentrate his forces as to assure maximum safety for the strongholds of Formosa and the Pescadores – although this was an important factor: at an emergency meeting on the 19th, Secretary Dulles argued that

It is unlikely that any of the off-shore islands can be defended without large-scale American armed help. Therefore, I believe we must modify our policy: we should assist in the evacuation of the Tachens, but as we do so we should declare that we will assist in holding Quemoy and possibly the Matsus, as long as the Chinese Communists profess their intention to attack Formosa.[73]

Equally important factors were the safety of the American hostages, the over-all stabilisation of the Straits, and the maintenance of Chinese Nationalist morale – but not necessarily prestige. The factor of morale depended to a large extent on the degree of publicity which the various off-shore islands had received – high for Quemoy and Matsu, low for the other off-shore islands: it was not difficult to save face – and morale – while giving up the little-known Tachens.[74]

In the course of the first Taiwan Straits crisis, then, Washington was perfectly ready to tolerate Taipei's surrender not only of Yikiang Shan but also of the Tachens which the ROC began to evacuate with US 'assistance' and under US 'protection' on 4 February. In fact, the evacuation of 20 000 civilians and 10 000 troops, not only from the Tachens but from neighbouring Yu Shan and Pen Shan as well, was carried out entirely by the US Navy and Air Force under the direction of Admiral Stump, Commander-in-Chief of the Pacific Fleet. In this operation, Stump was authorised 'to attack Red Chinese airfields, if self-defense so required'.[75] The fact that Washington announced both the operation and its protective role was a fairly reasonable indicator of the considerable pressure to which it had subjected Taipei. To Peking, the 'liberation' of the Tachens 'is a reliable guarantee showing the Chinese people are fully capable of completing their sacred task of liberating Taiwan', although because of 'fires and blasts set off by demolition groups of the US Navy, the Tachen Islands have been reduced to ruins'. (There was no hint, however, of the damage caused by PLA bombardment.) [76]

Two weeks later, Taipei transferred four thousand troops from Nanchi Shan to Matsu,[77] thereby relinquishing the base it had so carefully prepared over the winter.[i] At least the move enabled the Nationalists to consolidate their remaining off-shore positions opposite Foochow and (with Quemoy) opposite Amoy.[78] By this time, most US officials had persuaded themselves that their Chinese allies needed above all to concentrate their forces in fewer and closer island positions.[j]

In spite of Taipei's anger at apparent US betrayal, American appeasement was strictly provisional and temporary: the Administration was prepared to use any further Chinese Communist demands to rally public and Congressional opinion to a more active and concerted policy. On one side, Taipei secured an informal understanding from Washington that Quemoy and Matsu would be defended in return for the surrender of the Tachens.[80] On the other side, Peking soon came to the aid of the Administration – whose commitment to Quemoy and Matsu officially depended on their bearing to the security of Formosa and the Pescadores – by associating, predictably enough, its preliminary gains with its long-term objective of total liberation and re-unification. This was confirmed on 24 January, when Chou En-lai rejected the proposed cease-fire and reiterated his country's resolve to invade Taiwan.

On the same day, Eisenhower sent a special message to Congress, requesting emergency authorisation to protect Formosa, the Pescadores and related positions. This he justified because of their importance, in this view, for the 'island chain of the Western Pacific' and the 'existing balance of moral, economic and military forces upon which the peace of the Pacific depends'. To this vision of collective security he added the fear of further aggression: the Communists had undertaken 'a series of provoca-

---

[i] See note f p. 135. Although the Nationalist evacuated Nanchi Shan without overt US assistance, it is difficult to believe that they agreed to withdraw from both the Tachens and their planned substitute without being exposed to US pressure.

[j] A prominent exception was Admiral Carney, Chief of Naval Operations, who argued that it would be easier for the US to defend the Tachens than to evacuate the 30 000 troops and civilians on these islands. Although supported by the other Joint Chiefs (except Ridgway), he was unable to change Eisenhower's mind.[79]

tive political and military actions, establishing a pattern of aggressive purpose', and were in danger of 'misjudging our firm purpose and national unity' and even 'readiness to fight if necessary'.[81]

The net effect of the sequence of PRC successes – which the Administration had effectively underwritten – was not only Congressional approval of the Formosa Resolution in late January but also the Senate's consent to the Mutual Defense Treaty in early February – both by overwhelming margins.

The principal results of these two Legislative acts were threefold: first, to lend prestige to Executive decisions in the Taiwan Straits crises; second, to confirm the US guarantee of Formosa and the Pescadores in unequivocal terms; and third, to grant the President a 'predated authorisation', in Senator Morse's words, to extend this guarantee to other Nationalist-held territories if he considered them to be sufficiently related to the defence of Formosa and the Pescadores. Congress resolved

That the President of the United States be and he hereby is authorized to employ the Armed Forces of the United States as he deems necessary for the specific purpose of securing and protecting Formosa and the Pescadores against armed attack, this authority to include the securing and protection of such related positions and territories of that area now in friendly hands [i.e., the off-shore islands] and the taking of such other measures as he judges to be required or appropriate in assuring the defense of Formosa and the Pescadores.[82]

It is to the credit of certain Senators that they quickly recognised the dangers inherent in granting carte blanche to the Executive, whose Constitutional prerogatives were already sufficient for handling crises short of declaration of war. For example, in January Senator Humphrey argued, quite correctly, that there was not 'one iota of evidence' to show that Quemoy and Matsu, so close to the mainland and distant from Taiwan, had to be 'essential to the defense of Formosa'. The one-day debate over the Mutual Defense Treaty was even more pointed, because of the realisation that the Chinese Nationalist position would be both legitimised and given permanence (expressed by Senator Kefauver) and because of qualms ranging from Senator Morse's fear of the increased possibility of war, on the one hand, to Senator Lehman's complaint that the Formosa Resolution gave the President quite enough authority as it was: 'What contribution is made, what strength is taken on, what further pause is given to the Chinese Communists by virtue of this treaty?'[83]

Just as the surrender of Yikiang Shan ensured the near-unanimous approval of the Resolution, however, so the surrender of the Tachens, along with a PRC refusal to join the UN Security Council in discussing New Zealand's ill-fated cease-fire resolution [k] over-rode most objections to the Treaty. Most shared Senator Knowland's determination to 'serve notice that this area will not be used as a blue chip in an international poker game' – although they did not pause to reflect that such an injunction rubbed both ways – and some even agreed with Senator Wiley's view that 'Either we can defend the United States in the Straits of Formosa – now – or we can defend it later in San Francisco Bay.' [85] Against Secretary Dulles' generally accepted argument that 'In the face of Communist probing deeds and blustering words, the United States should remain calm, but it should remain firm in its purpose' of resisting international Communism,[86] the most that his critics could muster were three *non-binding* 'understandings' contained in the Foreign Relations Committee's report on the Mutual Defense Treaty to the Senate: first, that the Administration should seek Senate approval for US military action over the off-shore islands; second, that the Treaty did not imply any change in the legal status of Formosa (which remained theoretically under US occupation after the defeat of Japan); [87] third, that the US would be committed to defend the ROC 'only in the event of external armed attack and that military operations by either party . . . shall not be undertaken except by joint agreement'.[88]

The Treaty, and more particularly the Senators' failure explicitly to restrict its scope, was viewed by Peking with considerable misgiving as 'a serious provocation against the Chinese people (which) represents a new move by Washington to aggravate the situation in the Far East and step up preparations for a new world war . . . Nominally a treaty, it is really a deed of transfer designed to make the U.S. occupation of Taiwan permanent and "legitimate".' [89]

[k] A *Jen-min Jih-pao* leader of 29 January made abundantly clear why Peking opposed the resolution: 'To have a cease-fire with the Chiang Kai-shek nest of traitors is to sell out the interests of the Chinese people. It would mean allowing the United States to perpetuate its occupation of Taiwan and the Penghu Islands . . . (and) . . . the division of China . . . It would mean tolerating the establishment on Chinese territory of U.S. military bases that would be used as a springboard to extend aggression against China and prepare for a new war. No matter whether it is put forward by the United Nations or by any single state, this cease-fire plot contravenes the United Nations Charter and constitutes intervention in China's internal affairs.' [84]

Advocacy of forward defence and concern caused by such advocacy crystallised quite naturally over Quemoy and Matsu. Here were two groups of islands which, while not unimportant in view of their geographic position, were to assume a wholly disproportionate significance both for the Nationalists, who (like the French in Dienbienphu) invested the élite third of their forces in their defence, and for the Americans, who did not wish to jeopardise the morale of their ally and incur the onus of permitting another Dienbienphu. The awkward (to say the least) position in which the US found itself because of this ROC investment of manpower is revealed by a letter from Eisenhower to Churchill of 19 February, in which he agreed that

Diplomatically it would indeed be a great relief to us if the line between the Nationalists and the Communists were actually the broad Strait of Formosa instead of the narrow Straits between Quemoy and Matsu and the mainland. However, there are about 55 000 of the Nationalist troops on these coastal islands and the problem created thereby cannot, I fear, be solved by us merely announcing a desire to transplant them to Formosa.

The 'problem' to which Eisenhower was euphemistically referring was a case of neat Nationalist diplomatic blackmail, from which a discomfited Administration could not hope to extract itself unless it was prepared to abandon its Chinese ally, which it quite clearly was not: 'We must not lose Chiang's army and we must maintain its strength, efficiency and morale.' The succession of compromises with the Communists over peripheral areas could no longer continue, in the Administration's view, without risking a débâcle of the first order, given the Nationalist commitment to some off-shore presence and the determination which underlay that commitment. As Eisenhower put it to Churchill,

Only a few months back we had both Chiang and a strong, well-equipped French Army to support the free world's position in Southeast Asia. The French are gone – making it clearer than ever that we cannot afford the loss of Chiang unless all of us are to get completely out of that corner of the globe. This is unthinkable to us – I feel it must be to you.[90]

Phase of declension

The essential ambiguity of the extent and conditions of US commitment to Quemoy and Matsu, which the Administration intentionally wrote into the Formosa Resolution, disconcerted advocates both of forward ROC 'defence' and of a stable buffer zone between Taiwan and the mainland – the former because they suspected that the US commitment to Quemoy and Matsu could and should have been even more explicit,[1] and the latter because they feared that the US would be prepared to go to war over 'small islands', in Adlai Stevenson's words, 'that lie almost as close to the coast of China as Staten Island does to New York'. Stevenson went on to ask: 'Are the off-shore islands essential to the security of the U.S.? Are they, indeed, even essential to the defense of Formosa – which all Americans have agreed upon since Truman sent the Seventh Fleet there five years ago?' [92] Dulles' comment, on 12 April, that the titular Democratic leader 'suggests, as original ideas, the very approaches which the Government has been and is actively exploring', was not merely a querulous 'I'm-in-charge-here' rejoinder. It contained a hint of the Administration's preoccupation with being sufficiently committed both to deter any serious PRC risk-taking and to bolster ROC morale, while remaining sufficiently flexible both to encourage tacitly an eventual 'two-Chinas' outcome with the Straits as a buffer and to discourage Taipei, in the interim, from taking Quemoy and Matsu seriously as 'stepping-stones' for liberating the mainland.

In the end, this domestic debate had as little to do with the dénouement of the first crisis as a similar debate would with the second crisis in 1958. During the course of the debate, the crisis had become stalemated as Peking's tests revealed rapidly solidifying enemy commitments – both in terms of the energy with which the Nationalists reciprocated any seizure of islets, between the Tachens in the north and the Quemoys and Matsus in the south, and in terms of the increasing US verbal and physical support for the ROC defence. In the face of this solidifying commitment, Peking chose not to accept the high risk of US intervention which any test of its writ over Quemoy and Matsu would entail. This concrete decision was suitably disguised by rhetoric: in response to Eisenhower's renewed offer to end hostilities under the UN aegis, Radio Peking rejected the idea of a cease-fire and called on the UN rather to 'take steps to check US aggression against China', on 29 January.[93] On 3 February, Peking rejected

[1] Admiral Radford, for instance, felt that 'we should include the off-shore islands in our defense perimeter out there and just make it stick. In other words, we should eliminate the off-shore islands as a cause of friction by saying that we would defend them. Then the Communists wouldn't try to take them.' [91]

the UN Security Council invitation to attend a discussion of a cease-fire in the Straits, saying that they would only attend if they were given the ROC seat on the Council.[94]

Full impasse was reached, then, by the time of US ratification of the Mutual Defense Treaty with Nationalist China. During February and March, any hint of a break-through became quickly submerged in a series of denunciations and counter-denunciations. A good example of this state of affairs was the fate of Chou En-lai's offer, on 28 February, to negotiate the release of China's thirteen American prisoners with an unofficial US delegation. The Administration rejected the offer as inappropriate and demanded the immediate release of all prisoners; this response was supplemented by Secretary Dulles' warning to Peking, in a nationwide broadcast on 8 March, not to underestimate US determination to meet aggression in the Far East. Not only did SEATO 'possess plenty of strength' in this area, but also the US contribution of naval and air forces was 'equipped with new and powerful weapons of precision,[m] which can utterly destroy military targets without endangering unrelated civilian centers'.[95] And President Eisenhower privately revealed years afterward that 'Under certain conditions – if they (the Chinese Communists) got too aggressive and arrogant – we had selected targets that we would hit. And we never talked about strategic bombing in the sense of going at great populated areas. These were just airfields and supporting points around the Quemoy and Matsu complex.'[96]

The extent of US determination not to concede any further territory to the PRC, at least under crisis conditions, had by that time become clear, not least to American decision-makers themselves. Both Chiang Kai-shek and George K. C. Yeh assert that the ROC withdrawal from the Tachen Islands was made in return for a US guarantee of the Quemoys and Matsus[97] – according to Chiang, in the form of an oral promise made by Dulles; according to Yeh, in the form of a tacit understanding between Washington and Taipei. At a White House meeting on 10 March, following a two-week tour of southeast Asia and the western Pacific, Secretary Dulles took the US commitment to defend these off-shore islands sufficiently seriously to speak in terms of using atomic weapons which, in his judgment, 'alone will be effective against the mainland airfields'.[98]

Two weeks before, at a SEATO meeting in Bangkok, Dulles

[m] Dulles probably had howitzers and Sabre jets, both of which could be armed with tactical nuclear weapons, in mind.

had told Eden (on Eisenhower's instructions) that US logistic support would continue to be given to the ROC 'at all points, as long as there was no mutually agreed-upon or tacit cease-fire',[99] thereby hinting that the Administration might withdraw its support of Quemoy and Matsu if Peking would accept a cease-fire. This hint is confirmed in a secret memorandum which Dulles had prepared on his Government's position: 'If the Chinese Communists, while retaining their claims to Formosa, would give assurances that they would not seek a verdict by force, then the situation might be different.'[100] Nevertheless, he tried to assure Eden that the US 'had taken step after step to reduce the chance of war'.[101] None of the steps which Dulles cited could be said to reduce tension, however: the Formosa Resolution was sufficiently ambiguous to invite additional PRC probes of positions possibly unrelated to ROC security; the unpopularity of the UN cease-fire initiative with both Communists and Nationalists resulted in its having a neutral effect on the course of the crisis; and the existence of hostages served to maintain tension, although the decision not to retaliate prevented it from increasing further.

What did serve to reduce tension and control the crisis was a combination of impasse in the crisis system and the actors' ability to accept risks as well as communicate threats. The increased concentration of Nationalist forces, visibly supplied by US-ROC air and sea forces, reduced the prospects for a successful PRC invasion, especially after 25 March, by which time the Nationalist garrison had largely completed its fortification of Quemoy and Matsu. After that date, according to a report from Colonel Goodpaster, the White House Staff Secretary, all but the most sustained PRC amphibious attacks, backed by both artillery and air strikes, could be resisted by ROC forces. Before that date, the US would have been compelled to intervene at a much earlier stage on the side of its allies.[102]

Once the US had clarified its operational support of the Quemoy and Matsu garrisons, following the surrender of the Tachens, Peking was forced to face the risk of striking American forces and thereby provoking US retaliation against the mainland. This was an unacceptably high risk, in contrast with the relatively low risks which faced Washington, given the limitations on Chinese Communist sea and air power and the lack of Soviet operational support for the PRC. The US Administration sought to widen this risk-taking gap even further by making public its readiness to resort to atomic weapons *in extremis*. In a general war in Asia, the President told his 16 March press conference, he would authorise the use of atomic weapons against 'strictly military targets', such as shore batteries or airfields;[103] in such circumstances, he saw 'no reason why they shouldn't be used just exactly as you would use a bullet or anything else'. This information followed Secretary Dulles' statement, a week earlier, that 'if the Chinese Communists engage in open armed aggression this would probably mean that they have decided on general war in Asia'.[104] Taken together, these two statements maximised the risk of US intervention if Peking pressed its attack on Quemoy and Matsu. A fairly credible link from a PRC attempt to invade the remaining off-shore islands to a pre-declared US perception of general war in Asia, leading finally to the potential use of tactical nuclear weapons, was enough to discourage any concerted Chinese attempt to revise the situation in the Taiwan Straits by force.

On the other hand, Peking could still hope for eventual reunification by peaceful means, an outcome suggested both by Western initiatives for a cease-fire without prejudice to the contending claims of the Chinese parties and by the private communications between Washington and London. The Bandung Conference, as will be seen in the next chapter, proved to be an ideal forum for a face-saving PRC backdown from forceful confrontation with the US – and a pursuit of its aims by peaceful means. A tacit Sino-American bargain seemed to be emerging by the end of April, in which Peking and Washington were beginning to disengage simultaneously from counter-productive crisis confrontation and to search for viable alternatives. Both sides transmitted important signals at that time: on the 23rd, Chou En-lai publicly offered to negotiate a settlement with the US Government, and on the 26th Dulles responded, gruffly but nonetheless positively, agreeing to talk about a cease-fire but refusing to discuss ROC interests 'behind its back'.[105]

Concurrently, the Administration sent Admiral Radford and Assistant Secretary Robertson on a mission to Taiwan, to persuade Chiang Kai-shek to 'change the off-shore islands, by partial evacuation and intensive fortification, from population centres into defensive outposts',[106] according to Eisenhower's account. This would emphasise their role as defensive *shields* against a Communist invasion launched from Amoy and Foochow, instead of aggressive *springboards* for Nationalist attacks on Chekiang or Fukien. This was consistent with the President's

5 April memorandum to Secretary Dulles, which called for convincing Chiang to 'regard the off-shore islands as outposts and consequently to be garrisoned in accordance with the requirements of outpost positions'.[107] Predictably, Chiang Kai-shek refused to 'redistribute' his forces; even if the President's unlikely representatives had used all their persuasive powers, which seems doubtful, the most Washington could exact from Taipei was an abstention from any direct provocation of Peking – and hence any renewed destabilisation of the crisis system in the near future.

While this outcome was not the best of all possible worlds, the fears of a number of high Administration officials, in late March, that war would break out within a month,[108] remained unfulfilled. By mid-May, Dulles could urge Molotov in Vienna to match US influence over the ROC by exerting

a comparable influence on the Chinese Communists. I said that we needed a solution where as in Germany, Korea and Viet Nam, it was agreed that unification would not be sought by force.[n] Molotov said they wanted peace. He suggested a five-power conference. I said a six-power conference would be better. He said the Chinese Communists would not meet with the Nationalists. I said we would not meet with the Communists without the Nationalists.[109]

It was unfortunately true that Dulles had blocked any negotiated solution to the Taiwan problem. But in strategic terms, the acute crisis had been de-escalated and the chronic crisis re-stabilised. By 22 May, PRC vessels and aircraft were reportedly abstaining from attacks on their ROC counter-parts, and a lull had returned to the last stage in the Chinese civil war.

Implications of the crisis

An important concern of my comparative case study approach is the extent to which the sum total of the participants' actions, their 'crisis behaviour', is influenced by shared experiences from the past. Although the perceptual field of the decision-makers narrowed under stress in each one of the crisis sequences under study – to the point that they would concentrate on immediate issues and think only of the present – it is nevertheless true that their behaviour was conditioned by the course of previous crisis

[n] Dulles' statement also implied that a cease-fire would be a further step toward establishing two Chinas, as two Germanys, Koreas, and Vietnams had been created previously.

interactions and that each crisis would set precedents for future crisis behaviour as well.

The present case study is a good case in point, in view of the effect which the Korea and Indochina experiences had on Sino-American crisis behaviour in the mid-1950s and, in turn, the effect which the latter would have on the course of the second Taiwan Straits crisis in 1958. In 1954–5, the crisis activities of Peking and Washington had become highly responsive to each other. There was very little of the sequential escalation with minimal effective communication typical of Korea in 1950–1, or of the largely erratic and one-way threats from Washington to Peking typical of Indochina in 1954. Instead, the first Taiwan Straits crisis was characterised by a two-way exchange of threats, initiatives, and responses, highly co-ordinated throughout the phases of escalation, declension and de-escalation.

US decision-makers can be justly criticised for having impeded effective crisis management by excessive procrastination in defining their commitments. Yet the fact that they did extend the scope of their mutual security system, and that even their disturbing ambiguity over the off-shore islands was offset by successful resistance to Communist attack, seemed to enhance the stability of the area. Moreover, Secretary Dulles appeared more sensitive, toward the end of the crisis, to the factors which would result in such a relatively successful outcome, in spite of the inherently destabilising influence of the Nationalist presence on the off-shore islands. In a very carefully worded statement issued in Taipei on 3 March, he indicated that

The United States continues to evaluate the words and deeds of the Chinese Communist regime to ascertain whether their military actions, preparations and concentrations in the Formosa area constitute, in fact, the first phase of an attack directed against Taiwan and whether the United States must proceed on this assumption. If so, it cannot be assumed that the defense would be static and confined to Taiwan itself, or that the aggressor would enjoy immunity with respect to the areas from which he stages his offensive . . .

The Chinese Communists constantly profess a love of peace. They now have a chance to practice what they preach. The United States has no alternative but to stand firm.[110]

This statement reveals a degree of operational flexibility in the US position on the off-shore islands, once again signalling to Peking (1) American willingness to modify its posture on the off-shore islands if the PRC relinquished its objective of occupying Taiwan and the Pescadores by force if necessary, (2) US intent to retaliate against mainland military installations should these become staging areas for an intensified PLA attack, and (3) Washington's receptivity to a peaceful outcome, admittedly on the basis of continued US-ROC superiority in the PRC's coastal waters.

The Chinese Communists fell short of maximising their gains, failing to mobilise sufficiently rapidly and to achieve a fait accompli prior to the formalisation of the US commitment to Nationalist positions. Yet in view of the very real difficulties confronting any attempt to seize Quemoy and Matsu – not to mention Formosa and the Pescadores – and in view of the PRC's concern to repudiate any suggestion of a two-Chinas outcome, its occupation of the Tachens and related islands could be counted as a gain and a modest encouragement to try again later.

Most importantly, Sino-American crisis interactions had become sufficiently sophisticated to rub out any significant risk of war between Peking and Washington. Without either the benefit of a sizeable buffer zone (a deficiency which caused much concern in Opposition circles in the US as well as in the British Government)⁰ or the benefit of indirect participation by proxy, American and Chinese leaders engaged in coercive relations without very much fear of conflict on the scale of Korea, the last crisis area in which the moderating influence of buffer zones and proxies had been reduced to such a dangerously low level.

Indeed, in this crisis, Chinese Nationalist proxy tactics – including a certain amount of 'bridge-burning' over the issue of Quemoy's overly concentrated defence, combined with the support of the China Lobby in Congress and of the Committee of One Million at the grass roots level – threatened to compromise,

---

⁰ Dulles undoubtedly appreciated the strength of this argument.[111] On the other hand, he wrote in a private memorandum, prior to a meeting with Eden in February 1955, that 'to pressure the R. of C. into the surrender of Quemoy and Matsu would (1) importantly increase the attacking capacity of the Chinese Communists by making more available Amoy and Fuchow Harbors, the natural staging grounds for a sea attack; (2) greatly weaken the morale of the R. of C. in Formosa and increase the opportunity of Chinese Communist subversion; (3) probably increase the Chinese Communist intention to probe our resolution by putting it to the test of action'.[112] This list represents a mixture of well-chosen objective and subjective criteria, but should be considered more as a rationalisation of US policy than as a reliable guide to Dulles' crisis analysis, which would have taken into account the advantages as well as disadvantages of surrendering Quemoy and Matsu.

even endanger, the US position in the Taiwan Straits. Nevertheless, the forces of restraint successfuly resisted advocates of a
preventive war against the Communists. As in the case of Indochina, President Eisenhower's position played a very important
rôle. In August, he told a press conference that he would not
listen seriously to anyone who advocated first strike against the
PRC [113] (presumably short of general war). At a meeting of the
National Security Council in Denver on 12 September, Eisenhower was reported to have rejected out of hand a proposal to
bomb mainland lines of communication, in the event of a Communist attack on Quemoy,[114] in favourable contrast to his willingness to take extreme measures to defend the Red River Delta in
Indochina.

Chinese freedom of manoeuvre, on the other hand, was enhanced by Peking's independence from a proxy. Moscow's reluctance to follow verbal with concrete support deprived Peking of
much-needed backing,[p] but on the other hand, it did not amount
to the active Soviet discouragement of Chinese tactics which
would be experienced in 1958. In 1954–5, it was the Sino-American crisis system that was the main source of Chinese restraint; in
1958, the system would have to be expanded to include Moscow
in a more complex, triadic relationship. The presence or absence
of active proxies therefore results in a two-way power relationship, not only between primary and secondary powers but also
between the secondary powers themselves, which becomes a part
of the dynamics of the crisis system.

For this further development – and sophistication – in the
Sino-American crisis system, the crisis analyst can thank Peking,
which remained sufficiently dissatisfied with the status quo in
the Taiwan Straits to strive, by a variety of means, to make
further changes in it.

---

p The 12 October 1954 joint declaration on general policy denounced 'direct
acts of aggression' by the US against the PRC and deplored American
'support of the Chiang Kai-shek clique'; [115] on 15 December, the Soviet
government announced full support of Chinese demands that the US
withdraw all of its armed forces from Formosa; [116] but beyond these
gestures, there was no Soviet diplomatic thrust in Europe and no overt
Soviet military support in the Far East. East-west détente appeared, then
as now, to take precedence over total allied solidarity.

Part Three: The management of confrontation

7: Inter-crisis period: détente miscarried

In the inter-crisis period from 1955 to 1958, three major developments would influence the pattern of Sino-American crisis relations. First, the super-powers entered a period of over-all détente. Second, a 'third force' of neutralist, Afro-Asian states emerged in international society. Third, there was a major shift from increased possibilities for Sino-American détente – resulting mainly from the resolution of the first Taiwan Straits crisis but associated as well with the first two developments – to renewed Sino-American tension in the Far East. In this chapter, I will discuss each of these developments in turn, concentrating on the third, and I will then consider the implications of this three-year phase for Sino-American crisis relations.

East-West détente

The 18–23 July 1955 US-Soviet summit conference at Geneva marked an important shift toward East-West détente despite the fact that the summiteers made little concrete progress. It was the first conference of its kind in a decade and its atmosphere, by most accounts, was relatively friendly. The conference was also significant in the context of (1) great-power agreement at Geneva the year before, (2) reduction in Sino-American tension in the springtime, and (3) possibilities for peaceful co-existence that would arise in the future. As Sir Anthony Eden put it, 'The Geneva meeting was worthwhile if only for the discreet improvement it brought about in the Formosa Strait. By the end of the conference, the Foreign Secretary and I were convinced that all present would have been sincerely happy to see the off-shore islands sunk under the sea.'[1]

Possibilities for peaceful co-existence must be seen in terms of the mutual recognition by Moscow and Washington of the danger of nuclear war and of the need to reduce this danger by stabilising their deterrent relationship. This was easier to achieve than in the past, because both states were assuming an increasingly status quo position in international politics. Moreover, both capitals had a stake in maintaining the international order which made their privileged, super-power position possible. Thus Washington did not act to prevent the Soviet occupation of Hungary in 1956, nor did Moscow intervene in 1958 when the Eisenhower Doctrine was applied to the Lebanon in the form of intervention by over 14 000 soldiers and marines. It was simply not in the interests of either country to do more than verbally denounce the other's coercion in the defence of the existing political order.

The Soviet-American progress toward détente even entailed limited collaboration in crisis management by the super-powers at the expense of their allies. Thus both Moscow and Washington were opposed in 1956 to the Anglo-French-Israeli attack on Egypt over Suez, denouncing it as imperialist aggression; Washington's successful pressure on London created an intramural crisis of the first order. In 1958, Moscow was to be equally willing and successful in applying political-military pressure on Peking to prevent it from forcing the American hand over the Taiwan Straits – again provoking an intramural crisis which would escalate into the Sino-Soviet split.

The 'third force'

The 'third force' of non-aligned, neutralist and predominantly Afro-Asian states became an important factor in international affairs especially after the conference held at Bandung, Indonesia, from 18 to 24 April 1955. The admittedly weak Bandung coalition, consisting entirely of developing and mostly newly independent states, nevertheless helped to loosen the previously rigid East-West bipolarity of the international system – most immediately in the United Nations, where 1955 could be considered the divide between the earlier East-West debate and the later North-South debate.[2] Not only did Washington and Moscow modify their bloc-centred ideologies to make place for a third alternative road between the dogmatic options of Communism and Free Enterprise, but both sides proceeded to compete actively in granting foreign aid to and in trying to win the support of the neutralists.

Sponsored by the Colombo Powers (which, it will be recalled, influenced the course of the 1954 Geneva Conference), the

Bandung Conference included representatives of 29 countries and of 1500 million people. Since neither the United States nor the Soviet Union was permitted to attend and since Taiwan was excluded, Bandung offered an ideal opportunity for Peking to occupy centre stage. Perceiving that the 'third force' was a potential ally in revising the international order in favour of the world's countryside, Chou En-lai employed his considerable diplomatic skills to woo and impress the conference delegates. He showed considerable flexibility in the face of criticism of Peking's past policy toward its national minorities and with respect to Southeast Asia.

Chou was eminently successful, broadening his contacts, increasing the prestige of the PRC, and establishing China as an Afro-Asian power of the first order. One mark of this success was the fact that *panch shila,* the Five Principles of Peaceful Co-existence [a] which had originally formed the basis of Sino-Indian agreement, were expanded into ten similar principles which were adopted by the conference as a whole.

The Bandung phase

The de-escalation of the first Taiwan Straits crisis, occurring in the spring of 1955, ran parallel with a complex and indirect Sino-American bargaining process. The Nationalist withdrawal from the Tachens in February, the March invocations by Dulles and Eisenhower of the dangers of general war in Asia; the April refusal by Taipei, in spite of pressure to the contrary from Washington, to reduce its forces on the remaining off-shore islands; and Chou's famous 23 April offer at Bandung to negotiate Far Eastern and particularly Taiwan-related problems with the United States – all were moves connected to the dynamics of the crisis itself and based on tacit understandings emerging from the crisis interactions between Peking, Taipei and Washington. What were the possibilities for Sino-American détente, as a result of the spring reduction in tension, and what were the reasons behind its miscarriage?

Bandung was by far the most opportune setting for a more or less graceful Chinese back-down from confrontation with the more powerful and threatening United States, even if, in the

[a] (1) Mutual respect for each other's territorial integrity and sovereignty; (2) mutual nonaggression; (3) mutual non-interference in each other's internal affairs; (4) equality and mutual benefit; (5) peaceful co-existence.

Chinese mind, confrontation and negotiation are simply different aspects of the anti-imperialist struggle.[3] Chou En-lai, at his most reasonable, went as far as to say, in his 23 April Bandung speech, that

The Chinese people are friendly to the American people. The Chinese people do not want to have war with the United States of America. The Chinese Government is willing to sit down and enter into negotiations with the United States Government to discuss the question of relaxing tension in the Far East, and especially the question of relaxing tension in the Taiwan area.[4]

There were at least three immediate incentives for this peaceful initiative. First, such a conciliatory approach could serve as a vehicle for Chinese leadership of a broad anti-imperialist international front of the poor countries of the world by impressing the latter with the tactical flexibility and peaceful inclinations of the PRC – an important aim of the 'Bandung phase' of China's foreign policy. Second, Communist China's internal security already demanded lower tension levels than those suggested by US-ROC actions from December to March, and would demand even further reduction of these levels as China's Soviet model gave way to a more radical, Maoist model of economic development.

The third incentive, and probably the most persuasive from Peking's point of view, was the increased possibility of regaining maritime China by peaceful means, once the pressure on Washington was lifted, thereby requiring less risk and sacrifice than the bombardment and threatened invasion of the past autumn. This assessment depended, of course, on an accurate reading of US intentions, but we saw that American signals in the spring of 1955 encouraged at least a phased de-coupling of the US commitment to defend the off-shore islands.

Peking also hoped that if Washington could be neither coerced nor cajoled into leaving the Taiwan Straits, the Nationalists might alternatively be persuaded to rejoin the mainland of their own accord. For instance, on 30 January 1956 Chou En-lai stated that 'there are two ways for the Chinese people to liberate Taiwan, that is, by war or by peaceful means', but that 'At present, the possibility of peacefully liberating Taiwan is increasing.' He also recalled that 'the Chinese Communists and the Kuomintang members have twice fought shoulder to shoulder against (Japanese) imperialism' before the Revolution, implying that they could do so again: 'Although in the past few years, owing to U.S. armed intervention, we and the Kuomintang military and political personnel on Taiwan have taken different paths, yet so long as we all hold supreme the interests of our nation and motherland, we can still link arms again and unite.'[5] In a banquet which he gave for Soviet President Voroshilov on 16 April, Chou reiterated his Government's flexibility in even more explicit terms: 'From the liberation of Peiping to the liberation of Tibet, we have always . . . carried out negotiations with the other party . . . As long as we are not subjected to imperialist interference, deception and instigation, the internal questions of China can always be settled through consultation. Taiwan is no exception.'[6] These intriguing statements, along with subsequent CCP and 'Revolutionary Kuomintang' overtures to the Nationalists, amounted to a concerted effort to persuade Taipei that its future could not be indefinitely tied to Washington – and might be more profitably tied to Peking.

Détente miscarried

The 'Bandung phase' of PRC foreign policy became associated, then, with the flexible diplomacy which was the trademark of Premier and Foreign Minister Chou En-lai. It provided the greatest possible opportunity for Sino-American détente that would exist either in that decade or in the next. The return of greater inflexibility and of increased regional tension was to be a function of (a) continued American rigidity, (b) a dramatic swing leftwards in the pendulum of Chinese politics and (c) an apparent revision of the central balance of power tending to favour the East.

American rigidity. Among the unfortunate cases of missed opportunities for moderating the ideological divisions of the Cold War in the 1950s must be counted the American refusal – until too late – to take Peking's overtures seriously. Even the Sino-American ambassadorial talks, which began in Geneva in August 1955 and which were the most positive legacy of the period, were treated by Washington as primarily a device for the repatriation of prisoners, whereas Peking viewed them as a means of influencing the US to speedily reduce its military presence in the Taiwan Straits. The stretching out of the talks with almost no concrete progress on the Taiwan Straits issue, in spite of the 10 September 1955 agreement on the return of civilians of both sides, caused much dissatisfaction in Peking.[7]

In 1956 and 1957, Peking's initiatives for expanded bilateral contacts were rejected by the State Department, which insisted on prior acceptance of the principle of renunciation of force. The irony and tragedy of these talks, which were transferred to Warsaw in the fall of 1958, was that US policy would finally become more flexible and open to concrete measures, only to see Chinese policy become more rigid and insistent on matters of principle.[8]

It is of course true that Chou En-lai's offer to negotiate on a bilateral basis reflected Communist self-interest, especially since it could not fail to place US policy at an embarrassed disadvantage. On the one hand, the American perception of Chinese Communist enmity had hardened over five years, and a powerful China Lobby encouraged Congressional and public opposition to any positive movement in Sino-American relations. On the other hand, despite some slight movement in the official US position at the time (for example, Dulles admitted in his 2 August press conference that Chou's speeches 'indicated his going further in the renunciation of force than anything he said before'),[9] the policy of recognition and active support of Chiang Kai-shek had been almost irretrievably strengthened in the winter before. It can be readily argued, therefore, that the crisis interactions of 1954–5 and the imperatives of American domestic politics had pre-determined the realistic range of response for Dulles. At any rate, it came quite naturally to this 'preacher in a world of politics' (as Eden so nicely put it)[10] to impose a series of conditions on heathen coming from the outer regions of atheistic, aggressive Communism before they could be permitted to enter the rarefied atmosphere of what he called 'the civilized part of mankind'.[11]

To the PRC, the initial US terms for Sino-American talks were too harsh to be acceptable; the State Department, in a statement issued on 23 April 1955 (the same day as Chou's Bandung overtures), set the following preconditions: equal representation of Taipei at any Sino-American meeting, prior release of the forty-one civilians and fifteen airmen captured during the Korean War, and acceptance of the UN Security Council's invitation to 'participate in discussions to end hostilities in the Formosa region'.[12] The first precondition neither Peking nor Taipei would consider; the second would more appropriately have been part of any package deal which might emerge from such a meeting; and the third (while not impossible in view of the renewed efforts by the Soviet bloc to secure admission of Peking to the UN and expulsion of Taipei from the Security Council) was still difficult to accept because of the UN's refusal to withdraw the label of 'aggressor' that it had given the PRC four years earlier.

Even so harsh an offer ran into automatic opposition from Senator Knowland and his supporters. The Administration had the fifty-six prisoners to thank for forcing its supporters (and its own foreign policy establishment) to agree, reluctantly, to the Sino-American talks, just as it had had the fate of the thirteen earlier prisoners to thank for persuading its Right wing to tolerate a non-violent approach to the 1954–5 crisis.

The failure of American officials to exercise more positive leadership – especially with the potential support of the Democratic majority leaders in the Senate – suggested that dogmatic attitudes had combined with partisan ones to sabotage a more flexible response to Peking's initiatives. This failure, which no doubt Dulles saw as the only right response, would set back the possibilities for Sino-American détente by at least seven years, and this despite belated American overtures between 1959 and 1961. It would also possibly serve to weaken Chou's pragmatic supporters and to encourage Peking in its turn to become inflexible.

Most relevantly to this study, the rigidity of the American response became an important cause of the 1958 crisis, for it had become clear to Peking that there was no hope of coming to a peaceful settlement of outstanding differences or even of beginning to resolve 'certain other practical matters now at issue between both sides', to use the ungrammatical euphemism of the first agenda of the Sino-American talks. The hopeful overtures associated with Bandung were soon to be buried in a more militant phase of Chinese policy, both domestic and external, including a perilous determination to achieve the objective of national reunification by whatever means necessary. It was a long qualitative leap from Chou's 30 July 1955 address to the National People's Congress, in which he asserted: 'Provided that the U.S. does not interfere with China's internal problems, the possibility of peaceful liberation of Formosa will continue to increase',[13] to his ominous warning in an interview of 10 January 1958 that the more the United States 'exerts pressure on us, the more we will resist', and if the US 'insists on waging war, we will fight'.[14] This warning, following a greatly expanded programme of US military aid to Taiwan,[b] was to lead to the decision to 'liberate'

[b] One of the most disconcerting examples was the US decision to install Matador missiles, capable of carrying nuclear warheads, on Formosa on 7 May 1957.[15] Peking promptly denounced this as evidence of a plot to turn Taiwan into 'a United States dependency and a base for atomic war'.[16]

Taiwan 'at any moment', taken after an unprecedented conference convened by the Military Committee of the CCP Central Committee between 27 May and 22 July 1958.

Leftward swing in Chinese politics. This series of lost opportunities came at a particularly inopportune time in domestic Chinese politics. 1955 was the year of departure, for China, from the Stalinist economic model into a more ambitious collective programme of economic development. As the economy continued to respond favourably and the phase of political consolidation appeared to have been completed, Mao and his colleagues took the risk of permitting criticism of defects in Chinese society – the Hundred Flowers campaign – in the hope that this criticism would attack bureaucratic conservatism and lethargy and eventually strengthen the political fibre of the new China. What in fact occurred was a holocaust of criticism and abuse which challenged the fundamental basis of Communist power and revealed opposition in all walks of life, predictably strongest among the intelligentsia but surprisingly prevalent at all levels of the CCP. That reverses happened to manifest themselves almost simultaneously in both the internal and (as we have seen) the external spheres was not only an unfortunate coincidence: the double misfortune helped to prompt the introduction of a much more militant posture in the political, economic, foreign policy and eventually military spheres — roughly in that order.

The Hundred Flowers speedily gave way before a new rectification, an 'anti-Rightist' campaign which, from May 1957 to May 1958, counter-attacked (in a fashion similar to the 1942–3 *Cheng-feng* movement and 1954–5 Kao-Jao purge) the 'bourgeois' influences which expressed themselves inside and outside the Party. The relatively moderate pace of economic development gave way before the Great Leap Forward. The Great Leap, in making fantastic demands for mass mobilisation while at the same time shifting the entire economic orientation from collectives to communes, disorganised and in some cases turned back economic growth. As a result, the PRC entered a time of increased vulnerability, requiring a long period of economic recovery before rational economic planning could make a fresh start.

The east wind prevailing. Internal vulnerability – which could only be compared with that of the 1949–51 period – was not the only factor encouraging more uncompromising diplomatic and strategic posture. The other key factor in this hardening of external policy was the Maoist assessment of the world balance of forces. The military achievement of the USSR in successfully testing the world's first inter-continental ballistic missile (ICBM) on 26 August 1957, along with the parallel space spectacular of the launching of Sputnik on 4 October 1957, were used by Chinese strategists as further proof of the superiority of Communism over Capitalism. No less an authority than Chairman Mao himself declared in Moscow on 18 November, that 'the international situation has now reached a new turning point . . . I believe that it is characteristic of the situation today that the East Wind is prevailing over the West Wind. That is to say, the forces of socialism have become overwhelmingly superior to the forces of capitalism.' [17] This new assessment of the central balance of power would have serious implications: Peking would not only be willing to take risks regionally but would also expect Moscow to take similar risks on its behalf globally. Chinese strategists would use Soviet successes as further support of the cavalier thesis, put forward by Mao in February 1957, that in the event of a third world war, capitalism would be eradicated and socialism would triumph and prosper [18] – in spite of the Malenkov-Khrushchev prediction of disaster for all in a nuclear exchange, irrespective of social system. The more aggressive approach taken in 1957, then, accentuated the differences between a militant China and an increasingly conservative Russia. Similarly, this approach would adversely affect Chinese crisis behaviour over the Taiwan Straits in 1958, in that the PRC would count on a forthright Soviet commitment which would actually be either ambiguous or too late in coming.

In conclusion, the miscarriage of Sino-American détente was the cue for increased militancy in Chinese policy. This militancy, in turn, fed on the frustration of China's Bandung diplomacy and on signs of flux in the central balance of power. The stage was set for the final test of strength of the decade.

8: Second Taiwan Straits crisis, 1958

The second Taiwan Straits crisis can be interpreted as the 'spin-off' of a radically revised Sino-American assessment of the central balance of power. Not only in Peking did the East Wind appear to prevail. In Washington as well, one could sense growing fears of strategic vulnerability (garbed in what became known as the 'missile gap') which resulted in a crash programme to narrow the alleged technological and military gap between the US and the USSR.

International setting

A clear and important influence both on strategic calculations and on Sino-American crisis relations, this putative 'missile gap' dominated the international setting in 1958. Chinese proclamations of the gap [a] combined with an obvious Russian reluctance to disavow publicly strategic superiority: these postures in turn generated Western fears of the consequences of this imbalance for 'free world' security and global influence. Uncertainty about the state of the East-West balance contributed to – and was exacerbated by – the 1958 series of crises from the Middle East through the Taiwan Straits to Berlin.

Western perceptions of the 'missile gap' – and of its negative implications for crisis management – were exaggerated for at least three reasons. First, although this was far from obvious at the time, Moscow never accepted Peking's argument. Both its enhanced security (as opposed to outright superiority) and its increasing satisfaction with its leading international role induced the Soviet Union to display strategic caution and to support steps toward détente.[2]

[a] Mao's November proclamation that 'the East Wind is prevailing over the West Wind' was reiterated by Chou En-lai before the National People's Congress: 'a decisive change has taken place in the international situation that favours . . . the socialist camp.' [1]

The West, not at all reassured, proceeded to take steps to redress the power balance. American alliances, especially NATO, were revitalised as allies accepted the need for solidarity – in spite of the bitter legacy of Suez. In the United States, military, technological and scientific programmes were accelerated, spurred on by increased justification for their existence.

The arms race stemming from Western insecurity leads to a second consideration. If the USSR was in fact satisfied with its security at the end of 1957, by the middle of 1958 it too had greater cause for insecurity and for taking measures to counter those of the West. This cycle of measures and counter-measures was to have a de-stabilising effect up to the 1962 Cuban missile crisis. By that time, Moscow would have become so dissatisfied with its inter-continental missile capability that it would be willing to take considerable risks in order to install intermediate-range ballistic missiles in Cuba. If this widely-held interpretation of Soviet motives is to be accepted, it must also be added that in the Cuban crisis – as in the 1958 Taiwan Straits crisis – Chairman Khrushchev was to be notably unwilling to maintain his nuclear bluff beyond preliminary stages of escalation.

This consideration about Russian crisis behaviour over time is important for this study because it brings Sino-Soviet differences over crisis strategy into focus. When Peking would denounce Russian actions as 'adventurist' and 'capitulationist' in 1963, it would be clear that, at least in Peking's book, Moscow's immediate sins dated back to 1958. Just as Khrushchev would fall short of revising the status quo in the Western Atlantic in 1962, Mao would blame him for failing to have revised the status quo in the Western Pacific in 1958 – with the important difference that primary Chinese interests at stake in the Taiwan Straits would have been frustrated, whereas the primary US interests at stake in the Caribbean would have been respected. This emerging triangle of Peking, Moscow and Washington was perhaps the most fundamental strategic development underlying the second Taiwan Straits crisis.

At this point, we might recall the basis of the American and Chinese commitments in order to compare the regional balance of power system with the Soviet-American central balance. On the one hand, Americans were firmly committed to the defence of Formosa and the Pescadores as part of their security chain in the West Pacific. The Administration was also committed – albeit reluctantly – to the defence of the off-shore islands because, as a result of the first crisis, Quemoy and Matsu had become symbols of the US commitment to Chiang Kai-shek.

From 1955 on, Chiang had heavily reinforced the islands, investing approximately 500 million dollars and 100 000 élite troops [3] – making it virtually impossible for Eisenhower and Dulles to excuse the surrender of the islands as of no relevance to the security of Taiwan. And yet the 1958 crisis would dramatise the vulnerability of Quemoy and Matsu to PRC attack, particularly since Peking had completed its construction of jet airfields around Amoy and Foochow and had generally strengthened its communication, road and rail networks in Fukien and Chekiang Provinces.[4] The reciprocal build-up of PRC and ROC forces inevitably raised the question of how the United States could improve its position in the Taiwan Straits, especially since the Chinese of both sides remained dedicated to the goal of national reunification. The stationing of Nationalist troops on Quemoy and Matsu and the Communist refusal to distinguish between the off-shore and main islands were only incongruous from the Western point of view; for the Chinese, these have remained testaments to their rejection of a 'Two Chinas' solution to the problem, imposed from the outside.

Peking was especially apprehensive that Nationalist moves were directed toward an imminent attack – an attack which was an increased possibility as a result of Taipei's fears that the Communists would soon have Russian-supplied nuclear missiles which would deter a Nationalist landing. In February, ROC Foreign Minister Yeh warned that his Government might go so far as to abrogate its security pact with the United States 'if the terms of the pact prevent the Chinese Government from exercising its sovereignty' – a euphemism for invading the mainland. 'At present, however, the Chinese Government has no intention of doing this', Yeh conceded, 'because of the aggressive threat of the CCP bandit State',[5] which presumably made US protection more desirable than the lifting of the accompanying restrictions on ROC freedom of action. This cycle of mutual apprehension contributing to crisis escalation offers an interesting parallel to that occurring on the East-West level discussed above. The two levels of 'apprehension-escalation cycles' were linked as both Taipei and Peking became ever more committed to a revision of the status quo, and as their super-power patrons showed every sign of sustaining this status quo in the Western Pacific.

The foregoing discussion has implied the third reason for Western perceptions of the missile gap being exaggerated: Moscow's specific attitudes to the 1958 crisis in the Taiwan Straits. It will be seen that the USSR would not permit the PRC to employ the Sino-Soviet alliance, with its nuclear force, as an instrument in the manipulation of risk – at the very time that wholehearted support would be most urgently required by Peking. The Russians would furthermore prove to be quite prepared to sacrifice Chinese interests and to ignore Chinese advice on the Middle East and in disarmament talks, in favour of peaceful relations with the West.[b] Moscow's ambivalence during the Sino-American adversary crisis would be increased by CPSU criticism of the CCP's introduction of communes in the Great Leap Forward, which in effect advanced a Chinese claim to be the first to make the transition from socialism to communism.

Not only did the Chinese persist with the Great Leap over Russian objections; they also pursued a crisis course over Taiwan. This course was ensured by the victory of the militant 'modernisers' over the more cautious professionals at the May–July meetings of the CCP Military Committee. The former were fully prepared both to exploit what they considered to be the military superiority of the Communist bloc as a whole and to concentrate on the Great Leap Forward; the latter favoured a strong national military establishment, patiently built up over a long period of time and at the expense of rapid industrialisation, which would eventually permit the PRC to escape its military weakness.[6] All indications would be that the cautious professionals were forced to give way to the reckless exuberance of the Great Leap, whose main failing was that it prompted Chinese leaders to disregard basic obstacles, whether domestic, adversary or intramural. The second Taiwan Straits crisis can therefore be seen partly as a belated Chinese reaction to Russian stone-walling and hence as much a test of Russian as of American resolve under stress.[c]

[b] The intramural flavour of this crisis for the East was as strong as that of Indochina for the West. One might extend this comparison further by noting that just as the seeds of Anglo-American discord over Egypt (1956) must be found in 1954, so must those of Sino-Soviet discord over India (1962) be found in 1958.

[c] While American resolve appeared vulnerable because of growing internal difficulties (see pp. 175–7), Russian resolve was more a function of intramural issues, namely the aftermath of crises with Hungary and

Already strategically fluid in 1957–8, the international climate was further troubled by events in Latin America and the Middle East. In May, riots greeted Vice President Nixon and his wife on their Latin American tour, provoking President Eisenhower to order a thousand US troops to stand ready for a rescue operation in Caracas. In July, the overthrow of the Iraqi Hashemite monarchy was followed by the landing of American troops in Lebanon and of British troops in Jordan. The Anglo-American presence through October in the Middle East provoked mounting protests from Moscow and Peking, as well as from some Arab capitals. The US Administration's crisis behaviour over the Taiwan Straits seems to have been significantly influenced by these protests and by an almost instinctive fear of Communist retaliation elsewhere. For instance, Navy Secretary Thomas Gates felt that the Communist setback in the Middle East would force the Communist monolith (as he saw it at the time) to search for successes elsewhere, notably in the Far East. Gates took action accordingly by putting the Seventh Fleet on alert in the Pacific.[7] The Middle Eastern crisis would compound the stress experienced by American decision-makers during the intervening crisis in the Taiwan Straits and would increase their determination not to appear weak to their antagonists. In Secretary of Defense McElroy's view, 'the direct action taken by the United States in these two consecutive instances had to give the same sort of a signal to the Russians that President Eisenhower and his Government were not going to be stepped on in international affairs'.[8]

It is possible to interpret the extremely strong Chinese reaction to US intervention in the Lebanon as merely a reflection of Soviet views, but both the character and extent of PRC commentaries indicate that Peking was genuinely concerned not only about (1) the unequivocal American response to revisions of the status quo, but also about (2) the Soviet failure to prevent a collapse of revolutionary forces and about (3) the implications of such a disastrous set of events for PRC prospects in the Taiwan Straits. Mayor P'eng Chen's shrill (but representative) speech at a July mass rally in Peking becomes comprehensible in this context:

Poland and the impact both of those crises and of the de-Stalinisation programme on Sino-Soviet relations. Internally, Khrushchev had decisively strengthened his hand by purging the 'anti-party group' headed by Molotov, Kaganovich and Malenkov, relegating Premier Bulganin to the back seat, and even dismissing the military leader and war hero, Marshal Zhukov.

The U.S. forces of aggression must get out of Lebanon at once! The U.S.A. must stop its frenzied war of provocation at once! . . .

We Chinese people have long seen through the wolfish features of the U.S. imperialists. We have dealt heavy blows to their aggressive designs and won brilliant victories . . .

We Chinese people are determined to liberate Taiwan and have full confidence that we will achieve this. The U.S. forces must get out of our territory of Taiwan! We firmly believe that the people, with justice on their side, will triumph in the end and that, with the East Wind prevailing over the West Wind the imperialists are all the more definitely doomed to failure.[9]

The ensuing crisis in the Taiwan Straits can be seen, then, not only as a re-run of its 1954–5 predecessor, but also as a function of a parallel 'sub-crisis' in the Middle East. Peking was concerned not only with successfully asserting what it considered to be legitimate and pressing national interests, but also with applying its ideological view that as a representative of progressive, popular forces it could defeat an over-committed imperialist foe. A *Jen-min Jih-pao* leader expressed this aspiration well: 'The heroic people of the Middle East and all the Asian and African people who are fighting for freedom are preparing a big grave for the Western aggressors. Since they insist on entering it, let us unite and help them in.'[10] The incidental benefit of convincing an over-cautious Moscow of the advantages of militancy made a strategic initiative in the Taiwan Straits even more attractive to Peking. As *Jen-min Jih-pao* remonstrated, in rather pedantic terms, 'Nothing can be saved by yielding to evil, and coddling wrong only helps the devil . . . The imperialists have always bullied the weak and been afraid of the strong. The only language they understand is that of force.'[11]

Thus, the PRC accelerated its build-up of military forces in the coastal areas around Quemoy and Matsu in July, and on 17 July (the same day as P'eng's speech), ROC Premier Chen Cheng issued a 'special alert order' cancelling all military leave, 'in view of the present explosive situation in the Middle East'. Vice Admiral Doyle also put the Seventh Fleet on alert to be ready to cope with 'the serious international situation'.[12] 'While carrying out armed aggression in the Middle East', the New China News Agency charged, 'the U.S.A. has ordered the Chiang Kai-shek clique to create new tension in the Taiwan area'.[13] A process of mutual apprehension had been set in full motion by the end of July, which would result in accelerated escalation of the crisis in August.

Domestic developments

The Great Leap Forward is the key domestic development in 1958 with regard both to Chinese behaviour in the crisis and to Chinese foreign policy in general. Significant events co-incide in the internal and external spheres; the inter-relationship of these spheres is reflected in Chinese crisis behaviour as well as in Chinese ideology. In May, Liu Shao-ch'i proclaimed the general line of socialist construction – the grand strategy of the Great Leap – at the second session of the Eighth Party Congress. The following period, according to Franz Schurmann, 'was the most militant since the Korean War'.[14] In July, the people's militia was revived; arms were distributed to the peasantry, notably in the coastal province of Fukien; Agricultural Producers' Co-operatives which had been amalgamating led to the introduction of people's communes. At the end of the month, Communist and Nationalist planes clashed in force over the Straits while Khrushchev and Malinovsky urged caution in Peking.[d] In August, *Red Flag* called for the working people to 'Militarise Organisation, Turn Action Into Struggle, Collectivise Life!'[15] An enlarged Politburo met in Peitaiho from 17 to 30 August to formally launch communisation. On 23 August, the bombardment of Quemoy and Matsu began.

This rough chronology provides a record of radicalisation in Chinese politics and policy. The linkage between domestic and foreign policy can be established ideologically, in the sense that the Great Leap was designed to be not merely an instrument of economic development, but was also designed as a means of radical change which would serve as concrete proof of the superiority of the Chinese Communist model. Other approaches had been deemed inadequate, from the co-operative in economic life to peaceful change in foreign affairs.

Among the officially 'democratic' organisations which were the victims of the 'rectification' campaign following the Hundred Flowers movement, the Taiwan Democratic League was an outstanding example. Madame Hsieh Hsueh-hung, the League's Chairman, was dismissed and several Central Committee members expelled in January. A 'number of League members who were then in Peking' – undoubtedly a convenient euphemism for what was a rump faction – thereupon endorsed the proposal of their Secretary-General, Chen Yin-shen, to 'turn themselves into

d See pp. 182–5.

a political force which will render genuine service to the cause of Socialism and the liberation of Taiwan'.[16] The Taiwan Democratic League is not only an interesting case of internal radicalisation of the PRC's political system; it also serves as an important example of the linkage between Peking's internal and external militance, with Taiwan as an appropriate symbol of the unfulfilled aspirations of the CCP. The Bandung diplomacy of Chou En-lai had given way to the East Wind militance of Ch'en Yi,[e] which was in line with the apocalyptic mood of the Great Leap and the general conviction that anything was possible, given sufficient political fervour.

A second, and more generalised, link in the militancy of the internal and external spheres was the militarisation of Chinese life, which was on a scale comparable only to mid-1950 in the first decade of the PRC. The Army was being used more and more as the model for all organisation, much as it would be under different circumstances in the 1960s. This does not mean, however, that mobilisation was always advertised to the populace as being linked specifically with the events in the Taiwan Straits. If it had been, Peking would have been less capable of retreating easily from its probing action. It should also be noted that the initial distinction between the internal and external spheres is more an analytical device than a realistic representation: from the Chinese perspective, the Straits represented the final theatre in the protracted civil war between Communists and Nationalists – an internal matter.

In the United States, the internal-external distinction is much more clear-cut, both traditionally and in terms of the second Taiwan Straits crisis. In the first crisis, the link between Taipei and the China Lobby and the ideological demands of the first Eisenhower Administration tended to undermine this distinction, but in the second crisis, the political debate (although not necessarily Administration thinking) was formulated in terms far more of strategy (e.g., is American forward commitment in the best national interest?) than of ideology (e.g., can we tolerate any Communist gains?). In 1958, therefore, the co-incidence of internal and external events was not as close in the United States

---

[e] Ch'en Yi became Foreign Minister on 11 February 1958, permitting Chou En-lai to concentrate on the Prime Ministership. Chou's foreign reputation as a pragmatic diplomat was, as a result, preserved for opportune occasions in the future, although he did not shirk from making uncharacteristically extreme pronouncements in the domestic setting.

as it was in China, nor could it be expected to have been, in view of the pluralistic nature of American society.

Indeed, far from projecting an image of solidarity abroad, the United States appeared singularly vulnerable and divided in 1958. President Eisenhower was recovering from a serious heart attack which he had suffered the previous November. The Gold-fine furore monopolised attention in Congress in the summer and forced key presidential assistant Sherman Adams to resign in 1958. Several Cold Warriors left the Government, including AEC Chairman Strauss, Edward Teller and Senator Knowland, who lost the California gubernatorial race in November. General Nathan Twining (the Air Force Chief of Staff) had replaced the formidable Admiral Radford as JCS Chairman more than a year before. Secretary of State Dulles was in the penultimate stage of terminal cancer, which would force him to leave office in April 1959, a month before he died.

In addition to the reversals of personal fortunes in 1958, there were serious economic and political difficulties which confronted the Republican Administration. The 1957–8 recession was the most serious experienced by the US in the post-War period and was contrasted by Chinese Communist commentators with what they considered to be the economic dynamism of the socialist bloc. In May, for example, Liu Shao-ch'i asserted that 'This crisis is shaking the entire capitalist world, and has thoroughly exploded the myths spread since the war by bourgeois politicians and scholars, reformists and revisionists, that the capitalist economy can avoid crises.' [17]

The mid-term elections in November were to over-fulfill expectations of a resounding Republican defeat. Democrats outnumbered Republicans in both houses of the 86th Congress by nearly two to one. It must be recalled, however, that the most acute phase of the first Taiwan Straits crisis occurred *after* the mid-term elections in 1954, whereas that of the second crisis occurred *before* those in 1958. The Congressional parties were near-unanimous in supporting the Administration over the first crisis. In the second crisis, however, the campaign coincided with a crisis commitment of dubious value and, for many, appallingly high stakes.[f] As a result, many politicians could not

f In both crises, there was an under-current of Congressional uneasiness over the extent of Executive power over foreign policy which was most notably manifested in the attempt by Senator Bricker and others, in 1954 resist the temptation of making an election issue out of US China policy, as the following statements – all made in the first half of September 1958 – illustrate. Adlai Stevenson called recent foreign policy 'clumsy, erratic, and self-righteous'. Dean Acheson complained on 6 September that the US was 'drifting either dazed or indifferent, toward war with China, a war without friends or allies, and over issues which the Administration has not presented to the people, and which are not worth a single American life'.[18] Senator Wayne Morse, was, as usual, refreshingly peppery: 'The U.S. is being dragged into a war through the back door by a dictator, a Chinese warlord who was driven off the mainland of China.'[19]

To counter such attacks, Vice President Nixon asserted that the US 'could make no greater mistake than by appearing to be a paper tiger' in the Far East, because in dealing with dictatorship's you do not maintain peace by appearing to be weak but only by maintaining strength militarily and diplomatically'.[20] Former President Truman whole-heartedly agreed with this view: he said that the crisis 'should be treated as a major element in a global struggle for survival', and that 'It would be folly and dangerous for us to abandon Formosa to the Communists as long as they are aggression-minded.'[21]

This extended debate during the 1958 campaign reflected the conviction of many at the time, especially Vice President Nixon, that foreign policy had become a major election issue and that the mid-term elections amounted to a test of confidence in US foreign policy. Against this it can be argued that Nixon arbitrarily chose foreign policy as 'the' issue to distract the voters' minds from the economic recession. No doubt the prospect of a resounding Republican defeat – which in retrospect appears due mainly to the domestic recession rather than to foreign policy issues – proved to be an overwhelming temptation for a partisan debate over the Taiwan Straits. Even appeals for bipartisanship appeared to favour the beleaguered Administration. On 21 October, Senate Majority Leader Lyndon Johnson insisted that, in

and 1955, to amend the Constitution in order to wrest control of foreign policy from the President. What was new in 1958 was a Congressional willingness to deny the President the near-unanimous support that he had received in January and February 1955. This time, the stress of events in Lebanon and Quemoy increased rather than allayed domestic opposition.

foreign policy, 'Bipartisanship should be a two-way street, and it should not run one way during a national crisis and another way during a political crisis.' [22]

The significant point to query is the extent to which this partisan debate affected US crisis behaviour. Contemporary observers were inclined to give the opposition the credit for the peaceful outcome of the second Taiwan Straits crisis. Secretary Dulles' sensitivity on this point is often used as evidence supporting such a view: it is true that Dulles would have an interest in generating political support for his China policies, which were controversial enough with America's allies.[g] Continuing this line of reasoning, many would argue that Washington was persuaded – or tricked – by Taipei into bringing a local disturbance to the brink of general war, and that the critics would serve an essential role in forcing the Administration to abandon both its risky manipulation of ambiguity and its predilection for brinkmanship.

There is little evidence to support this contention. It is true that the US commitment was to become more explicit, that the United States would be cautious in countering the Communist blockade, and that restraint, combined with resolve, would contribute to a peaceful resolution of the crisis. But the opposition's criticism would never relate to the day-to-day responses which made such crisis behaviour possible. Its criticism was rather more broadly gauged, directed against the general course of US Far Eastern policy, or concerned simply with the unfortunate facts of the islands' existence and/or of the American commitment to Chiang's forces.[23]

A further obvious but important point about American crisis behaviour was that Washington *would* manage, after all, to preserve the status quo in the Taiwan Straits, in spite of the generally negative and divisive political debate which increased America's pre-existing vulnerability as a crisis manager in 1958. For an explanation of this interesting paradox, one must turn to

[g] One example of this intramural tension was the insistence of Labour Party Leader Hugh Gaitskell that Britain should dissociate itself from US policy over Quemoy and Matsu. Prime Minister Macmillan continued to support US opposition to Chinese force (as he put it) but this did not extend to military support, which at any rate was not requested by Washington. Unlike the allied controversy over differentiating permissible trade with the USSR from that with the PRC, there is no evidence that such disagreement as there was over the Taiwan Straits affected Sino-American crisis relations in any significant way.

the record of crisis interactions in the summer and autumn of 1958, for neither international nor domestic settings could alone provide a satisfactory explanation for the stand-off which occurred.

Pre-crisis phase

Both international and domestic factors contributed an essential context for this as well as the other crises which I have examined. It remained, as it were, for the crisis actors to play the part that domestic and international politics had prepared for them, to test the validity of the assessment by Li Chun-ching, Vice Chairman of the Taiwan Democratic League, that in spring 1958, 'The present domestic and foreign situation is favourable for the liberation of Taiwan.' [24]

It was up to Peking to initiate the second 'run-through' of the Taiwan Straits crisis. Taipei had been led to accept the status quo, and Washington had come to endorse it, during the first crisis and the inter-crisis period. As the first crisis drew to its end, the Administration had become increasingly reluctant to further appease what it considered an aggressive, expansionist regime. During the inter-crisis period, its predilection for defusing the off-shore islands issue had been dissipated both by its respect for Taipei's commitment to Quemoy and Matsu and, ironically, by the lack of any sense of urgency.

Peking could rightly conclude that 'you're damned if you do and you're damned if you don't' exert coercive pressure for a revision of this status quo. It felt dissatisfied as well as threatened by the American military presence on its maritime flank and by the existence of a Nationalist alternative in Taipei. By mid-1958, it had become quite clear that the PRC's attempts to achieve reunification by peaceful means, either by securing US military withdrawal or by appealing to Taipei over the head of its American patron, were unavailing. One of the most energetic appeals from Peking to Taipei prior to the second crisis appeared in February 1958:

peaceful liberation is to the advantage of both the people on Taiwan and the people on the mainland. The Kuomintang military and government functionaries will have a bright future after the liberation of Taiwan. The people in the motherland believe that the people on Taiwan will sooner or later realise their sincerity in this endeavor and will see through the ugly countenance of the US aggressors and respond to the motherland's call to return to this big family of fraternity and unity of the motherland, freeing themselves from the grasp of the vicious American talons.[25]

Understandably, Taipei rejected Peking's overtures as ploys to 'soften up' Taiwan and then seize it by force – 'peace' and 'force' being compared to the two edges of a Communist knife.[26] Peking's reaction seemed to be that, in that case, it would opt for sharpening the forceful edge, holding the peaceful edge in abeyance during the acute crisis period which would ensue.

However, Peking could not afford to disregard the risks entailed in excessive provocation of the United States – especially while the PRC lacked the benefit of a credible and effective Soviet nuclear umbrella. Alice Hsieh has written of a high-level PRC nuclear policy review occurring in the spring of 1958, as a result of which

the Chinese, aware that they could not depend on an immediate grant of a nuclear capability from the Soviet Union, had realised that they had no alternative but to rely on their own indigenous production of nuclear weapons through stepped up efforts for industrial and scientific development and to continue to adhere to a transitional strategy based on the acceptance of their own military weakness.[27]

In view of the ambiguity of the Soviet commitment and their own country's vulnerability, Chinese leaders reacted in an emphatically negative manner to American missile bases located around the periphery of the PRC, including Taiwan, following the emplacement of the Matador guided missiles in 1957. In March, the Chinese Government denounced these bases in the strongest terms, timing its declaration to coincide with the SEATO Council's meeting in Manila:

The setting up by the U.S.A. of bases for launching rockets with nuclear warheads on China's territory of Taiwan, which it occupies, and in South Korea and Japan has aggravated tension in the Far East . . . The setting up of such bases in more countries not only will tighten U.S. control over these countries and increase the danger of war, but will bring inestimable disaster upon these countries first of all, should war be started by the U.S.A.[28]

Joint military exercises which US forces conducted with those of the ROK and the ROC in April and May, including the test-firing of the Matador missiles, predictably provoked further PRC denunciations. *Jen-min Jih-pao* condemned these 'attempts to intimidate the people and to boost the low morale of the U.S.

lackeys, Chiang Kai-shek and Syngman Rhee. The Chinese and Korean people, however, have never been afraid of the aggressors.' [29]

An early signal of Peking's disposition to test Taipei's strength and Washington's commitments further – and possibly in a major way – emerged in the immediate aftermath of the Anti-Rightist campaign, in the context of the Sino-American talks in Geneva. The Geneva talks, the only forum for direct Sino-American communication, had been established following the first Taiwan Straits crisis, but were suspended in December 1957 – shortly before Ambassador Johnson was to be transferred from Geneva to Bangkok. After much procrastination in choosing Johnson's successor, the State Department finally nominated Edwin Martin, the First Secretary in its London embassy, as Johnson's temporary successor, a nomination which Peking rejected as an inadmissible downgrading of the talks. In March, it emerged in a letter from Martin to Ambassador Wang Ping-nan that the unsatisfactory nature of the talks was due to Peking's retention of six US prisoners, in spite of the 1955 agreement on exchange of nationals. This Lai Ya-li, Martin's counterpart in status, rejected on the grounds that the prisoners were not ordinary civilians but war criminals, whereas Washington remained allegedly guilty of 'obstruct[ing] thousands of Chinese in the United States from returning to their motherland'.[30] Finally, on 30 June, Peking warned that it would abandon the talks altogether unless the US agreed to resume them on an ambassadorial level within fifteen days, an ultimatum which Washington rejected along with a denial that it was trying either to downgrade or to terminate the discussions.[31]

On 1st July, Secretary Dulles announced that the Administration 'would not bow to any such ultimatum from the Chinese', but that, provided that Peking would agree to transferring the talks from Geneva to Warsaw, Ambassador to Poland Jacob Beam would 'presumably' be designated as the US representative in due course.[32] The expiration of the PRC's deadline resulted not in further denunciations from Peking, but rather in a relatively mild Foreign Ministry statement which seemed directed to making a resumption of the talks a fairly graceful exercise for both sides: 'That the United States should want to save a little face is understandable . . . Since the United States has declared its intention to resume the Sino-American ambassadorial talks soon, a few days' delay is not so objectionable.' [33] US officials continued to delay sending the memorandum on Sino-American talks, which Dulles had claimed was about to be sent when Peking first issued its ultimatum. The advent of the Middle East crisis was used to justify further US delay – State Department scribes claimed that 'We are just too busy nowadays' [34] – and it was not until the end of July, when high-level Sino-Soviet talks were about to begin in Peking, that the Department got around to designating Ambassador Beam as the US representative.

The course of events in July had made it quite clear that Washington was content with Sino-American consular contacts at the lowest level in Geneva and that, in fact, it was in no hurry to resume ambassadorial talks in spite of increasing East-West tension in mid-1958. It is possible that a more responsive US approach to the talks might have mitigated the more radical tone of PRC policy and strategy in the summer of 1958, but by the time Dulles and the State Department had overcome their political and institutional inertia, Peking had irrevocably entered the most extreme phases of its policies, internal and external.

Just as the initiation of the Sino-American talks in 1955 had been a signal of mild thaw in relations between the two states, so their suspension and resumption would prove to be accurate signs of important transformations between phases of chronic and acute crisis thereafter. This proved to be the case in 1958 and again in the late 1960s, with the escalation of the Vietnam War and the 'Great Proletarian Cultural Revolution'. However, the suspension of the talks during the most acute phases of Sino-American crisis forced both Washington and Peking to rely primarily on, and therefore refine the technique of, strategic rather than diplomatic communications.

Just a month after Peking's warning on the talks and only a few days after Washington's intentionally delayed offer to resume them, Premier Khrushchev and his Minister of Defence, Marshal Malinovsky, led a high-level Soviet delegation to Peking, where they met with Mao, Chou, their Minister of National Defence P'eng Teh-huai and equally high-ranking officials.[h] The presence of such important Government, Party and Army leaders at a four-day conference (from 31 July to 3 August) indicated that issues

[h] The other participants in the talks were Acting Foreign Minister V. V. Kuznetsov and Central Committee member B. N. Fonomarev, on the Russian side, and Foreign Minister Ch'en Yi and Central Committee Secretariat member Wang Chia-hsiang.

of the greatest import for Sino-Soviet relations and strategy must have been carefully considered. The communiqué emerging from the talks was singularly unenlightening about the specific decisions which were made. Instead, it vaguely alluded to 'all-round discussions on the urgent and important questions in the present international situation', recorded that 'China and the Soviet Union sternly denounce the flagrant aggression carried out by the United States and Britain in the Near and Middle East', and announced that the parties 'reached unanimous agreement on measures to be taken to oppose aggression and safeguard peace'. In its most scintillating (if still hopelessly over-generalised) section, the communiqué warned that: 'if the imperialist war maniacs should dare to impose war on the people of the world, all the countries and people who love peace and freedom will unite closely to wipe out clean the imperialist aggressors and so establish an everlasting peace'.[35] In spite of the difficulties that this document presents to the analyst, it is clear that Moscow and Peking were sufficiently infuriated by Middle Eastern reverses in July to prepare for political-military counter-offensives, whether over the Taiwan Straits or over Berlin. Moreover, the fact that the Chinese stepped up their threats immediately after this visit suggests that the Taiwan Straits question was high on the agenda of Sino-Soviet consultation. (The issue was not specifically mentioned in the communiqué, but this intentional omission probably reflected an unwillingness to disclose the Sino-Soviet hand – including possible disagreements – prematurely.)

It is not known whether the Russians actively discouraged or equivocated about a PRC probe of ROC and US commitments, but the course of the ensuing crisis did make it clear that Peking was concerned with Moscow as much as with Washington in its crisis behaviour. If Khrushchev and Malinovsky discouraged Mao in the beginning of August (as both Alice Hsieh and Donald Zagoria have tended to argue) [36] then PRC actions in August and September represented a tacit declaration of independence from Soviet control, as well as an effort to embarrass the Russians into supporting Chinese demands. This is the most likely possibility, for two reasons – one procedural and one substantive: first, such a high-level Soviet delegation would probably not have been called for at that time, unless there were serious disagreements too hot for normal inter-state or inter-party channels to handle;

second, Peking and Moscow differed, as we have seen, over the Communist camp's strategic superiority,[1] and especially over the manner in which any such apparent advantage should be translated into action.

On the strength of the hypothesis of Sino-Soviet dissension over anti-imperialist strategy prior to the re-escalating of the Taiwan Straits crisis, a lengthy *Jen-min Jih-pao* leader appearing on 8 August becomes far more comprehensible. Entitled 'Only Through Resolute Struggle May Peace Be Defended', it first hailed the Sino-Soviet communiqué and then alleged that 'Some soft-hearted advocates of peace' – without explicitly identifying who those advocates were – 'even naively believe that in order to relax tension at all costs the enemy must not be provoked. They dare not denounce the war provokers, they are unwilling to trace the responsibility of war and war danger and to differentiate between right and wrong on the issue of war and peace.'[38] When the New China News Agency publicised this leader, it omitted this section from its English edition. A not unreasonable inference is that Peking was concerned not to advertise the existence of an intramural dispute to its principal adversary, but to persuade its main ally to make a less accommodating analysis, and to take a more militant stand against 'imperialist aggression'. Citing in another untranslated section 'the historical experience of the Chinese people' against Japan and in Korea and Indochina, 'when resolute resistance against the aggressors forced them to accept the armistice', the leader argued that 'The results of these struggles show that so long as the forces of peace unite and reliance is placed in the people the ferocious U.S. imperialists can be beaten. They have nothing to be feared. There should be no compromise in dealing with the imperialists because this will end in submission.' This important leader amounted, then, to an elaborate defence of unity and uncompromising struggle, on the basis of both historical experience and up-to-date strategic estimates. It attacked 'the policy of "let each person take care of his own house, and pay no attention to the frost on the roof-top of another person"' – in yet another untranslated section — as doomed 'to cause the disintegration of the forces of peace' and 'to facilitate the oppression of the countries which, fearing war, oppose union with others and thus become isolated and helpless'.[39]

[1] Two weeks before, President Tito charged Chinese leaders with attempting to subvert world peace and dominate Asia through war.[37] He might well have been reflecting and/or encouraging similar Russian misgivings.

It broke ground for China's militant initiative in the Taiwan Straits a fortnight later, on the basis of a crisis analysis which was deemed to be consistent with the superiority of a united East over a vulnerable West.

It should be noted, however, that even if Peking and Moscow were far less divided than this discussion leads one to believe, PRC declaratory and operational behaviour in the pre-crisis period still served similar functions in preparing for the adversary crisis which ensued. For instance, if the Russians equivocated – perhaps limiting themselves to a plea that Peking should not push Washington too far – then the Chinese must have hoped to secure at least as rapid and effective support as in 1954–5. It is also conceivable that the Russians encouraged their allies to challenge the Americans within limits, partly to retaliate against Anglo-American intervention in Jordan and the Lebanon, and partly to keep the US off-balance in the Middle East and in Europe, where Khrushchev was preparing a further test over Berlin. In that case, their subsequent reluctance to support and identify themselves fully with the Chinese campaign to liberate Taiwan amounted to an act of betrayal, as Peking was to tell the world when the Sino-Soviet split came into the open in the 1960s.[40]

In any event, on 1st August, the PLA was hailed as 'invincible and irresistible', having 'no match in the whole world'. The Nationalist Air Force was considered so inferior – allegedly depending 'on U.S. imperialism for the supply of some old and obsolescent aircraft' – that 'it cannot be compared at all to the Air Force, P.L.A.'. Even the primitive 'People's Navy' claimed to 'have the necessary strength and will surely liberate Taiwan', although the writer understandably did not elaborate on how it proposed to overcome the Seventh Fleet.[41]

On its own, this was all good Armed Forces Day rhetoric, but all indications were that in the radicalised political climate of August 1958, Chinese Communist decision-makers were coming perilously close to believing their own propaganda. In the following week, Communist activity was on the increase in the Straits, and on the 6th Taipei declared a state of emergency. On the 8th, the State Department declared that Peking was 'trying to increase tension and raise the specter of war' in the Formosa Straits by increasing its air force strength on the mainland nearest Formosa.

The following day, the State Department issued a lengthy

circular to all its embassies which was a clear example of how *not* to defuse a crisis in the offing. The memorandum offered an elaborate justification of the Administration's policy of non-recognition of the PRC and declared that 'The Chinese Communist Party which holds mainland China in its grip is a tiny minority comprising less than 2 per cent of the Chinese people, and the regimentation, brutal repression, and forced sacrifices that have characterised its rule have resulted in extensive popular unrest.' It went on to predict 'that communism's rule in China is not permanent and that it one day will pass' and made the point that by 'withholding diplomatic recognition from Peiping, [the US] seeks to hasten that passing'.[42] Reacting one week later to the memorandum, *Ta Kung Pao* claimed that it reflected the 'isolation of the United States in the world today', which nevertheless failed to prevent the Administration from maintaining 'its bankrupt policy', and reiterated Chinese determination to liberate Taiwan.[43] By contrast, an approving leader in the *New York Times* warned that 'Our recognition of Red China would, in effect, aid and abet the Communist conspiracy for world domination'[44] – a reminder of that newspaper's traditional conservatism in foreign affairs prior to its liberal conversion in the 1960s.

On the 15th, an authoritative leader appearing in *Jen-min Jih-pao* confirmed the partial reaction which had appeared in *Ta Kung Pao* previously. It declared that the State Department memorandum 'exposes still more clearly the aggressiveness and ambition of U.S. imperialism' and it concluded that 'The liberation of Taiwan is a sacred responsibility of the Chinese people. We are determined and have the strength to liberate the last of our territory', notwithstanding the 'aggressive policy of U.S. imperialism'.[45]

At the same time, short-term strategies in the national interest continued to be related to Chinese Communist claims to the intrinsic superiority of the East over the West. An article entitled 'The Forces of the New Are Bound to Defeat the Forces of Decay', appearing in the 16 August issue of *Hung Ch'i* (Red Flag), pressed the thesis that 'Developments in the current international situation further confirm Comrade Mao Tse-tung's famous dictum: "The east wind prevails over the west wind". It is now abundantly clear that the forces of socialism are overwhelmingly superior to those of imperialism.' The 'U.S. bourgeoisie', 'rotten to the core', was seen as 'beyond recovery'; as a whole, 'The U.S. imperialists are isolated as never before . . .

over-extended on too long a front, they lack the necessary strength and are vulnerable at many points . . . the imperialist aggressive bloc that once made such a continuous hullabaloo about a third world war, is shaking in its shoes and worrying about its future.' As for the nuclear threat, the writer quoted Mao Tse-tung's comment to Anna Louise Strong that 'The atomic bomb is a paper tiger' and reiterated the view that 'The U.S. policy of atomic blackmail has never daunted the revolutionary people.' While downgrading the importance of the Bomb on the one hand, he proceeded to contradict this view by underscoring the significance of the Soviet nuclear and missile capability in deterring the imperialist threat.[46]

In spite of the article's internal inconsistencies, however, it is another revealing instance of the atmosphere of optimism about the superiority of socialism and of Chinese power which enveloped PRC preparations to reassert its challenge of US-ROC positions in the Taiwan Straits.[47]

Rapid escalation of the crisis

Unlike the initially gradual escalation of the first crisis, the second crisis over the Taiwan Straits escalated fairly rapidly after the first few weeks of military preparation and exchange of threats and abuse. On 23 August, three to five hundred PLA artillery pieces began intensive shelling of the Quemoys and Tan Island just to the south. This met with Nationalist reprisals in kind: between Communists and Nationalists, the military exchange amounted almost entirely to an artillery duel, with a small amount of strafing but no bombing undertaken by either side [48] – probably in recognition of the unacceptable penalties which reciprocal bombing could entail.

As far as the PLA was concerned, its commanders seemed to expect that a strategy of interdiction would (a) prevent enough supplies from reaching the Nationalist garrisons, (b) sufficiently isolate the ROC forces to make them susceptible to appeals to defect or surrender, and (c) if necessary, sufficiently weaken them to make an eventual invasion of the off-shore islands relatively uncostly. In line with these expectations, Fukien Front PLA Headquarters warned the ROC Quemoy Defence Headquarters on 28 August that:

The lone island of Quemoy is facing its doom under the serious assault of our powerful air force, navy and artillery . . . Not only will there be no hope for you to hold on and await reinforcements, but your withdrawal will be most difficult. Your attempt to rely on your defence works to carry out stubborn resistance will be futile . . .

The landing on Quemoy is imminent. You have reached the last critical stage of your fate. For your own sakes . . . you should immediately issue orders to surrender and lead your men to defect and come over to our side.[49]

The immediate rejoinders of the super-power patrons to the escalation of the crisis were relatively limited. On the US side, Congressman Morgan received a letter from Secretary Dulles, written before but disclosed on the same day as the first shelling, stating that an invasion of the off-shore islands would be a 'threat to peace in the area'. Dulles carefully left options open, however, on the extent of US commitment: it would be up to the President, he wrote, to determine the 'value of certain coastal positions' to Formosa if the Communists did attack, although he thereupon stated that 'over the last four years the ties between these islands and Formosa have been closer and their interdependence increased'.[50] On the 27th, President Eisenhower restricted himself to a statement of general support: the Administration would not 'desert our responsibilities or the statements that we have already made', but this could not deceive anyone who was familiar with the intentionally ambiguous phrasing of the Formosa Resolution. The most to which the President would commit himself was to note that the Nationalist commitment of a third of their forces to the off-shore islands 'makes a closer interlocking between the defense systems of the islands with Formosa than was the case before that'.[51]

On the side of the USSR, the commitment was similarly impressive on the surface and open-ended in substance: on the 31st, *Pravda* promised 'the necessary moral and material aid' to help Peking 'in its just struggle' against the imperialist 'aggressors', but offered no details about types of aid or extent of commitment.[52]

Three main forces acted toward escalating the crisis and implicating the super-powers more rapidly and effectively than in 1954–5. First, the sheer momentum of crisis escalation was more powerful as a result of the intensity of local initiatives and responses from the start. Second, the local actors were both pressing hard for super-power support: Peking, to deter US intervention if not support, and failing that, to be able to press its attack more militantly under Soviet nuclear protection against massive retaliation; Taipei, to deter a PRC attempt to invade any more off-shore islands, and failing that, to be able to rely on

American logistic support and if necessary Marines to hold the line. Third, all of the parties could draw on past crisis experience, both in the Straits and elsewhere, as well as on contingency planning in August, to respond more quickly to challenges or threats.

The Soviet Union by and large resisted these pressures; the United States did not. On 27 August, both the *Essex* and four destroyers from the Sixth Fleet were dispatched to reinforce the Seventh Fleet in the Taiwan Straits. News reports indicated that US nuclear forces were being strengthened in the area – a development which the Defense Department confirmed on the 29th, and which the State Department accompanied with the ominous (if somewhat cryptic) warning that any Communist attempt to revise the status quo could not be limited. The Nationalist Chinese were making sure, in the meantime, that the US commitment to all of their territory would be as clear-cut as possible. The very considerable talents of Wellesley-educated Mme Chiang Kai-shek (sister, incidentally, of Soong Ching-ling) were deployed in this direction, when she told the American Legion convention in Chicago on 3 September that 'a clear-cut, strong stand by the U.S. . . . will stop the Communists short in their tracks', whereas 'no amount of appeasement will do any good'.[53]

It was not so much Mme Chiang's charm, however, as it was the combination of crisis pressures from the Straits which decided the nature of US response. As long as Nationalist forces could withstand Communist attacks on their own, the Americans could maintain an indirect role in the crisis, helping to strengthen the defences of Formosa and the Pescadores without becoming involved over the off-shore islands. As Communist pressure increased, Washington could step up its military supplies – particularly howitzers, Sabre jets and finally Sidewinder air-to-air missiles – while remaining in the background. If PLA artillery interdiction and blockade threatened to cut off the off-shore islands, the Seventh Fleet could – and did – convoy ROC supply vessels under air cover from the 13th Air Force. This is the closest that the Administration would move toward direct involvement in the conflict, and yet it is noteworthy that it would abstain from bringing the war to the Chinese mainland, even from bombing the Fukien coast, while retaining Quemoy and Matsu in Nationalist hands.[54]

This would be no mean achievement at a time when pressures

to retaliate more massively or to relinquish coastal positions willingly were building up in Washington. It must be recognised, however, that Peking would share the responsibility, and the credit, for this outcome. By and large, the PLA would refrain from air attacks on Quemoy, and would not build up sufficient numbers of men and amphibious equipment to invade the off-shore islands. It could have attempted to do both, but a combination of factors dictated its reliance on a limited strategy of interdiction and blockade. First, of course, Chinese Communist military commanders expected this strategy to succeed in and of itself. Secondly, they did not wish gratuitously to provoke retaliatory air strikes against their coastal positions (shore batteries, jet airfields, and urban centres) or even further into the mainland. Thirdly, their objective was to secure US non-intervention and a collapse of Nationalist resistance, prior to a take-over of Taiwan and the Penghus, not to capture a few coastal islands through a disproportionate sacrifice of their own strength and of the symbolic value of these islands themselves.

The first few days of September produced a momentary lull in the crisis, probably related to Peking's reluctance to press an attack without Soviet reassurances against possible US retaliation. While the Russians remained notably unforthcoming about their commitments, the Americans were yielding somewhat to pressures – from both Taipei and Peking, contrary to the latter's intentions – to strengthen their commitment to Nationalist positions. On 4 September, Secretary Dulles issued an important statement, cleared with Eisenhower at the summer White House in Newport, Rhode Island, warning Peking that the President 'would not hesitate' to use armed force 'in insuring the defence of Formosa', if he deemed such action to be necessary. 'Military dispositions have been made by the United States so that a Presidential determination, if made, would be followed by action both timely and effective.' Along with offering the reassuring implication that any significant change in US tactics (such as the use of tactical nuclear weapons) would require prior Presidential approval, the statement also indicated that the defence of Quemoy and Matsu has 'increasingly become related to the defence of Taiwan'. It then put the issue in the general context of US interests in the region: 'any naked use of force', said Dulles, would 'forecast a widespread use of force in the Far East which would endanger vital free world positions and the security of the United States'.[55]

The US was still not fully committed to defending the off-shore islands, although Washington provided sufficiently strong hints of the serious consequences of any PRC attempt to forcefully seize Quemoy and Matsu, minimally satisfying Taipei and giving further pause to Peking. As such, the Newport statement represented quite a departure from the predisposition of the Administration in its early years to rely on crude threats of massive and even nuclear retaliation. If this was brinkmanship, it was brinkmanship with kid gloves, carefully modulated to correspond with the extent of Nationalist commitment and Communist threat. Instead of treating Peking (and US right-wingers) to inflated, muscle-flexing rhetoric, Dulles and Eisenhower relied on more subtle intimations of threat. This was a direct benefit of past crisis experience.

One might still argue that Washington could and should have enforced a more clear-cut division between the two Chinas – a division running through the centre of the Taiwan Straits rather than along the mainland's coast. Such a course might have better served US interests and stability in the area, but the Administration preferred a status quo option where the dangers it knew seemed safer than those it did not. The course it adopted led neither to a major psychological blow for Taipei, nor to the risk of an important reverse for Washington, which would hurt the Administration far more during the mid-term elections than would charges of lack of imagination and innovation. In retrospect, Dulles' relatively cautious strategy succeeded in striking a neat balance between the need to compel the recalcitrant Nationalists to reduce their forces on the off-shore islands, and the need to deter the Communists from attacking and putting into jeopardy such a substantial proportion of expensively equipped ROC troops.

The success of US strategy was ensured on 14 September when a Seventh Fleet convoy of ROC supply vessels succeeded in breaking the previously highly effective PRC blockade (enforced by artillery barrages and torpedo boat raids). Whereas the blockade had successfully cut into as much as 80 per cent of Nationalist supplies prior to that date, neither deep-penetration shells nor PLA Air Force strafing significantly altered the ROC military advantage after that date.[56] A major contribution to the continuous supply of the islands was the introduction of highly mobile LSTs (landing ship/tanks) and LVTs (amphibious tractors), whose versatility and small size eluded PLA guns.

Besides the intervention of the Seventh Fleet and the effectiveness of its 'small ship operation', rapid, qualitative improvements in Nationalist ground and air forces ensured their off-shore superiority. The entrenchment of ROC artillery in Quemoy granite made it invulnerable to all but the most direct and powerful PRC strikes. Moreover, the US-supplied eight-inch howitzers (the smallest guns capable of firing nuclear shells) signalled a US willingness to supply tactical nuclear weapons to the Quemoy garrison in extreme circumstances.[57] This implication did not escape Peking; if anything, the Chinese tended to exaggerate their significance. According to *Jen-min Jih-pao*, 'U.S. imperialism has now confronted mankind with the danger of guided missile and nuclear warfare.'[58]

While the howitzers related more to the threat of what *might* happen, the US-provided Sabre jets and Sidewinder missiles (with their lethal accuracy) very much affected what *did* happen, by establishing Nationalist air superiority over the PLA's air force. Even the Russian-supplied MIG-15s began to evade engagements. This was especially the case after 24 September, when thirty-two Sabre jets, armed with Sidewinders, succeeded both in shooting down over ten MIGs and in fighting their way out of a trap set by over a hundred others.[59] As former Defense Secretary McElroy modestly put it in retrospect, 'The Communist Chinese just folded up like a tent.'

Just as the howitzers spared the Americans the need to intervene directly on the ground, the Sabre jets and Sidewinders spared them the need to engage in direct combat with the PLA in the air. This McElroy confirmed when he told me that 'we were flying up and down the Strait, but we never got into combat'.[60] The Administration succeeded, therefore, in demonstrating its power at the ringside [j] while its Nationalist proxies put it into good effect in direct engagements with the Communists.

Declension and de-escalation of the crisis

Thomas Schelling reminds us that deterrence is far easier to implement than compellence. This is true if only because the former

---

[j] There are indications that US forces occasionally forsook their position as enrapt spectators and became prejudiced referees. American pilots frequently flew close to and occasionally within the three-mile limit.[61] The latter could generally be ascribed to ordinary navigational error but obviously could have been avoided if flights did not occur so near the PRC

is governed by a reasonable degree of doubt while the latter must depend on mutual agreement or physical coercion. In the second Taiwan Straits crisis, the continued indeterminacy of Soviet commitments was enough to transform the doubt raised by US actions and declarations into a credible deterrent against such a high-risk operation as a military invasion of Quemoy and Matsu. Peking decided to resort to lower-risk means, both political and military, to try to achieve its aims; this resort from escalatory to de-escalatory tactics, combined with super-power caution, permitted the crisis to enter a phase of declension prior to de-escalation. As for the US, it was unable to do much about Chiang Kai-shek's polite strategic blackmail, when ROC forces (90 000 on the Quemoys, 10 000 on the Matsus) were concentrated as much to force Washington's hand as to defend the off-shore islands: Walter Lippmann wrote that as a result of the crisis 'it has become brutally clear that Chiang thinks he has the opportunity, and is determined to seize it, to embroil the United States in a war with the Chinese mainland'.[62] As soon as the crisis began to de-escalate, however, Washington resumed its pressure on Taipei to redistribute its forces to reflect more closely the American view of strategic priorities in the area.

The phase of declension was signalled on the same day as the Newport statement, when Peking laid formal claim to all waters and islands within twelve miles of its coasts.[63] This was in effect a legalistic substitute for the military course which the PRC had announced in August, but it had no direct effect since the US declared that it would only respect a three-mile limit. A further, more realistic Chinese initiative met with a positive US response: after a lengthy recapitulation and defence of past policy and a ritualistic affirmation that 'The Chinese people's determination to liberate their own territory of Taiwan and the Penghu Islands is unshakeable', Chou En-lai offered, on 6 September, to resume ambassadorial talks to discuss the Taiwan question, in spite of 'the fact that the U.S. Government often acts otherwise than it says and often uses peaceful negotiation as a smokescreen to cover up its actual deed of continuously expanding aggression'[64] – a perception which was the mirror image of the American view of PRC manipulation of negotiations at Panmunjom and Geneva.

At any rate, President Eisenhower 'himself accepted Chou

territorial limit. The proximity of the flights was clearly linked, however, to a US refusal to accept what it considered to be arbitrary PRC interference in international waters and airspace up to an alleged twelve-mile limit.

En-lai's proposal with greater alacrity than Chou had shown in his response to Dulles' gesture', according to Ambassador Kenneth Young's account.[65] The White House announced, the same day, that US Ambassador to Poland Jacob Beam 'stands ready promptly to meet' with Wang Ping-nan, the Chinese Ambassador to Poland who had conducted the talks for China since they began in Geneva. Washington entered a careful proviso that it would not be 'a party to any arrangement which would prejudice the rights of our ally, the Republic of China',[66] but this attempt to reassure Taipei did not obscure the fact that the resumption (again in its absence) of the ambassadorial talks, transferred from Geneva to Warsaw, represented a significant decline in the level of Sino-American tension.

Confirmation of the change in the PRC's approach to the Taiwan question came from Mao Tse-tung himself, speaking at the Supreme State Conference on 8 September. Instead of emphasising the PLA's role in forcing America's hand, Mao professed to take the longer view and rely on the contradictions confronting the imperialists, including progressive, popular forces, for ultimate victory.

China's territory of Taiwan, Lebanon and all U.S. military bases on foreign territories are like nooses round the necks of U.S. imperialists. The Americans themselves, and nobody else, made their nooses, and they themselves put them round their necks and handed the ends of the ropes to the Chinese people, the people of the Arab countries and all peoples who love peace and oppose aggression. The longer the U.S. aggressors remain in their places the tighter the nooses round their necks will become.[67]

When Wang Ping-nan returned to Warsaw four days later, after consultations in Peking and Moscow, he disclosed that 'Chairman Mao Tse-tung has said [also at the Supreme State Conference] that the (Sino-American) talks might lead to some results provided that both sides had the sincere desire to settle the (Taiwan) question', and added that 'I look forward even more to seeing these results brought about soon in Warsaw.' [68]

As tension declined, it became much easier for all parties to assume impressive declaratory postures without having to support them on an operational level. This was blatantly clear on the Soviet side: it was only on 8 September that President Eisenhower received a letter from Chairman Khrushchev, calling for moderation and warning that 'an attack on the Chinese People's

Republic, which is a great friend, ally and neighbour of our country, is an attack on the Soviet Union'.[69] President Eisenhower's reply on 12 September reiterated previous White House statements that the best way to ensure peace would be to persuade the Chinese Communists to 'discontinue their military operations and to turn to a policy of peaceful settlement of the Taiwan dispute'.[70]

After Ambassadors Beam and Wang opened talks on the crisis on 15 September, Khrushchev wrote to Eisenhower that neither Moscow nor Peking were intimidated by Washington's 'atomic blackmail' and 'may no one doubt that we shall completely honour our commitments' to the PRC; [71] the White House rejected the Kremlin's 'false accusations' as 'abusive and intemperate' on 20 September.[72] By then, it was clear that effective Soviet support for China had been delayed until the de-escalation of the crisis, when it was no longer much use: the less the danger, the bolder Khrushchev could afford to appear. Indeed, the latter admitted to a TASS correspondent that 'The USSR will come to the help of the CPR if the latter is attacked from without; speaking more concretely, if the United States attacks the CPR.' [73] This explanation dramatised the *partial* character of the Soviet commitment throughout the crisis: Moscow would not necessarily come to Peking's aid if the latter attacked first or if Sino-American conflict did not encompass PRC territory, both conditions remaining subject to the cautious interpretation of the Kremlin.

A second interesting development in the phase of de-escalation was Washington's endeavour to make Taipei adopt a less aggressive posture in the off-shore islands. Partly in relation to such an endeavour, US officials tended to issue bolder statements as the danger of war with Peking receded. For instance, Defense Secretary McElroy stated on the 11th that the US had 'made it clear that we would resist an assault on Quemoy by the Chinese Communists' and on the 12th, he added that all possibilities for supplying the Quemoys, in the face of PLA bombardment, had not been exhausted – comments which well-placed sources interpreted as a warning that the US would retaliate against coastal artillery with tactical nuclear weapons if necessary.[74] A week later, the Pentagon announced that US pilots were authorised to engage in 'hot pursuit', even into enemy territory, of any attacking PRC aircraft.[75] Even Eisenhower coupled an expressed belief that 'negotiations and conciliation should never be abandoned in favour of force and strife' with the more combative assertion that the US could not be 'either lured or frightened into appeasement', in his radio-television address of 11 September.[76]

These reassurances helped to allay Nationalist fears of a US sell-out to the Communists in the Warsaw talks, although such fears remained near the surface. To emphasise this fact, George Yeh, now ROC Ambassador to Washington, told newsmen on his arrival that his Government would never accept a cease-fire or a renunciation of force, and Premier Chen Cheng warned on the 19th that Taipei would 'not accept any resolution reached in Warsaw that might prejudice the rights of (Nationalist) China'. The continued US emphasis on not discussing any such resolution (dating back to Dulles' provisos to this effect on the 6th as well as in 1955) made this much less of an issue, therefore, than the future of ROC forces on the off-shore islands. In the same speech, Chen Cheng declared: 'Nobody has the right to make us demilitarise these islands. Communist occupation of Quemoy and Matsu would pose a serious threat to the security of all the Far East area.' [77]

Under US pressure, with the 1954 Dulles-Yeh correspondence limiting ROC freedom of action anyway, Chiang Kai-shek conceded on 29 September that the off-shore islands had become a 'shield' for the protection of Taiwan, rather than a springboard for invasion of the mainland.[78] For the ROC, this was a crucial change in emphasis, but in reality it represented a psychological readjustment to a state of affairs which had existed at least since 1955 – namely a ROC inability to do more than partially destabilise strategic interactions between Peking and Washington, further limited by its agreement not to use force without American consent, and finally controlled by the US refusal to support any attempt to invade the mainland.

It had become clear that the Communists had so fortified those positions of the Fukien and Chekiang coasts opposite Nationalist territory that the 'springboard' function of Quemoy and Matsu had disappeared. This Secretary Dulles recognised in a very revealing memorandum at the time: 'these mainland areas are so heavily militarised and so forbidding in their geographical formation that they do not serve as a useful place for staging commando raids or introducing intelligence agents, much less for an invasion in aid of a future revolt'.[79]

The greatest importance of the change of mission for the off-shore islands is that it implied a reduction of Nationalist forces so as to approximate their defensive role. Washington lost no time in pressing this point – in his 30 September news conference, Secretary Dulles signalled uncharacteristic flexibility on the Taiwan Straits issue. He not only confirmed that his Government had 'no commitment of any kind' to help Chiang return to the mainland, but he also implied that the Administration would favour reducing ROC forces on Quemoy and Matsu if the Communists agreed to a cease-fire in the Straits. In the bluntest public statement yet to emerge from a high American official, Dulles told the press: 'If there were a cease-fire in the area which seemed to be reasonably dependable, I think it would be foolish to keep these forces on these islands. We thought that it was rather foolish to put them there.' [80] Moreover, Dulles by no means excluded a tacit and mutual acceptance of a *de facto* cease-fire in the Taiwan Straits; in fact, he rather favoured such an outcome. He observed in the same memorandum that 'the formation which best serves our purposes is, on *our* side, along the area of close contact, i.e. the off-shore islands, to do what we would presumably do if there were an armistice, as in Korea and Vietnam; and thus, we would hope, build up a *de facto* armistice condition on *both* sides'. 'Under the conditions suggested', Dulles concluded, 'some appreciable reduction of forces . . . would give comparable security to what now exists. There would be enough forces left not only to maintain internal security, but to put up a substantial resistance. The number left behind could at any time be augmented from Taiwan.' [81] What is important to emphasise in this context is that no high American official, and certainly not Secretary Dulles, advocated a total withdrawal from any of the off-shore islands remaining in ROC hands in 1958. The lone dissenter, General Ridgway, had retired; Dulles and his associates viewed a concentration of ROC forces on Taiwan instead of the off-shore islands as a contribution to allied strategic mobility against the PRC, rather than as part of a more flexible diplomatic overture to Peking. In Dulles' words, 'The ability of the Chinese would be increased with less diffusion of their forces, with more located at a focal point such as Taiwan. From there they could be either re-deployed to the off-shore islands or elsewhere, rather than be immobilised on the off-shore islands.' [82] On 1 October, the President told his news conference that

We want a peaceful solution, and fundamentally anyone can see that the two islands (Quemoy and Matsu) as of themselves, as two pieces of territory, are not greatly vital to Formosa. But of course the Chinese Nationalists hold that if you give way to that, you have a way to exposing us to great attack and that is a different thing than just concluding that two pieces of territory are the vital issue.[83]

Almost as quickly, however, Chiang Kai-shek announced his opposition to reducing the island garrisons as the price of a cease-fire, and Dulles hastily instructed Ambassador Drumright to 'straighten out' misconceptions that 'gave an exaggerated idea of a shift of position on our part'.[84]

In spite of the Nationalist attempt to deprive the State Department of its bargaining counter for a cease-fire, the Americans adopted a mechanism for strategic communication with Peking more directly under their control: the Seventh Fleet suspended its convoys of supplies to the off-shore islands when the Fukien coastal batteries suspended their bombardment, and resumed the convoy when bombardment was renewed. This was a response to Defense Minister P'eng Teh-huai's 6 October announcement of a one-week cease-fire in the Straits, during which Nationalists would be 'fully free to ship in supplies on condition that there would be no American escort'. P'eng had reiterated the PRC view that 'the question of a cease-fire does not arise' between Peking and Washington, since the crisis was 'an internal Chinese matter' which should be settled among the Chinese themselves, on the basis of a one-China formula.[85]

Thus began another curious phase of Communist overtures both to Taipei and to 'our compatriots on Quemoy', in which the PRC attempted unsuccessfully to exclude the US from an eventual settlement of the crisis and, more generally, of the civil war. In the same message of 6 October, P'eng emphasised that 'We all are Chinese. Of all choices, peace is the best . . . There is only one China, not two in the world. To this, you also agree, as proved by the documents issued by your leaders.' He then contrasted the advantages of reunification with the risks of continued alignment with America, in much the same terms employed by Peking vis-à-vis Taipei in 1973: 'The day will certainly come when the Americans will abandon you. Do you not believe it? . . . The clue is already there in the statement made by Dulles on 30 September. Placed in such circumstances, do you not feel wary? In the last analysis, the American imperialists are our common enemy.'[86] On 8 October, the US halted its convoys of

ROC supply vessels to Quemoy for the period of the cease-fire; on the 13th, Peking extended the cease-fire for two additional weeks and Washington continued with its halt until the PLA's resumption of the bombardment on 21 October, one week ahead of schedule, in honour of Dulles' visit to Chiang Kai-shek.[87] On the 25th, the Communists began alternate-day bombardment of the off-shore islands, as a further twist in their tactics. Admiral Arleigh Burke, the Chief of Naval Operations at the time, went rather overboard when he attacked this 'off-again-on-again routine', designed to 'wear down the free world will to resist'. 'The world needs no better demonstration', said he, 'of the barbarism and brutality of Communism than this.' [88] To the contrary, it is clear that Peking was prepared to permit supplies to reach the Nationalist garrisons, but was not prepared to relinquish its demonstration of dissatisfaction with a *de facto* cease-fire which only confirmed the *status quo ante*. In fact, these methods were relatively sophisticated albeit coercive; they were hardly barbarous.

The October period of bombardment alternating with cease-fire might superficially appear to be a further escalation of the crisis, following the period from 23 August to 6 September. It makes more sense, however, to consider it in the context of crisis de-escalation, and of consolidation of Sino-American communications. At no time in October did either Washington or Peking betray the kind of crisis behaviour which was characteristic of August and September: rapid escalation of threats and actions; relative loss of independent control over the course of events in the Straits; suspension of diplomatic in favour of strategic interactions; and fear of a broadening of the conflict. Instead, both the Warsaw talks and deliberated control of their strategic activities in the Straits proceeded hand-in-hand, in much the same way that they have over the subsequent years of chronic crisis.

Outcome of the crisis

In retrospect, it is clear that the crisis served to freeze a remarkably fluid situation. Although alternate-day Chinese Communist bombardment began on 20 October, and although there would be a brief flare-up over the Straits in June 1962, the period following the 1958 crisis has been characterised by only moderate tension and primarily political interactions.

Many people hoped that the return of Quemoy and Matsu to

a fitting obscurity would permit the United States to de-couple its commitment to their defence. They overlooked the cardinal fact that these islands symbolised the future unification of China – to both Taipei and Peking.[k] They also overlooked the sheer force of inertia, permitting bureaucracies to retain policies that are more notable for their ambiguity and duration than for clarity or enlightened self-interest.

In more immediate terms, the crisis has been seen to have three main effects. First, it was a blow to the Sino-Soviet alliance, which provided for unqualified mutual assistance. Moreover, it had a jarring effect on Peking's view of past Soviet contributions, by putting them in a more accurate, and less favourable, light.

Second, the crisis induced Washington to insist on the defensive character of its alliance with the Chinese Nationalists. It also forced Taipei, on 23 October, to renounce the use of force in returning to the mainland. A joint communiqué following a conference between Foster Dulles and Chiang Kai-shek, issued that day, stated that:

The Government of the Republic of China considers that the restoration of freedom to its people on the mainland is its sacred mission. It believes that the foundation of this mission resides in the hearts and minds of the Chinese people and that the principal means of successfully achieving its mission is the implementation of Dr. Sun Yat-sen's three people's principles [nationalism, democracy and social well-being] and not the use of force.[90]

This communiqué essentially represented a ROC surrender to the conclusions which Secretary Dulles had reached prior to his visit. In a secret memorandum prepared for his 22 October meeting with Chiang Kai-shek, Dulles had written that most free world countries felt (and he did not disagree with this) 'that the relationship between the GRC [Government of the Republic of China] and CPR not only endangers the peace but that the GRC *wants* it to endanger the peace and involve the US as the only

---

[k] Cf. Anna Louise Strong's interpretation of Peking's thinking: 'To take Tsinmentao [Quemoy] at present would isolate Taiwan and thus assist Dulles in his policy of building "two Chinas". It would deprive the Chinese on Taiwan of their hopes of "return to mainland", hopes that Peking will realise for them, but in its own way. It would throw Taiwan on the mercy of Washington. Hence Peking strengthens Tsinmentao and attaches it firmly to Taiwan, hoping later to take them both in a "package deal".' [89] Although something of a rationalisation, this interpretation seems to have some substance, in view of Peking's curious appeal to Taipei to make a common front against the Americans.

means of returning to the mainland'. He then insisted that the ROC's long-term future depended on its being able to shed its image 'as a civil war survival essentially militaristic in its outlook', and to this end he pressed Chiang to 'make it clear to the world that the bases for GRC counter-attack against the mainland are not in the armed might of the GRC or in its off-shore positions, but rather in the minds and souls of the 600 million Chinese people on the mainland who hope and pray for delivery from their present bondage'. His memorandum concluded with a list of 'acts which might be taken in an effort to dramatise the larger and enduring role of the GRC', which included (1) armistice at least on a basis of *de facto* reciprocity, (2) no ROC 'attempt forcibly to return to the mainland', (3) no Nationalist commando raids, overflights and 'like provocations', (4) retention of the off-shore islands but abandonment of the 'use (of) these islands for prosecution of the civil war, e.g. for blockading the Ports of Amoy and Foochow, or "jumping off" to the mainland', (5) following a cease-fire, 'adjustments' of ROC forces 'in an effort to achieve greater mobility' – undoubtedly a euphemism for force reduction along the mainland's coast, and amusingly if not gratuitously, (6) 'increasing emphasis on Chinese education, art and . . . culture'.[91]

It is remarkable that Secretary Dulles became so committed not only to a *stabilisation* of the ROC-PRC balance in the Taiwan Straits but also to an *amelioration* of that balance – in his words, to a condition of 'stabilised tranquillity'.[92] It is at least equally remarkable that his determination was strong enough to extract, from such a recalcitrant ally, an endorsement of a public statement which explicitly supported the essence of his personal views and implicitly subscribed to even the more controversial consequences of these views. Assistant Secretary Robertson was quite right when he wrote (probably with a sense of personal regret) to Elmo Roper on 31 October that 'The present policies of the Chinese Government should remove any lingering fear that we might be drawn involuntarily into hostilities by a free Chinese attempt to overthrow the Communist regime by an attack on the mainland.'[93]

It is true that Lincoln White, the State Department spokesman, introduced the qualification on 31 October that Taipei would still use force 'for self-defense or in the case of a large-scale uprising' on the mainland,[94] and that Premier Chen Cheng and other Nationalist leaders spoke of the need to stage a 'counter-attack' and of the imminence of popular revolt in the PRC.[95] Yet it was abundantly clear by November 1958 that, in practical terms, the Eisenhower Administration had completed the long-winded process of re-leashing the Chiang regime, which it had begun three long years before with the negotiation of the Mutual Defense Treaty. Taipei, for its part, would have to remain content (1) with having successfully rebuffed Peking's probe, (2) with being able to retain Quemoy and Matsu under US protection, and (3) with continuing to resist successfully US pressures to reduce the number of its forces on the off-shore islands.[96]

The third effect, from Peking's point of view, was that there was a salutary change away from the Nationalists' initial threats of imminent attack across the Straits. The PRC's probing action did not reveal the anticipated weakness on the other side, but potential PRC losses were clearly minimised by its prior decision not to attempt an invasion of the off-shore islands. (The facts that landing craft were not assembled and that the typhoon season was imminent bear this out.) [97] Peking had demonstrated its freedom of manoeuvre, but it had also revealed its inability to press its claims to a successful conclusion.

Theoretical implications of the crisis

The second Taiwan Straits crisis has helped to highlight many theoretical issues which have been discussed in the context of the previous crises.

Structure: action and actors. One of the most important points about the second crisis in the Taiwan Straits is that its 'action structure' was determined in large part by its 1954–5 predecessor. The Sino-American test of strength was conducted in essentially the same way in both crises, except that in the 1958 crisis the Americans did not permit the Nationalists to use their air force over the mainland, even to strike the Communists' shore batteries; the Communists reciprocated by restricting their bombardment of Quemoy to artillery.

This development is in line with my earlier observation that Taipei was no longer the autonomous proxy of yesteryear: its political influence on Washington had declined considerably since the early 1950s and its field of independent action was seriously limited as a result of strong US pressure. Ever since the 1954 Dulles-Yeh agreement, it had become increasingly clear that armed invasion of the mainland was no longer an option for Taipei. This new position was confirmed officially by the joint Chiang-Dulles undertaking, on 23 October 1958, to renounce the use of force in the Kuomintang's sacred mission to return to the mainland.

The main American problem at this time was no longer the remote contingency of a Nationalist invasion of the mainland. The new problem was two-fold, relating to whether the United States could (1) soothe Nationalist sensitivities and deter future PRC attacks, and (2) diminish the strategic status of the off-shore islands even further, from that of 'shield' to that of 'military outpost'. Some may have seen these efforts as initial steps toward the eventual de-coupling of the US commitment, but they were most likely intended simply to forestall a major military defeat in the event of a massive PRC attack on Quemoy and Matsu. Whatever the intention, the net effect was a partial – and therefore unreliable and potentially unstable – paring of the commitment.

This ambivalent outcome arose from the contradiction between US efforts, which suffered because of the lack of a definite ultimate purpose, and Nationalist commitments, which were resistant to change. In 1958, the Defense Department had reversed its earlier position and accepted the JCS recommendation that, because of their exposed position, Quemoy and Matsu 'should be vacated (or lightly manned as outposts only)'. Defense Secretary McElroy had urged this view on President Eisenhower (on 11 September), and had also warned that Chiang Kai-shek hoped to 'promote a fight between the United States and the Chinese Communists as a prelude to a Chinese Nationalist invasion of the mainland'.[98] When Mr McElroy pressed Chiang to reduce the number of Nationalist troops on Quemoy and Matsu, however, he was as unsuccessful as his colleagues had been – and would continue to be. The record of these efforts is a good example of the extent to which a client state can hope to limit the concessions required by its patron.

Finally, the US failure to tailor its commitment to its liking can be explained by the perceived dominance of the crisis system and, consequently, by reduced US freedom of action. A State Department 'Memorandum Re Formosa Strait Situation', dated 4 September 1958, put this bluntly to President Eisenhower: 'Once we intervened to save the off-shore islands, we could not abandon that result without unacceptable damage to the safety of the free world and our influence in it.'[99] The successful US deterrence of further PRC escalation was due, in the meantime, to Peking's unwillingness to risk attacking the American convoy or following up its ineffectual bombardment of the Nationalist garrison on Quemoy with an amphibious landing. Here, the accuracy of the Sidewinder missiles and the nuclear potential of the howitzers seemed to be decisive in Peking's assessment of risks.

Crisis triad and dyad. The other side of this issue of 'client control' was that American control over Taipei was matched by Russian control over Peking. The 1958 crisis, in this sense, consisted of a Chinese test of the resolve of both the US and the USSR. It was therefore noteworthy that Khrushchev's bellicose support of Peking, in the form of notes to Eisenhower, came only *after* the Chinese offer to resume the Sino-American talks on 6 September, and that Russian support increased to the nuclear level only as the danger of East–West conflict receded. After the Sino-Soviet conflict broke out into open polemics in 1963, the Chinese would observe bitterly that

The Soviet leaders expressed their support for China on 7 and 19 September respectively. Although at that time the situation in the Taiwan Straits was tense, there was no possibility that a nuclear war would break out and no need for the Soviet Union to support China with its nuclear weapons. It was only when they were clear that this was the situation that the Soviet leaders expressed their support for China.[100]

The emergence of this new crisis triad, consisting of Moscow, Peking and Washington,[1] augmented the degree of each actor's doubt about the extent of the others' commitments in the crisis. This doubt was successfully manipulated by Moscow and Washington vis-à-vis Peking, so that a crisis which might well have gone out of control, under the instigation of the local parties, entered relatively smoothly and rapidly into a phase of declension and then de-escalation.

[1] As I have already indicated, Taipei's role was rather more restricted to de-stabilising the triangular system at the peak of crisis, than to becoming fully engaged in strategic interactions throughout the crisis. Tang Tsou's analysis, by contrast, places Taipei much more in the centre of the second Taiwan Straits crisis and seems to underestimate the deterrent role of Sino-American crisis interactions and the inhibiting effect of Sino-Soviet relations.[101]

Perhaps the most compelling reason for Russia's role being so significant in the 1958 crisis in the Taiwan Straits is that the crisis threshold was initially so weak in this case. There was hardly any buffer between Chinese and American forces, and both Taipei and Peking refused to play the proxy roles of the French and Vietnamese in Indochina. Soviet inhibitions seemed to fulfill the crisis control roles vacated by the buffers and proxies of previous crises. In this sense, this crisis is the first to offer lessons on the prospects for world order after the breakdown of Cold War bipolarity. Whereas the international setting was sufficiently stable in 1955 to permit the Sino-American crisis system to be self-directing and self-controlling, the changing balance of power in the late 1950s entailed an increase in the number of primary strategic actors, both globally and regionally.

A further issue, which remains largely hypothetical, is whether the original crisis *dyad* could have reached the stage of de-escalation without the intervention of a third (supernumerary) party, Russia. From the record of increased Sino-American sophistication in crisis-handling, one can infer that the crisis dyad would ultimately have become self-controlling. On one side, the Chinese Communists displayed both operational caution in the Straits and strategic flexibility vis-à-vis Nationalists and Americans. On the other side, the Americans were able to regulate their commitment and taper it to the demands of the crisis: their rôle ranged from indirect participation as a source of essential supplies to more direct involvement in breaking the PRC blockade and effectively guaranteeing the off-shore islands against massive attacks. Nevertheless, the refusal of Moscow to support Peking fully and unconditionally undoubtedly reduced the risks provoked by the most direct Sino-American crisis interactions since the Korean War.

Communication. As in the previous cases, the 1958 crisis also raises the issue of Sino-American communications. The interplay between diplomatic interactions in Warsaw and strategic interactions in the Taiwan Straits is particularly striking in this case. In terms of timing alone, the fact that the talks, suspended by the United States in December 1957, were not resumed during the escalation phase of crisis was a source of serious alarm both to Peking and to many Americans, in spite of the fact that the actual content of the talks was rather sterile.

A second communications relationship which has been ex-

amined is that between PRC bombardment and US convoy of
Nationalist supply ships up to three miles from the mainland.
Two striking examples of this link are (1) the US halt in convoys on 8 October, two days after the PRC cease-fire, and
(2) the resumed PRC bombardment on 21 October, one day after
the US had allegedly broken the truce by escorting a Nationalist
vessel to Quemoy but more likely timed to coincide with Dulles'
visit to Chiang Kai-shek. This relationship is relevant to theories
about the place of signalling and tacit bargaining in crisis
dynamics.[m]

Another aspect of communication, the exercise of ambiguity,
was again apparent in the 1958 crisis. The day before the shelling
of Quemoy began, White House Press Secretary James Hagerty
said: 'The Chinese Communists have been trying to find out
for years what we might do if they tried to take over Matsu and
Quemoy on the way to Formosa. As far as I'm concerned, they
can keep on guessing.' [103] After 23 August, the Administration
took a 'wait and see' attitude, knowing that the President could
invoke at will the Formosa Resolution to defend 'related positions and territories'. Ambiguity was a function of the desire to
create uncertainty in Peking over the risks involved in an attempt
to take over Quemoy and Matsu, but it was also a function of
the Administration's own hesitation over the wisdom of becoming over-committed. Moreover, the Administration was eager to
induce caution on the part of Chiang Kai-shek by leaving some
doubt in his mind as to the limits of its support. As Eisenhower
put it,

a statement of unqualified support would encourage [Chiang] to
attack. A statement expressing less would be harmful to him and helpful to the enemy.
    Therefore at the moment nothing was put out.[104]

Ambiguity as a tactic became – and might have been all along
– counter-productive, however, because of the chance that Peking might underestimate the extent of the American commitment and spark off a general war. (Eisenhower noted in his
memoirs that this was the essential difference from the 1954–5

[m] Charles McClelland has argued that the crisis over Quemoy 'offers an
unusual instance of crisis resolution by tacit communication through
actions taken in its central arena rather than by diplomacy at the conference table.' [102] I have been demonstrating how this has characterised
Sino-American crisis handling (none of the crises was actually resolved)
and how the Quemoy crisis is far from being an unusual case.

crisis, as far as he was concerned.)ⁿ The problem in 1958 was the necessity to clearly signal the facts of strength and resolve to Peking. In this respect, it is noteworthy that Secretary Dulles was the exponent of 'an immediate, strong statement of United States intentions', while the Joint Chiefs of Staff – and at the beginning, the President – favoured the idea of 'keeping the Communists guessing'.[107] After Secretary Dulles' Newport statement that Quemoy and Matsu 'had become increasingly related to the defence of Taiwan', and that the US had taken military dispositions permitting 'action both timely and effective' if the President were to decide that the threat to Taiwan was real,° the forward-defence character of the American commitment became more explicit, both in terms of US restraints on Taipei (such as they were) and in terms of its deterrence of Peking.

* * *

It was clear in the aftermath of the Taiwan Straits crisis that the Sino-American impasse had not contained as high a risk of war as had originally been feared. More or less moderate levels of tension were secured, and Sino-American relations could once again return to their 'chronic crisis' levels.

Personalities changed as well. The death of Dulles in May 1959 was perhaps as significant an event for the decade as the death of Stalin six years before. The previous January, Mao Tse-tung retired as Chairman of the PRC, retaining his chairmanship of the Party.ᵖ

ⁿ 'I did not doubt our total superiority, but any large-scale conflict stimulated here was now less likely to remain limited to a conventional use of power.'[105] This view dove-tailed with the Russian concern about escalation and their fear, in particular, that local violence in the Straits would act as a powerful catalyst.[106]

° This statement retained an important element of ambiguity, in spite of the widespread interpretation of it at the time as an unqualified commitment. I agree with Charles McClelland that Tang Tsou is quite mistaken in classifying this as an unambiguous act of (adversary) brinkmanship and (intramural) commitment.[108]

ᵖ It is still debatable whether Ch'en Yi was telling the truth when he denied that the failure of the Great Leap Forward and of the Taiwan Straits effort had anything to do with Mao's decision. It is possible that Ch'en was not truthful in the latter case; in the former case, it is certain that Mao was influenced by the decision of the 28 November–10 December Wuchang Plenum of the Central Committee to begin the retreat from the extremes of the previous summer. In military matters, Mao's summer decision to militarise the peasants and resurrect the militia was reversed by P'eng Teh-huai from January until September 1959, when he was

The de-escalation of the Quemoy crisis, along with the 31 October 1958 moratorium on nuclear testing and the uneventful passing of Khrushchev's 27 May 1959 ultimatum over Berlin, broadened the basis for eventual Soviet-American détente. Khrushchev's visit to the United States in September and the 'spirit of Camp David' which emanated from his meetings with Eisenhower suggested to suspicious allies, and especially to Peking, that peaceful co-existence was more important to Moscow and Washington than full accord within their respective alliances. The promising 'Eisenhower phase' of foreign policy was set back by the collapse of the Paris summit in May 1960, but expectations of better times to come would survive this reverse and be confirmed in the aftermath of the Cuban missile crisis.

In the Sino-American case, however, the 1960s were to mean mainly a series of false hopes and bitter frustrations. These would result both in a failure in many quarters to look beyond Peking's hostility to the New Frontiersmen, and in a tendency to underestimate the positive function of Sino-American crisis interactions in the 1950s. By establishing limits on the types, intensity and extent of crisis interactions, the experiences of Korea, Indochina and the Taiwan Straits had in fact acted to significantly reduce the risk of Sino-American conflict in the 1960s.

dismissed for trying to 'abolish the local armed forces and the militia' and for his open attack on the Great Leap policies during the Eighth Plenum, held in August at Lushan.[109] Since P'eng is also known to have outmanoeuvred General Su Yü, the militant Chief of Staff, in successfully ordering a cease-fire, it is possible that his position in the Taiwan Straits crisis also figured in his dismissal.

9: Principal findings

In this study of Sino-American crisis interactions in the 1950s, I have tried to show how substantial and important developments occurred in the relations between China and America during a period which is all too commonly dismissed as a sterile phase of Sino-American relations. Instead of adopting a traditional, 'diplomatic' approach to this field, concentrating on the negative area of commercial and diplomatic impasse, I have used – and elaborated – the 'strategic' approach of crisis analysis, which makes it possible (1) to define a Sino-American crisis system, (2) to determine how this system functions in the course of critical crises in Korea, Indochina and the Taiwan Straits, and (3) to evaluate the effect of these crises on the evolution of Sino-American strategic relations.

Definition of the Sino-American crisis system

The Sino-American crisis system can be defined both historically and analytically. Historically, it was the consequence of the first watershed period in post-War relations between the two countries – the product both of the Chinese Communist Revolution and of events in Korea. The bitter legacy of an abortive (if well-intentioned) US China policy in the late 1940s combined with rising CCP antagonism to freeze long-standing traditional relations, but more than this legacy was needed to transform Sino-American relations from a condition of hostility to one of conflict. Essentially, Far Eastern regional instability in the context of East-West polarisation and stalemate in Europe, together with an at first too narrow and imprecise definition of American commitments in Asia, were key factors in guaranteeing Sino-American conflict around the periphery of China.

The process of strategic interactions provoked by the testing of commitments in Korea is best seen as a function not only of the domestic and international contexts but also of the life cycle of each crisis which implicated the interests and participation of the US and the PRC. By describing and explaining this process, not only in the Korean case but in the cases of Indochina and the Taiwan Straits, I have sought to define the Sino-American crisis system analytically.

In each case, it is apparent that no single one of these three factors – domestic, international and strategic – can provide a sufficient basis for an explanation of how Sino-American strategic relations function and evolve: single-factor explanations must be abandoned in favour of more precise and complex (if less elegant) theories of behaviour and interactions. Of these three factors, however, I would argue that the crisis system occupies a central position, for in it are concentrated the most powerful forces for stability and change in the domestic and international environments. Almost by definition, a crisis is the consequence of a test of wills, one bent on challenging, the other on preserving, the existing order; in the case of China and America, it has been a test of national wills vying between maintenance and upheaval of the strategic order in the Far East. While China's bitter memories of imperial domination enhanced its dedication to protracted, anti-imperialist struggle, America's fears of Communist conspiracy strengthened its commitment to enforcing a *Pax Americana* in the name of collective security for the free world.

These images contrasted with significant realities of national interest. Although in the spring of 1950, neither Peking nor Washington anticipated squandering precious men and national treasure over Korea, in the end they did just that, if only to defend their positions in Manchuria and Japan. The Korean War forced Peking to postpone its cherished aim of final victory over the Kuomintang in Taiwan: it also forced Washington to stand committed to a forward defence of the Asian rimlands, and thus to abandon plans for merely defending the islands and seas of the West Pacific. In this respect, the Sino-American crises over Korea ensured succeeding crises over Formosa and the Pescadores. American political and military leaders came to consider them indispensable to their strategic position in the Far East and, by implication, to 'the common defence'. Nor could Chinese leaders of either side be persuaded to de-couple the status of the off-shore islands from that of Taiwan and the Penghus: the former were all-too-powerful symbols of eventual Chinese re-unification; belated US pressure only succeeded in paring them down to the Quemoy and Matsu groups, by the end of the first Taiwan Straits crisis.

Next to Korea and Taiwan, Indochina in 1954 was of secondary importance to both the US and PRC. Basically a Franco-Vietnamese conflict with strong indigenous causes, it presented both states with an opportunity to play the role of patrons without feeling impelled to transform their participation into an all-important test of strength. Peking could remain content with the low-cost and low-risk character of 'sublimited war' which its proxies were winning quite well on their own; Washington did not directly intervene because it could escape neither domestic and intramural pressures nor the lack of any incontrovertible evidence of Chinese aggression in Southeast Asia.

The frustrating but temperate outcomes, in all three areas of Sino-American contest, were by no means easily achieved. On the contrary, they were the product of crisis interactions whose development was fraught with difficulties and, at the peak of each escalation, with high danger.

Functioning of the Sino-American crisis system

Over time, the Sino-American crisis system functioned less and less primitively. At the beginning of the 1950s, the Korean crises were characterised (a) by unilateral and sequential escalation, first on the part of the Americans and then on the part of the Chinese, (b) by asymmetric declension, in which both sides alternately assumed flexible and then inflexible postures, and finally (c) by strategic stalemate, which forced both sides to turn away from increasingly counter-productive violence to a grudging acceptance of each other's gains in the battlefield. The key factors making for such unsatisfactory crisis handling were distorted perceptions and inadequate communications.[1] Each side viewed the other's behaviour as aggressive, motivated by unswerving ambitions for further conquest; neither paused to consider whether such ambitions, if they had existed in the first place, had not given way to more defensive considerations, such as the security of their forces or territory. These perceptions were magnified by significant communications failures, in which messages and signals were seldom taken at face value even when monitored in the first place, and in which threats were almost invariably characterised as signs of bluff disguising strategic weakness.

The Indochina crisis was a positive change following Korea's dialogue of the deaf. Crisis interactions became more bilateral and responsive; each crisis phase – escalation, declension, and de-escalation – was experienced by the US and the PRC simultaneously; and messages and signals, threats and warnings were exchanged with less exaggerated responses, at least in operational terms. Ironically, there was a far greater degree of bluff in 1954 than in 1950–1, but reassuringly, both sides resisted the temptation to escalate the crisis into an outright test case of guerrilla or people's war. This was relatively easier for the PRC than for the US, because the crisis appeared to be much more acute and critical to the latter, on the losing side, than it did to the former, on the winning side. At any rate, the finer points of both American counter-insurgency strategy (with its disastrous consequences) and Lin Piao's *Long Live the Victory of the People's War!* were to be almost exclusively the domain of the 1960s.

The Sino-American crisis system attained a relatively sophisticated level of interactions with the two Taiwan Straits crises. No longer did Washington and Peking need a tangible crisis threshold to contain crisis escalation between them – whether in the form of sanctuaries in Manchuria, Yunnan and, if Soviet capabilities are to be taken into account up through 1955, just possibly Japan and even Europe or, alternatively, in the form of buffers as in the case of French and Vietnamese proxies or DPRK and DRV territory. Rather, crisis participation varied between the indirect form of Communist-Nationalist interactions, on the model of Indochina or the Chinese civil war, and the more direct form generated by more active US involvement, approaching but never reaching the direct engagement typical of the second Korean crisis. Yet in spite of the apparent lack of structural safeguards against crisis escalation – in the form of buffers or proxies – both sides demonstrated impressive flexibility of action as well as appreciation of desirable, self-imposed limits on their crisis behaviour. This was the rationale behind American willingness to sacrifice Yikiang Shan and the Tachen Islands in 1955 and Chinese willingness to adopt a wide variety of diplomatic and strategic tactics to press their quest for total reunification. It was also the rationale not only behind general US respect of PRC territorial limits within three miles of the mainland coast, but also, to a certain extent, behind PRC reluctance to make an all-out attempt to wrest the Quemoys and Matsus from the Nationalists, as long as the Americans remained so clearly committed to protecting Taiwan and, by extension, those areas which had so implicated ROC manpower and morale. Commenting on the memorandum developed between State Department and

White House in September 1958, President Eisenhower observed later that 'I was determined that by every possible means we should avoid expanding hostilities more than absolutely necessary. I was by no means convinced that the Chinese Communists would be willing to risk war with us.' [2]

The fact that Sino-American crisis interactions reached a stalemate, here as elsewhere, is no reason to dismiss them as an exercise doomed to futility. When measured against the lack of definition of Chinese and American commitments at the beginning of the decade, or against the very real possibilities that the post-Korean crises would escalate into all-out warfare, the Sino-American crisis system was perhaps the only viable strategic alternative in the Far Eastern context of the 1950s.

Evolution of Sino-American strategic relations [3]

Over the 1950s, Sino-American crisis interactions developed into a pattern in which the life cycle of each crisis became increasingly self-regulated and in which the ability of each actor to handle crises with the other became increasingly sophisticated. By the end of the decade, each important area of strategic relations between Peking and Washington had been sufficiently contested, so that any future interactions in that area would be more in the nature of probes confirming existing US and PRC commitments. While the international order established by those interactions was not considered just by either American or Chinese criteria, it was nevertheless stable, because neither side considered it worth taking the risks of revising that order to approximate more closely to their ideal international system. Moreover, as a result of a shared experience of dealing with each other in crisis conditions, both sides learned to respect each other's commitments in the area, because to challenge them directly would lead to disproportionate costs similar to those suffered in the Korean crises.

Another way of putting this fundamental outcome is to argue that in spite of the veneer of diplomatic stalemate and of East-West polemic, the cumulative effect of Sino-American crisis interactions is a case of deterrence at work. Even at present, nuclear parity between China and the super-powers remains a distant prospect. At the end of the 1950s, the power differential between the United States, a global super-power, and Communist China, a regional great power, was even more overwhelming than in the 1970s. If one bears in mind, however, the nuclear, air and sea superiority of America as opposed to the land strength and revolutionary dynamism of China, one can observe far more accurately the development of an uneasy regional balance of power. This balance has permitted the United States to extend its sphere of influence through the Western Pacific to the Asian rimlands, where the American presence has been contested ever since the Korean War. On the other side, this regional balance has allowed China to consolidate its control over the mainland, to protect the buffer states of North Korea and North Vietnam and – by indirect means – to challenge established US (and more recently Soviet) power.

The development of Sino-American deterrence often entailed the transformation of peripheral commitments into core commitments. The outstanding example of this process was the increasing US determination to defend Chinese Nationalist-held piles of rock off the Communist mainland's shore. It was not necessarily desirable for this to occur: we have seen how, in objective terms, these islands had only a remote – and primarily symbolic – bearing for the security of the United States and its allies. But the delineation of power and the securing of commitments undoubtedly made for a more orderly strategic relationship. John Foster Dulles, having recovered from his prolonged bout of roll-backitis and indiscriminate brinkmanship, expressed this live-and-let-live outcome well; in an interview with the British ITV in October 1958, he said: 'We are not going to attack or tolerate attacks against the Chinese Communists, but, when they attack, then I think we have to stand firm. If we don't, I think that there will be a breach in the line . . . and that whole portion of the free world in the Western Pacific will be lost.' [4]

At the same time as Sino-American strategic relations were assuming a pattern of deterrence, American and Chinese decision-makers were improving their skills as crisis handlers. This was rather ironic as an outcome, for neither side openly subscribed to explicit strategies of crisis handling at the time. Yet in operational as opposed to declaratory terms – and it is, after all, the former and not the latter that are the essential test of the character of a strategic relationship – Americans and Chinese demonstrated increasing creativity and flexibility in coping with each other during crisis conditions.

They were able to orchestrate physical and verbal actions more sensibly and more imaginatively. The contrast between

Dulles' empty warnings against Chinese intervention in Indochina, in September 1953, and his carefully worded Newport statement, accompanied by Seventh Fleet convoys and logistical support, in September 1958, is one striking example. That between Peking's expectation of a swift take-over of the off-shore islands in January 1955 and its coming to terms with more long-term pressures – as, for example, Mao's reliance on the contradictions confronting imperialism and P'eng's cease-fire announcement accompanied by alternate-day bombardment – is another case in point.

Peking and Washington also came to transmit more effective messages and signals.[5] At Bandung, instead of relying primarily on Soviet representatives and Indian go-betweens, as in 1950, Chou made it his business to make a dramatic personal overture. In contrast with the confusing signals of Acheson and MacArthur during the Korean crises, Eisenhower relied on Sabre jets and Sidewinder missiles to substantiate US commitments in the Taiwan Straits – a forcible but unquestionably effective signal.

Moreover, Sino-American understanding of the utility of clear threats and commitments at some times and ambiguous ones at others seemed to increase. One example was the ambiguous Chinese commitment to the Viet Minh, a contradiction between the internationalist duty of socialist countries to support people's war and the obligation of indigenous revolutionary forces to be self-reliant in waging people's war.[6] Even closer to home, Peking has been ambiguous in its commitment to liberate Taiwan by whatever means necessary, however clearly that commitment may be phrased in principle. Thus, on the one hand, appeals have been addressed to the Chinese Nationalists (always excluding the 'Chiang Kai-shek clique') stressing either past co-operation between the two parties or Kuomintang fears of eventual desertion by the United States. On the other hand, the off-shore islands have been subjected to varying degrees of shelling – to the tune of over a million explosive shells over the years – and to matching declaratory abuse.

It would appear that ambiguity is positively useful to the weaker of the two parties, if only because it allows China to undertake probes without great cost or great risk. However, Chinese ambiguity has been counter-productive to a certain extent, both because it has led to a positive US commitment to Taipei which did not exist before 1955 and because the Americans, and later the Soviets, have learned to take Chinese threats with a good deal of skepticism. While recognising this important flaw, Chinese leaders have realised that there is very little that they can do about it while the PRC remains strategically weak. They have therefore concentrated on rapidly increasing their state's military power. In the long term their antagonists might turn into 'paper tigers', but in the short term, they remain 'living tigers, iron tigers, real tigers which can eat people'.[7]

In order to resolve this issue of ambiguity versus clarity, one might be inclined to say that at least it is not in the interests of the stronger power to be ambiguous in its commitments, as was learned in the case of Korea. Also, in the case of the Taiwan Straits, Peking had high hopes of following its capture of Yikiang Shan and the Tachen Islands in January and February of 1955 with the capture of the Quemoy and Matsu groups because American ambiguity seemed a sign of weakness or vacillation. Objectively, the conclusion that clarity, expressed in a forthright US commitment to, or preferably exclusion of, the off-shore islands under the terms of the Sino-American Mutual Defence Treaty, seems far more attractive than determining, on each and every occasion, whether the defence of Quemoy and Matsu is or is not related to the defence of Formosa and the Pescadores. This is what Adlai Stevenson and other Democrats argued in the 1950s, and they concluded that withdrawal from the off-shore islands would be an important contribution to the stability of the Taiwan Straits area. But such private opinions never became US policy, and perhaps more importantly, never became Chinese Nationalist policy.

It is clear, from an examination of the papers and statements of Secretary Dulles, that he was aware of the force of these arguments and that he acted to minimise the negative implications of his Government's exercise of ambiguity. Yet he was also aware of the argument in favour of US ambiguity, for it enabled Washington to hint broadly to Peking that trading the off-shore islands for a permanent cease-fire remained a live possibility. As he put it in a secret memorandum prepared in October 1958, 'a situation might in fact be created comparable to that along the Korean and Vietnam armistice lines, where there is close [Sino-American] contact but no provocations across the line, and at least some appreciable reduction of forces'.[8] The Republicans shared some common ground with Democratic advocates of a 'Two Chinas' policy – the difference being that they would not abandon Quemoy and Matsu without a *quid pro quo* and at the expense of Chinese Nationalist morale. At any rate, neither Peking nor Taipei was receptive to such an outcome: the Nationalist-held off-shore islands served not only as a powerful symbol of eventual reunification under one system or the other but also as a symbol of the rejection of a 'Two Chinas' solution by both Chinas – a rejection which the United States would accept officially in the 1972 Shanghai Communiqué.

○　○　○

In sum, this study has defined the Sino-American crisis system in historical and analytical terms, shown how this system functions through a comparative case study of crises in Korea, Indochina and the Taiwan Straits in their phases of escalation, declension and de-escalation, and indicated what has been the cumulative effect of these crises on the evolution of the strategic relationship between Washington and Peking, in the context of the central balance of power. The analyst is left with an over-all impression of increasing stabilisation on the system level and of learning on the actor level. It becomes possible to suggest a learning curve of crisis handling, which describes the progress in Sino-American crisis behaviour and interactions in an impressionistic fashion (Fig. 7). Korea, 1950–1, was undoubtedly the low point in this curve because of its intra-war crises, with

Fig. 7. Learning curve of US-PRC crisis handling

Indochina 1954 occupying an intermediate position as, on the one hand, a relatively salutary crisis experience in terms of indirect Sino-American participation and, on the other hand, as the representation of mutual misapprehension regarding the character and extent of Sino-American commitments. The Taiwan Straits crises represent the most satisfactory model of Sino-American crisis behaviour and interactions, for they became self-limiting without requiring either buffers or proxies to blunt unilateral escalation or mutual misapprehension.

A 'diplomatic' analyst might well insist that the most striking feature about each one of the Sino-American crises in the 1950s is that none of the political differences inherent in them was in any sense resolved, in spite of the Panmunjom armistice, the Geneva Accords, and the resumption of the ambassadorial talks in Warsaw. The rejoinder of the 'strategic' analyst would be that something equally fundamental was achieved through and by these crises: the establishment and relative stabilisation of a balance of power system in the Far East. This was a far more positive legacy than continued Sino-American hostility would lead one otherwise to believe.

NOTES

Introduction

1 Lewis A. Coser, *The Functions of Social Conflict* (Glencoe, Ill.: Free Press, 1956), p. 8.
2 James A. Robinson, 'Crisis', in David L. Sills (ed.), *International Encyclopedia of the Social Sciences* (New York: Macmillan, 1968), vol. 3, p. 310.
3 William R. Kintner, David C. Schwartz, et al. *A Study on Crisis Management* (Philadelphia: University of Pennsylvania Foreign Policy Research Institute, 1965), p. I–1. Cf. David C. Schwartz, 'Decision Theories and Crisis Behavior: An Empirical Study of Nuclear Deterrence in International Political Crises', *Orbis*, Summer 1967, pp. 459–90.
4 Herman Kahn and Anthony J. Wiener (eds.), *Crisis and Arms Control* (Harmon-on-Hudson, N.Y.: Hudson Institute, 1962), pp. 7–11.
5 Karl W. Deutsch, *The Nerves of Government: Models of Political Communication and Control* (New York: Free Press, 1966), chapter 11.
6 Charles A. McClelland, 'Systems and History in Internation Relations', in *General Systems Yearbook* (1958), p. 201.
7 Cf. John T. Lanzetta, 'Group Behavior Under Stress', in J. David Singer (ed.), *Human Behavior and International Relations: Contributions from the Social-Psychological Sciences* (Chicago: Rand McNally, 1965), pp. 218–19.
8 Oran Young, *The Politics of Force: Bargaining during International Crises* (Princeton: Princeton University Press, 1968), pp. 16–17.

Chapter 1

1 *New York Times*, 6, 7 and 10 August 1949.
2 Senate Committees on Armed Services and Foreign Relations, 82nd Congress, 1st Session, *Hearings to Conduct an Inquiry into the Military Situation in the Far East and the Facts Surrounding the Relief of General of the Army Douglas MacArthur from his Assignments in that Area* (Washington, D.C.: Government Printing Office, 1951) [hereinafter cited as *Military Situation in the Far East*], pp. 187–8.
3 Department of State *Bulletin* [hereinafter abbreviated DSB], 16 January 1950, p. 79.
4 Stuart Schram, *The Political Thought of Mao Tse-tung* (Harmondsworth, Middx.: Penguin, 1969), p. 419.
5 Liu Shao-ch'i, *On Internationalism and Nationalism* (Peking: Foreign Languages Press, 1949), p. 32.
6 Cf. Louis J. Halle, *The Cold War as History* (London: Chatto & Windus, 1967), chapter xix.
7 Liu Shao-ch'i declared on 13 February 1953, for instance, that 'it would

be impossible for American imperialism or any other imperialist power to launch a large-scale aggressive war in the Far East without Japan as a base'. 'Third Anniversary of the Sino-Soviet Treaty of Friendship, Alliance, and Mutual Assistance', *Current Background* (Hong Kong: U.S. Consulate-General) [hereinafter abbreviated CB] 229, 20 February 1953. Cf. A. Doak Barnett, *Communist China and Asia* (New York: Random House, 1960), chapter 10.

8 *Shih-chieh Chih-shih* [World Culture] supplement, 'A Chronicle of Principal Events Relating to the Indo-China Question', New China News Agency [hereinafter abbreviated NCNA], 23 April 1954, in CB 285, 5 May 1954, p. 24.

9 John Foster Dulles, *War or Peace* (London: Harrap, 1950), p. 245.

10 Read into the Senate Foreign Relations Committee record by Ambassador Jessup on 4 October 1951, *New York Times,* 5 October 1951.

11 Cf. McGeorge Bundy (ed.), *The Pattern of Responsibility* (Boston: Houghton Mifflin, 1952), p. 190.

Chapter 2

1 Indirectly quoted by the *New York Times,* from the President's 1 June press conference, 2 June 1950.

2 *New York Times,* 2 March 1949.

3 DSB, 16 January 1950, p. 116.

4 *Ibid.*

5 Dean Acheson, *Present at the Creation* (New York: Norton, 1969), p. 358. Also cf. Department of State Press Release No. 761, 26 September 1952, in which Acheson tried to defend his National Press Club speech as an adequate warning against potential aggression.

6 Roy E. Appleman, *South to the Naktong, North to the Yalu (June–November 1950),* US Army in the Korean War (Washington, D.C.: Government Printing Office, 1960), pp. 16–17. Cf. G. F. Hudson, *The Hard and Bitter Peace: World Politics since 1945* (London: Pall Mall, 1966), p. 81. General Ridgway spoke of the rapid demobilisation of American occupation forces and described 'our lack of readiness' as 'lamentable. But I don't know that there was any force that could have stopped it.' Interview with author, 10 August 1970.

7 Carl Berger, *The Korean Knot: A Military-Political History* (Philadelphia: University of Pennsylvania Press, 1957), p. 94.

8 *New York Times,* 15 October 1949.

9 See I. F. Stone, *The Hidden History of the Korean War* (London: Turnstile Press, 1952), p. 8, and chapters 8 and 9.

10 *Military Situation in the Far East,* p. 1991.

11 *Pravda,* Current Digest of the Soviet Press (Ann Arbor: University of Michigan Press) [hereinafter abbreviated CDSP], 2 January 1950.

12 *Jen-min Jih-pao,* Survey of the China Mainland Press (Hong Kong: US Consulate-General) [hereinafter abbreviated SCMP], 21 May 1950.

13 Quoted in *People's China,* 16 February 1950, p. 5.

14 *Ibid.* 1 April 1950, p. 5.

15 Allen Whiting, *China Crosses the Yalu* (New York: Macmillan, 1960), p. 23. I am indebted to Whiting both for his analytical approach to Chinese Communist strategy and for his empirical evidence on PRC attitudes and behaviour during the Korean conflict.

16 NCNA, 23 November 1949.

17 Department of State, *North Korea, A Case Study in the Techniques of Violence* (Washington, D.C.: Government Printing Office, 1961), p. 117.

18 Allen Whiting, *op. cit.* p. 45.

19 Strobe Talbott (ed.), *Khrushchev Remembers* (Boston: Little, Brown and Co., 1970), p. 368.

20 Cf. Max Beloff, *Soviet Policy in the Far East* (London: Oxford University Press, 1953), p. 180; *New York Times,* 7 October 1949; Manchester *Guardian,* 2 March 1950.

21 Allen Whiting, *op. cit.* p. 43.

22 *Ibid.* Cf. Chin Szu-k'ai, 'Foreign Relations', in Union Research Institute, *Communist China 1949–1959* (Hong Kong: URI, 1969), p. 109.

23 Carl Berger, *op. cit.* p. 100.

24 Glenn Paige in Cyril Black and Thomas Thornton (eds.), *Communism and Revolution: The Strategic Uses of Political Violence* (Princeton: Princeton University Press, 1964), p. 227.

25 Dean Acheson, *Present at the Creation,* p. 412. On the military side, Robert Lovett believed the transportation problem posed too many logistical problems, both in bringing them to Korea and in taking them away. Interview with author, 27 July 1970.

26 Dean Acheson, *Present at the Creation,* p. 369.

27 Lin Piao, 'Hold High the Red Banner of the Party's General Line and Chairman Mao Tse-tung's Military Thought and Advance in Big Strides', NCNA, 20 September 1959 in CB 569, 7 October 1959, p. 1. Cf. C.P.V. Commander Yang Yung's reference to the 'wild attempt to wipe out the Korean Democratic People's Republic at one stroke, to extend the war to China and to spread the flames of war to the whole world. The most powerful and irrefutable proof that they were out to do this was given by the fact that U.S. imperialism sent its troops to occupy our territory of Taiwan while embarking on its war of aggression in Korea', in his 'Report on the Work of the Chinese People's Volunteers During the Eight Years of Resistance to U.S. Aggression and Aid to Korea', NCNA, 30 October 1958, in CB 535, 11 November 1958, p. 1.

28 Harold Hinton, *Communist China in World Politics* (London, Macmillan, 1966), pp. 208–9.

29 DSB, 3 July 1950, p. 5.

30 McGeorge Bundy (ed.), *The Pattern of Responsibility* (Boston: Houghton Mifflin, 1952), p. 190.

31 DSB, 16 January 1950, p. 79.

32 Dean Acheson, *Present at the Creation,* p. 351; DSB, 16 January 1950, p. 80.

33 *People's China,* 16 February 1950, pp. 8 and 9; 'Prologue to Taiwan', *People's China,* 16 May 1950, p. 4.

34 Dean Acheson, *Present at the Creation,* pp. 350–1.

35 DSB, 16 January 1950, p. 81.

36 DSB, 19 March 1950, p. 469. That intolerant Congressional anti-Communists affected the Administration's attitude toward both Chinas is reflected in an article (following the neutralisation) by James Reston: 'When President Truman on June 27 ordered the United States Seventh Fleet to prevent any attack on Formosa, he had several things in mind. He wanted to localize the Korean War by neutralizing Formosa, and to minimize the political opposition to the Korean War by neutralizing

Senators Taft, Knowland, Smith of New Jersey and others who had been condemning his "hands-off Formosa" policy.' *New York Times,* 28 July 1950.

37 Chou En-lai, 'Statement on Acheson's Speech', *People's China,* 1 April 1950, p. 5. Cf. editorials, 'A Mosquito and the Fortress of Peace', *ibid.* pp. 3–4 and 'Let the Warmongers Beware!', *People's China,* 1 June 1950, pp. 3–4.

38 ROK Commander-in-Chief (subsequently Premier) Chung Il Kwon, Oral History Collection, John Foster Dulles Library of Diplomatic History, Princeton University Library [hereinafter abbreviated Dulles OHC] transcript of a tape-recorded interview conducted by Spencer Davis (1964), p. 5.

39 DSB, 22 May 1950, p. 821 and 3 July 1950, p. 5.

40 Karl Rankin, *China Assignment* (Seattle: University of Washington Press, 1964), p. 56.

41 NCNA, 30 June 1950, in Margaret Carlyle (ed.), *Documents on International Affairs, 1949–50* (London: Oxford University Press for the Royal Institute of International Affairs, 1953), pp. 633–4. Cf. Tang Tsou, *America's Failure in China: 1949–50* (Chicago, Ill.: University of Chicago Press, 1963), p. 564.

Chapter 3

1 Malcolm W. Cagle and Frank A. Manson, *The Sea War in Korea* (Annapolis: United States Naval Institute, 1957), p. 31.

2 Glenn Paige, *The Korean Decision: June 24–30, 1950* (New York: The Free Press, 1968), pp. 98–9.

3 In his memoirs, General Ridgway wrote, 'The thought, of course, had flashed through my mind that this was the beginning of World War III. The Sino-Soviet treaty had been signed only a few months before and here, it seemed to me, could well be the beginning of Armageddon, the last great battle between East and West.' General Matthew B. Ridgway, *Soldier: The Memoirs of Matthew B. Ridgway* (New York: Harper, 1956), p. 192. Also in interview with author, 10 August 1970.

4 John D. Hickerson, interview with Glenn Paige, 6 November 1958, in Glenn Paige, *op. cit.* p. 92.

5 Harry S Truman, *Years of Trial and Hope* (London: Hodder and Stoughton, 1955), pp. 332–5.

6 *Military Situation in the Far East,* p. 1715.

7 Joseph de Rivera, *The Psychological Dimension of Foreign Policy* (Columbus, Ohio: Merrill, 1968), pp. 68–9.

8 Dean Acheson, *op. cit.* p. 406.

9 *Ibid.* p. 408.

10 United Nations Document S/1508 Rev. 1, 27 June 1950.

11 DSB, 10 July 1950, p. 46.

12 *New York Times,* 28 June 1950; *Military Situation in the Far East,* p. 2609.

13 Quoted by Defense Secretary Marshall in *ibid.* p. 536.

14 *Ibid.* p. 1012.

15 Harry S Truman, *op. cit.* p. 343.

16 Dean Acheson, *op. cit.* p. 411.

17 Cf. Allen Whiting, *China Crosses the Yalu* (Stanford: Stanford University Press, 1960), chapters 4 and 5.

18 Hanson Baldwin, *New York Times,* 28 June 1950.
19 *Military Situation in the Far East,* p. 2621. Cf. Allen Whiting, *op. cit.* p. 48.
20 *Jen-min Jih-pao,* 29 June 1950, in NCNA, 30 June 1950.
21 *Ibid.* 27 July 1950, in NCNA, 28 July 1950.
22 *Shih-chieh Chih-shih,* 5 August 1950, in NCNA, 6 August 1950.
23 *Jen-min Jih-pao,* 2 August 1950, in NCNA, 3 August 1950.
24 *Ibid.* 15 August 1950, in NCNA, 16 August 1950.
25 Trygve Lie, *In the Cause of Peace* (New York: Macmillan, 1954), pp. 333–4.
26 *Military Situation in the Far East,* p. 10.
27 United Nations Document S/1509, 27 June 1950.
28 United Nations Document S/1503, 26 June 1950.
29 Leland Goodrich, *op. cit.* p. 122; J. C. Kundra, *Indian Foreign Policy, 1947–1954* (Gronigen, Netherlands: Walters, 1955), p. 130; DSB, 31 July 1950, pp. 170–1. Dean Acheson, *op. cit.* p. 417.
30 Cf. W. Phillips Davison, *The Berlin Blockade* (Princeton: Princeton University Press, 1958), pp. 254ff.; Allen Whiting, *op. cit.* p. 73.
31 *New York Times,* 3 August 1950.
32 Dean Acheson, *op. cit.* pp. 422–3.
33 *Jen-min Jih-pao,* 5 August 1950, in NCNA, 6 August 1950.
34 *Military Situation in the Far East,* pp. 3479–80. Full text in *New York Times,* 29 August 1950.
35 *Shih-chieh Chih-shih,* 26 August 1950, in Allen Whiting, *op. cit.* pp. 84–5.
36 Robert Lovett, interview with author, 27 July 1970.
37 Allen Whiting, *op. cit.* pp. 98–9.
38 Quoted in Colonel G. Stanton Babcock to John Foster Dulles, hand-written draft memorandum, 'Chinese Communist Participation in Military Operations in Korea', December 1950, in File IX, 'UN-Korea', Dulles Papers, John Foster Dulles Library of Diplomatic History, Princeton University Library.
39 Allen Whiting, *op. cit.* p. 98–9.
40 Department of State, *US Policy in the Korean Conflict,* p. 12.
41 *New York Times,* 20 September 1951.
42 Dean Acheson, *op. cit.* pp. 445–6, 451.
43 Matthew Ridgway, interview with author, 10 August 1970.
44 RAD JCS 92801 to MacArthur, 27 September 1950, quoted in James F. Schnabel, *Policy and Direction: The First Year* (Washington, D.C.: Department of the Army, Office of Chief of Military History, 1967) and in Dean Acheson, *op. cit.* pp. 452–3.
45 *Ibid.* p. 453.
46 DSB, 9 October 1950, p. 579.
47 U.N. General Assembly Resolution 376 (V), 7 October 1950.
48 K. M. Panikkar, *In Two Chinas* (London: Allen and Unwin, 1955), p. 108.
49 Chou En-lai, 'Report to cadres convened by the National Committee of the Chinese People's Political Consultative Committee to commemorate the first anniversary of the founding of the People's Republic of China', 30 September 1950, in CB 12, 5 October 1950.
50 Allen Whiting, *op. cit.* p. 111.
51 Quoted in Leland Goodrich, *Korea: A Study of U.S. Policy in the United Nations* (New York: Carnegie Endowment, 1956), p. 134.

52 Radio Peking, Chinese International Service in English, 11 October 1950.
53 *New York Times*, 5 October 1950.
54 Cf. Chou En-lai's notes to Dean Acheson, 27 August 1950, and to the United Nations, 27 and 30 August, 10, 16, 17, 24 September 1950, in *People's China*, 16 September 1950, pp. 26–7, and 10 October 1950, pp. 26–7. See also NCNA, 28 October 1950, quoted in SCMP, 1 November 1950, p. 9.
55 Joseph de Rivera, *op. cit.* p. 146.
56 *Military Situation in the Far East*, p. 1241; Harry S Truman, *op. cit.* p. 372.
57 *New York Times*, 28 October 1950.
58 Admiral Arthur Radford, Dulles OHC transcript of a tape-recorded interview conducted by Philip Crowl (1965), p. 32.
59 General Matthew Ridgway, *Soldier*, p. 220.
60 United Nations Document S/1884.
61 Joseph de Rivera, *op. cit.* p. 426.
62 Yang Yung, 'Report on the Work of the Chinese People's Volunteers During the Eight Years of Resistance to U.S. Aggression and Aid to Korea', in CB 535, 11 November 1958, p. 2.
63 NCNA, 6 November 1950. Cf. *Jen-min Jih-pao's* attack on Washington the week before, NCNA, 31 October 1950; and C. C. Fang, 'Into the Boots of Japanese Imperialism', *People's China*, 1 December 1950, pp. 10–11.
64 Cf. Fan Po-ch'uan, 'American Aggression Against China', NCNA, 22 November 1950, in CB 33, 30 November 1950.
65 *Shih-shih Shou-ts'e*, 5 November 1950, in CB 210, 18 September 1952, pp. 2–3.
66 NCNA, 20 November 1950, in SCMP 14, 21 November 1950, pp. 5–7.
67 *New York Times*, 1 October 1950.
68 *Military Situation in the Far East*, p. 1835.
69 *Ibid.* p. 1933.
70 Roy E. Appleman, *South to the Naktong, North to the Yalu (June–November 1950)*, US Army in the Korean War (Washington, D.C.: Government Printing Office, 1960), p. 759. Martin Lichterman, noting that on 6 November MacArthur spoke in three communiqués 'of the flood of men and materials pouring into North Korea from Manchuria which "not only jeopardize but threaten the ultimate destruction of the forces under my command"', goes on to state, 'Why General MacArthur chose to discount or forget such a jeopardy and such a threat [two weeks later] is unclear; why he chose not to prepare at all for such an eventuality is baffling.' Martin Lichterman, 'To the Yalu and Back' in Harold Stein (ed.), *American Civil-Military Decisions: A Book of Case Studies* (Birmingham, Alabama: University of Alabama Press, 1963), p. 612. Washington's failure to attach great significance to the communiqués of 6 November may well be put down to the sheer force of numbers: so many cables were being received daily, over MacArthur's signature, of which very few portended disaster. MacArthur's success in dismissing earlier doubts seems a function of what Leon Festinger calls 'cognitive dissonance' – faced with information working against the success of the project for which he had taken responsibility, the General preferred to ignore hints of unpalatable

reality, to exclude them from his perceptions because he so wanted a rapid and successful campaign with the 'boys home by Christmas'. Cf. Leon Festinger, *Conflict, Decision and Dissonance* (Stanford, California: Stanford University Press – Stanford Studies in Psychology: 3, 1964).

71 Allen Whiting, *op. cit.* p. 118. Tang Tsou writes, 'On November 25, Eighth Army intelligence put the enemy strength on its front at 149,000, an increase of 95,000 from its estimate of the day before. Three days later the strength of Chinese Communist forces in Korea was put at 200,000. There were actually 300,000 Chinese troops.' Tang Tsou, *op. cit.* pp. 584–5. Cf. Lynn Montross and Nicholas A. Canzona, *The Chosun Reservoir Campaign*, vol. III of *U.S. Marine Operations in Korea, 1950–53* (Washington: Historical Branch, U.S. Marine Corps, 1957), p. 140, and Roy L. Appleman, *op. cit.* p. 768.

72 Babcock-Dulles memorandum, *op. cit.*

73 *Ibid.* Throughout this period, CPV field reports proved very optimistic. General P'eng Teh-huai's cables were described by Khrushchev as declaring categorically 'that the enemy would be surrounded and finished off by decisive flanking strikes. The American troops were crushed and the war ended many times in these battle reports which P'eng sent to Mao, who then sent them along to Stalin.' Strobe Talbott (ed.), *Khrushchev Remembers* (Boston: Little, Brown and Co., 1970), p. 372.

74 Radio Peking, English Morse, 29 October 1950; *Shih-chieh Chih-shih*, 28 October 1950, p. 1. Allen Whiting, *op. cit.* p. 129.

75 Mao Tse-tung, *On Protracted War*, in *Selected Works*, vol. II (Peking: Foreign Languages Press, 1967), pp. 113–94.

76 Dean Acheson, *op. cit.* pp. 465–6.

77 United States Air Force Historical Study Number 72, *United States Air Force Operations in the Korean Conflict, 1 November 1950–30 June 1953* (Washington, D.C.: USAF Historical Division, 1955), p. 22.

78 Quoted in Harry S Truman, *op. cit.* p. 376.

79 Dean Acheson, *op. cit.* p. 463.

80 *Military Situation in the Far East*, p. 3493.

81 Mao Tse-tung, *op. cit.* p. 172.

82 United Nations Security Council, *Official Records*, 16 November 1950, p. 30.

83 Quoted in Leland Goodrich, *op. cit.* p. 154.

84 Matthew Ridgway, interview with author, 10 August 1970.

85 *Shih-chieh Chih-shih*, NCNA, 31 October 1950, in SCMP, 1 November 1950, pp. 4–5; Allen Whiting, *op. cit.* p. 134. When interviewed in 1970 former Defense Secretary Lovett emphatically agreed with this analysis. Interview with author, 27 July 1970.

86 Mao Tse-Tung, *op. cit.* p. 159.

87 *Military Situation in the Far East*, pp. 3532–3; Harry S Truman, *op. cit.* p. 384.

88 *Ibid.* pp. 385–7.

89 Dean Acheson, *op. cit.* p. 467.

90 DSB, 18 December 1950.

91 *New York Times*, 1 December 1950.

92 K. M. Panikkar, *op. cit.* p. 108.

93 Dean Acheson, *op. cit.* pp. 473–4.

94 *Ibid.* pp. 481–4; Harry S Truman, *op. cit.* pp. 398, 411–12.
95 Trumbull Higgins, *Korea and the Fall of MacArthur: A Précis in Limited War* (New York: Oxford University Press, 1960), p. 80.
96 *Military Situation in the Far East*, pp. 907, 2180–1; Harry S Truman, *op. cit.* pp. 433–4.
97 Robert Leckie, *Conflict, The History of the Korean War, 1950–53* (New York: Putnam's, 1962), p. 203. As Tang Tsou notes, 'Just as American officials before him, Chou in his hour of victory overestimated his military strength.' Tang Tsou, *America's Failure in China: 1941–50* (Chicago: University of Chicago Press, 1963), p. 586.
98 US Department of State, *The Record of Korean Unification* (Washington, D.C.: Government Printing Office, 1960), pp. 114–16.
99 *New York Times*, 23 January 1951.
100 Quoted in U.S. Congress, Senate Committee on Foreign Relations, *The United States and the Korean Problem* (Washington, D.C.: Government Printing Office, 1953), p. 57.
101 Harry S Truman, *op. cit.* p. 362.
102 *People's China*, 16 November 1950, p. 23; *Hsin-hua Yüeh-pao* [New China Monthly], November 1950.
103 Letter to the author from former Assistant (subsequently Under) Secretary of State Livingston T. Merchant, 5 October 1970.

Chapter 4

1 *New York Times*, 3 October 1952. On 22 January, *Jen-min Jih-pao* asserted that this 'Asians fight Asians' policy was another phase in Washington's 'global plan of aggression' whose 'general objective . . . is the formation of a new "crusade" for the subjugation of the camp of peace and democracy', in NCNA, 25 January 1953.
2 John Foster Dulles, 'A Policy of Boldness', *Life*, 19 May 1952.
3 *New York Times*, 16 May 1952.
4 *Ibid.* 14 August 1952.
5 David Rees, *Korea: The Limited War* (London: Macmillan, 1964), p. 404.
6 *London Times*, 15 December 1952. Curiously, Admiral Radford disclaimed any knowledge of discussions about military policy on the *Helena*, although he was on board from Guam to Wake. Dulles OHC transcript of a tape-recorded interview conducted by Philip Crowl (1965), p. 6.
7 Dwight D. Eisenhower, Dulles OHC transcript of a tape-recorded interview conducted by Philip Crowl (1964), p. 28. Sherman Adams, *First Hand Report: The Story of the Eisenhower Administration* (New York: Harper, 1961), p. 48.
8 Roscoe Drummond and Gaston Coblentz, *Duel at the Brink: John Foster Dulles' Command of American Power* (London: Weidenfeld and Nicolson, 1961), p. 113. President Eisenhower later told Sherman Adams that 'danger of an atomic war' had 'kept (the Communists) under some control' in 1953. Sherman Adams, *op. cit.* p. 49.
9 Cf. Morton H. Halperin, *Contemporary Military Strategy* (London: Faber, 1968), chapter 4; and Dwight D. Eisenhower, *The White House Years: Mandate for Change, 1953–1956* (Garden City: Doubleday, 1963), p. 451.
10 *New York Times*, 27 December 1953.

11 DSB, 25 January 1954, pp. 107–8.

12 *New York Times*, 1 August 1953.

13 *Ibid.* 3 September 1953.

14 *Ibid.* 30 December 1953.

15 *New York Times*, 18 July 1953.

16 A 4 June 1953 National Intelligence Estimate included the judgment that the 'Communist leadership is aware that the West, and in particular the US, would probably retaliate against Communist China if Chinese Communist forces should invade Indochina. We believe that fear of such retaliation and of the major war which might result are important deterrents to open Chinese Communist intervention in Indochina.' Document 15, *The Pentagon Papers*, Senator Gravel edition (Boston: Beacon Press, 1971), vol. 1, p. 399.

17 'Talking Paper for Use in Clarifying United States Position Regarding Atomic and Hydrogen Weapons During Course of NATO Meeting in Paris on 23 April 1954', pp. 9–10 in File ix, 'London and Paris – April 10–15/54', Dulles Papers, John Foster Dulles Library of Diplomatic History, Princeton University Library. De-classified.

18 James Hagerty, interview with author, 21 July 1970.

19 *New York Times*, 3 February 1953.

20 Robert J. Donovan, *Eisenhower: The Inside Story* (New York: Harper, 1956), p. 30. Assistant Secretary of State Robertson characteristically went further and told a House Appropriations subcommittee that 'The heart of the present policy toward China and Formosa is that there is to be kept alive a constant threat of military action vis-à-vis Red China in the hope that at some point there will be an internal breakdown.' Quoted in O. E. Clubb, Jnr., *The United States and the Sino-Soviet Bloc in Southeast Asia* (Washington, D.C.: Brookings, 1962), p. 55. It is interesting that even Press Secretary James Hagerty, one of the more uncritical officials in the Eisenhower Administration, admitted that 'a military landing by the Nationalists on the China main coast would be touching off a major war'. Interview with author, 21 July 1970.

21 At the time, PLA sources in Foochow claimed 2664 Nationalists killed, 715 taken prisoner, 3 ROC landing craft sunk, 2 planes shot down, and a number of mortars, bazookas, guns and ammunition captured, between 16 and 18 July. NCNA, 19 July 1953, in SCMP, 18–20 July 1953, p. 1. By the following February, the PLA were claiming that their July successes had included annihilating 3300 Kuomintang troops invading Tungshan Island and Kuomintang 'gangs' on coastal islands; they further claimed to have recovered some twenty islands off the Chekiang and Fukien coasts, including Taluyueh, Hsiaolu Shan, Jienyuehtao, Hsiyang, Luying, and Chiku Shan. NCNA, 2 April 1954, Chinese code, in British Broadcasting Corporation, *Summary of World Broadcasts* – Part v: *The Far East* (Reading, Berks.: BBC Monitoring Service) [hereinafter abbreviated BBC/FE] 327, 11 February 1954, p. 36.

22 Arthur Radford, Dulles OHC transcript of a tape-recorded interview conducted by Philip Crowl (1965), p. 36.

23 Anthony Eden, *Full Circle: The Memoirs of Anthony Eden* (London: Cassell, 1960), p. 109.

24 United Nations Release of 23 October 1953, quoted in David Rees, *op. cit.* p. 461. Cf. Chiang I-shan, 'The Military Affairs of Communist China', in *Communist China 1949–1959*, vol. I (Kowloon, Hong Kong: Union Research Institute, 1961), pp. 228–9, and Po I-po, 'Three Years

of Achievement of the People's Republic of China', *Cheng-ch'ü Ch'ih-chiu Ho-ping, Cheng-ch'ü Jen-min Min-chu* [For a Lasting Peace, For a People's Democracy] in NCNA, 1 October 1952.

25 SCMP, 12–14 September 1953, quoted in Samuel Griffith II, *op. cit.* p. 173.

26 David Rees, *op. cit.* p. 245.

27 Theodore Shi-en Chen and Wen-hui C. Chen, 'The "Three-Anti" and "Five-Anti" Movements in Communist China', *Pacific Affairs,* March 1953, p. 18; Alexander Eckstein, *Communist China's Economic Growth and Foreign Trade: Implications for US Policy* (New York: McGraw-Hill, for the Council on Foreign Relations, 1966), p. 28.

28 Slogan for the 1954 Vietnamese-Soviet-Chinese Friendship Month, Radio Peking, 9 January 1954, Chinese language broadcast in BBC/FE 320, 19 January 1954, p. 53.

29 Voice of Viet Nam, 16 July 1950, quoted in *Shih-chieh Chih-shih,* CB 285, 5 May 1954, p. 30.

30 Bernard Fall, *The Two Viet-Nams: A Political and Military Analysis* (New York: Praeger, 1963), p. 109.

31 *New York Times,* 6 April 1954.

32 NCNA, 23 November 1949.

33 John Foster Dulles, *op. cit.* p. 147.

Chapter 5

1 Robert Murphy asserts that 'Eisenhower, having been through so many of those things, *knew* you could lose, and if he erred, it was on the side of having twice or three times what he needed to ensure success. And then he would have gone all-out for a win, whether that meant destruction of Haiphong or Hanoi or anything, but I know he wouldn't have gone into the thing at all unless some combination of events had forced him to go in.' Interview with author, 21 July 1970.

2 DSB, 13 February 1950, p. 244.

3 John Foster Dulles, *War or Peace* (London: Harrap, 1950), p. 231.

4 DSB, 30 June 1952, p. 1010.

5 Chungking *Hsin-hua Jih-pao,* 29 February 1954, in SCMP 773, 24 March 1954, limited circulation supplement, pp. xi–xiii.

6 Peter Calvocoressi *et al. Survey of International Affairs, 1949–1950* (London: Oxford University Press, for the Royal Institute of International Affairs, 1953), p. 434.

7 Cf. Peter Lyon, *War and Peace in South-east Asia* (London: Oxford University Press, for the Royal Institute of International Affairs, 1969), pp. 67–70; I. Milton Sacks, 'Marxism in Vietnam', in Frank N. Trager (ed.), *Marxism in Southeast Asia* (Stanford, Calif.: Stanford University Press, 1959), pp. 102–70.

8 Richard P. Stebbins, *The United States in World Affairs, 1954* (New York: Harper, for the Council on Foreign Relations, 1956), pp. 198–9.

9 Walter P. McConaughy, in DSB, 11 January 1954, pp. 40, 42.

10 *Pravda* and *Izvestia,* CDSP, 9 August 1953 in Melvin Gurtov, *The First Vietnam Crisis: Chinese Communist Strategy and United States Involvement, 1953–1954* (New York: Columbia University Press, 1967), p. 61.

11 *Pravda,* CDSP, 23 February 1953, in *idem.* I am indebted to Gurtov for background to the Sino-Soviet debate on Malenkov's international outlook.

12 *Jen-min Jih-pao,* NCNA, 18 November 1953, in SCMP 691, 19 November 1953, p. 19.
13 *Ibid.* NCNA, 9 October 1953, in SCMP 666, 9–13 October 1953, p. 17.
14 *Ibid.* NCNA, 4 January 1953.
15 Alice Langley Hsieh, *Communist China's Strategy in the Nuclear Era* (Englewood Cliffs, N.J.: Prentice-Hall, 1962), p. 7.
16 Sherman Adams, interview with author, 28 September 1970.
17 *New York Times,* 24 March 1954.
18 *Ibid.* 11 February 1954.
19 Radio Peking, 27 February 1954, Chinese language broadcast, in BBC/FE economic supplement 103, 9 March 1954, p. 22. Cf. NCNA, 11 January and 16 February 1954, coded transmissions, in BBC/FE economic supplements 96 and 101, 19 January and 25 February 1954, pp. 6 and 12, respectively.
20 *Jen-min Jih-pao* leader, 14 February 1954, in BBC/FE 330, 23 February 1954, p. 19. Cf. *Pravda* article by Wu Yu-chiang (Vice President of the Sino-Soviet Friendship Association), *ibid.,* pp. 20–21.
21 Anthony Eden, *Full Circle: The Memoirs of Anthony Eden* (London: Cassell, 1960), p. 88.
22 *Ibid.* p. 89.
23 DSB, 15 March 1954. Secretary Dulles said previously that the 'Chinese Communist regime will not come to Geneva to be honored by us but rather to account before the bar of world opinion'. *Ibid.* 8 March 1954.
24 NCNA, 26 October 1954.
25 *Ibid.* 25 March 1954.
26 *New York Times,* 28 March 1954.
27 NCNA, 28 March 1954, in SCMP 776, 27–29 March 1954, p. 1.
28 *New York Times,* 30 March 1954, and DSB, 12 April 1954, pp. 539–40.
29 New York *Herald Tribune,* 31 March 1954.
30 NCNA, 1 April 1954, which also labelled the March 29th speech 'an open manoeuvre to exert pressure and coercion on the allies of the United States to join in obstructing a Geneva agreement on the restoration of peace in Indo-China, while intensifying the Indo-China war and aggravating tension in Asia'. Cf. *Ta Kung Pao* in SCMP 782, 6 April 1954, pp. 2–3.
31 *New York Times,* 30 March 1954, and DSB, 12 April 1954, pp. 539–40.
32 Anthony Eden, *op. cit.* p. 93. Cf. Document 19, *The Pentagon Papers,* Senator Gravel edition (Boston: Beacon Press, 1971) vol. 1, pp. 429–33.
33 General Paul Ély, *Mémoires: L'Indochine dans la tourmente* (Paris: Blon, 1964), p. 32. Admiral Radford surprised me by denying that he favoured any plan for the US to intervene at that late stage, including that of General Ély. It is hard to believe that all of the accounts (and the available evidence in the *Pentagon Papers*) on the Admiral's position is consistent with his own strategic outlook. Interview with author, 15 September 1970. Cf. Document 26, *The Pentagon Papers, op. cit.* pp. 455–60.
34 *New York Times,* 30 March 1954.
35 Robert Bowie, Dulles OHC transcript of a tape-recorded interview conducted by Richard D. Challener (1964), p. 26.
36 John Foster Dulles, 'Policy for Security and Peace', *Foreign Affairs,* April 1954, p. 359.
37 DSB, 25 January 1954, p. 108. Selective retaliation represented an attempt to reconcile US strategic limitations with US external ambitions,

which far exceeded those of the Truman Administration four years previously. In this context, Dulles dramatised his initiative by timing it for the fourth anniversary of Dean Acheson's ill-fated National Press Club speech: both were delivered on 12 January.

38 Chalmers Roberts, 'The Day We Didn't Go to War', *The Reporter*, 14 September 1954.

39 *New York Times*, 13 April 1954.

40 *Ibid.* 7 April 1954. Document 29, *The Pentagon Papers, op. cit.* p. 462.

41 NCNA, 8 April 1954.

42 Richard Rovere, *Affairs of State: The Eisenhower Years* (New York: Farrar, Straus and Cudahy, 1956), p. 191.

43 Interview with John Foster Dulles in James Shepley, 'How Dulles Averted War', *Life*, 16 January 1956. According to Foreign Minister Bidault, Dulles went as far as to offer to use one or more A-Bombs to destroy Sino-Vietnamese supply lines and two A-Bombs against the Communist besiegers of Dienbienphu, and Bidault requested 'something much less grave', such as a conventional air strike, which was refused. Roscoe Drummond and Gaston Coblentz, *Duel at the Brink: John Foster Dulles' Command of American Power* (London: Weidenfeld & Nicolson, 1961), p. 122. No evidence corroborates Bidault's claim. It would appear that the most that can be said for it is that Dulles was possibly interested in testing French reactions to even the most far-fetched JCS recommendations before arriving at a much more conservative conclusion himself.

44 James Shepley, *op. cit.* With the possibility of the use of MIGs in the Red River Delta in mind, Eisenhower categorically stated in his memoirs that 'Had the Chinese adopted a policy of regular air support for the Vietminh, we would have assuredly moved in to eliminate this blatant aggression from without. This would have necessitated striking Chinese airfields and would have created some risk of general war with China. As it was, I feel confident that our ability to operate in this fashion had a decisively deterrent effect on the Chinese.' Dwight D. Eisenhower, *op. cit.* p. 313. Cf. Document 20, *The Pentagon Papers, op. cit.* pp. 442–3. I take issue with this assessment in my analysis, on the grounds that the low probability of direct Chinese involvement made such contingency plans highly hypothetical and not worth communicating.

45 Dwight D. Eisenhower, *The White House Years: Mandate for Change, 1953–1956* (London: Heinemann, 1963), pp. 346–7.

46 Dwight D. Eisenhower, *op. cit.* p. 347.

47 In the same statement, Eisenhower stated that 'Asia, after all, has already lost some 450 million of its peoples to the Communist dictatorship, and we simply can't afford greater losses'. Press and Radio Conference, Dwight D. Eisenhower, 7 April 1954, Official File 101-L, Dwight D. Eisenhower Presidential Library.

48 Dwight D. Eisenhower, *op. cit.* p. 347.

49 Eleanor Lansing Dulles, 'Time and Decisions', *Foreign Military Commitments*, *The Forensic Quarterly* (August 1969), p. 277. Cf. Richard Goold-Adams, *John Foster Dulles, A Reappraisal* (New York: Appleton-Century-Crofts, 1962), pp. 125–6.

50 Department of State, *American Foreign Policy, 1950–1955, Basic Documents* (Washington, D.C.: Government Printing Office, 1957), p. 1704.

51 Anthony Eden, 'Indo-China: Attitude of Her Majesty's Government', Cmnd. 2834, April 1954, p. 67.

52 Louis J. Halle, Jnr., *The Cold War as History* (London: Chatto & Windus, 1967), p. 297.
53 Matthew B. Ridgway, *Soldier: The Memoirs of Matthew B. Ridgway* (New York: Harper 1956), p. 276. According to a State Department official, deeply involved at the time in the efforts for 'united action', 'the Ridgway report was given real weight' (unattributable letter). Admiral Radford insisted, on the other hand, that 'the Report was irrelevant because there was no chance of massive troop involvement in Indochina at that time anyway'. Interview with author, 15 September 1970.
54 Quoted in Roscoe Crummond and Gaston Coblentz, *op. cit.* p. 119.
55 *New York Times,* 18 April 1954.
56 *Ibid.* 6 April 1954. On 7 April Secretary Dulles reiterated this view at the Republican Women's Centennial Conference, Department of State Press Release 182, 7 April 1954.
57 *New York Times,* 20 and 21 April 1954.
58 'Nixon's War Cry', *Jen-min Jih-pao,* 20 April 1954, in SCMP 792, 21–2 April 1954, p. 11.
59 Chu Jung-fu, quoted by NCNA, 20 April 1954.
60 *Ibid.* pp. 101–3; John R. Beal, *John Foster Dulles, 1888–1959* (New York: Harper, 1959), pp. 211–12.
61 *Jen-min Jih-pao,* 16 April 1954, in NCNA, 16 April 1954.
62 Anthony Eden, *op. cit.* p. 163.
63 Nathan Twining, Dulles OHC transcript of a tape-recorded interview conducted by Philip Crowl (1965), p. 29.
64 According to an Administration poll in April and the Gallup poll in March. Coral Bell, *op. cit.* p. 41.
65 Anthony Eden, *Full Circle,* p. 127.
66 James Shepley, *op. cit.*
67 *Jen-min Jih-pao,* 20 April 1954, in NCNA, 20 April 1954.
68 Louis Halle agrees somewhat reluctantly with this conclusion, 'Who can say, then, that a great power's deliberate affectation of international irresponsibility, however dangerous such a result might be, and however damaging to its credit in the long run, does not have its uses?' Louis Halle, *op. cit.* p. 298.
69 *Pravda* and *Izvestia,* CDSP, 13 March 1954, cited in Herbert S. Dinerstein, *War and the Soviet Union: Nuclear Weapons and the Revolution in Soviet Military and Political Thinking,* revised edition (New York: Praeger, 1962), p. 71; *Shih-chieh Chih-shih Shou-ts'e 1954 nien* [Handbook of World Knowledge, 1954] (Peking: Chih-shih Ch'u-pan she, 20 February 1954), p. 8, cited in Melvin Gurtov, *op. cit.* p. 65.
70 Final Declaration of the Geneva Conference, 21 July 1954, in Cmd. 9239, pp. 83–5. Cf. G. F. Hudson, 'The Final Declaration of the Geneva Conference on Indo-China, 1954', in *Far Eastern Affairs,* Number Four, St Antony's Papers, Number 20 (London: Oxford University Press, 1967), pp. 73–87.

Chapter 6

1 Mao Tse-tung, *Selected Works,* Vol. 1 (Peking: Foreign Languages Press, 1965), p. 236, and Stuart Schram, *The Political Thought of Mao Tse-tung* (Harmondsworth, Middx.: Penguin, 1969), p. 280.
2 John Foster Dulles, 'Summary of U.S. Position Regarding Taiwan', in

File IX, *Materials Concerning the Chinese Communist Regime* (June 1956), Dulles Papers, John Foster Dulles Library of Diplomatic History, Princeton University Library.

3 DSB, 28 June 1954, p. 971.

4 Remarks at Manila press conference, 2 March 1955, in File IX, 'Bangkok Trip', Dulles Papers, *loc. cit.*

5 *Ta Kung Pao*, 12 November 1954, in SCMP 927, 13–15 November 1954, p. 3.

6 New York *Times*, 24 and 28 November 1954.

7 *Ibid.* 30 November and 2 December 1954.

8 'The Little China War', *The Straits Times*, 26 November 1954.

9 Edgar Snow, *Red Star Over China* (New York: Modern Library, 1944), p. 96.

10 NCNA, 24 November 1954, in SCMP 935, 25 November 1954, p. 7.

11 Exchange of notes between John Foster Dulles and George K. C. Yeh, December 1954, in Peter V. Curl (ed.), *Documents on American Foreign Relations, 1954* (New York: Harper, for the Council on Foreign Relations, 1955), p. 10.

12 NCNA, 9 December 1954.

13 Chou En-lai, 'Report on Foreign Affairs to the Central People's Government Council', 11 August 1954, in *Important Documents Concerning the Question of Taiwan* (Peking: Foreign Languages Press, 1955), pp. 110–11. Cf. Chou En-lai, 'Report on the Work of the Government to the First Session of the First National People's Congress', 23 September 1954, in Chung-kuo jen-min chiao hsüeh hui, *Oppose U.S. Occupation of Taiwan and 'Two Chinas' Plot* (Peking: Foreign Languages Press, 1958), pp. 15–17.

14 Neal Stanford, 'Defense Bloc for Free Asia', *Christian Science Monitor*, 6 May 1954.

15 *Jen-min Jih-pao*, 8 August 1954, in SCMP 864, 7–9 August 1954, p. 10.

16 *New York Times*, 4 August 1954.

17 South China *Morning Post*, 26 May 1954. Cf. *Free China Information Bulletin*, 2 June 1954.

18 'Oppose U.S. Military Intrigues in Asia', *Jen-min Jih-pao*, 9 July 1954, in NCNA, 12 July 1954.

19 Harold Hinton, *Communist China in World Politics* (London: Macmillan, 1966), p. 261.

20 Cf. George F. Kennan, *American Diplomacy: 1900–1950* (New York: New American Library, 1951), pp. 34–6.

21 Chou En-lai, 'Report on Foreign Affairs to the Central People's Government Council', 11 August 1954, *op. cit.* pp. 111, 123–4.

22 NCNA, 1 August 1954, in SCMP 860, 31 July–2 August 1954, p. 2. Cf. Su Yü, in *Jen-min Jih-pao*, 31 July 1954, *ibid.* p. 3.

23 'Justice Is Certain To Triumph', *Jen-min Jih-pao*, 20 August 1954, in SCMP 874, 21–3 August 1954, pp. 5–9, and Chang Hsi-jo's *Jen-min Jih-pao* article in SCMP 876, 25 August 1954, p. 4.

24 E.g. *Jen-min Jih-pao*, 26 August 1954, in SCMP 878, 27 August 1954, p. 1.

25 NCNA, 22 August 1954, in SCMP 874, 21–3 August 1954, p. 1. The Joint Declaration was hailed as 'the voice of justice that resounds through the world' by *Kuang-ming Jih-pao*, 23 August 1954, in SCMP 875, 24 August 1954, p. 8.

26 Ho Cheng, 'Taiwan Must Be Liberated', *People's China*, 1 September 1954, p. 6. Also in NCNA, 29 August 1954.

27 NCNA, 7 September 1954, in SCMP 884, 8–9 September 1954, p. 20.
28 New York *Herald Tribune,* 3 February 1954.
29 Coral Bell, *Survey of International Affairs, 1954* (London: Oxford University Press, for the Royal Institute of International Affairs, 1957), p. 92.
30 *New York Times,* 2 April 1954.
31 *Ibid.* 13 April 1954.
32 SCMP 789, 15 April 1954, p. 1.
33 New York *Herald Tribune,* 19 July 1954.
34 *New York Times,* 17 August 1954.
35 Cf. the 'memorandum on the program for world revolution', purportedly prepared by Mao Tse-tung and carried to Moscow by Chou En-lai, which Senator Knowland entered into the *Congressional Record* on 29 April, in US Information Service press release, London, 4 June 1954. Initially reported in the New York *Herald Tribune* on 1 June, the recommendations for 'internal revolution, effective infiltration, or intimidation into inaction or submission' in Asia and the prediction that 'Twenty years from now, world revolution will be an accomplished fact' were further publicised in newspapers around the world (including *Le Monde, Il Popolo,* and *Free China Information Bulletin*). Huang Hua, then a counsellor for the PRC delegation at Geneva, angrily denounced the document as 'an out-and-out fabrication, forged by none other than Knowland and his partners on Taiwan'. NCNA, 11 June 1954. *Le Monde* came to take the same view on 3 June. The document itself does not seem to contain any typical Chinese Communist terminology; it most probably is an inept attempt to engineer 'misinformation', but it is revealing as a quasi-official assessment of the Chinese menace to both the Far East and the world. Cf. Bedell Smith's CBS-TV broadcast on August 1st, 'The Communists now would like to lull the world into a false sense of security . . . If they are able to do so, they can, behind the screen, pursue their tactics of subversion, infiltration and propaganda . . . in the face of this record of Chinese Communist hostility towards the United States, and indeed toward the independent governments of Asia, it is very hard for me to believe that whatever professions of friendship they might make can be regarded as more than complete hypocrisy, or at least as a temporary tactical move.' US Information Service press release, London, 3 August 1954.
36 *New York Times,* 16 September 1954.
37 *Jen-min Jih-pao,* 24 July 1954, in SCMP 855, 24–6 July 1954, p. 1.
38 New York *Herald Tribune,* 24 August 1954.
39 News report from Taipei, London *Times,* 30 September 1954.
40 News report from Taipei, *New York Times,* 30 September 1954.
41 Thomas Schelling, *Arms and Influence* (New Haven, Conn.: Yale University Press, 1966), p. 124.
42 Homer Bigart, 'Chiang Builds a New "Anchor" Island', New York *Herald Tribune,* 1 December 1954. Cf. Henry Lieberman, 'Anti-Red Chinese Build a New Base', *New York Times,* 1 December 1954.
43 Dwight D. Eisenhower, *The White House Years: Mandate for Change, 1953–1956* (Garden City, New York: Doubleday, 1963), p. 463.
44 *Ibid.* p. 464. Cf. Stewart Alsop, 'Another Great Debate', New York *Herald Tribune,* 2 January 1955.
45 Senator Mike Mansfield, Dulles OHC transcript of a tape-recorded interview conducted by Richard D. Challener (1966), pp. 5–6, on the

basis of information given to him by Secretary Dulles in Manila in September 1954. Cf. the less well-informed but nonetheless perceptive analysis of Stewart Alsop, who contrasted the Eisenhower-Ridgway search for a *modus vivendi* with the Knowland-Radford-Robertson attempt to 'strangle the Chinese Communist baby in its cradle'. 'The Inner Crisis', *Matter of Fact*, New York *Herald Tribune*, 29 November and 1 December 1954.

46 Dwight D. Eisenhower, *op. cit.* p. 464.

47 NCNA, in SCMP 903, 7 October 1954, p. 16, and SCMP 912, 21 October 1954.

48 NCNA, Peking, 2 November 1954, English language broadcast, in SCMP 921, 3 November 1954, p. 25; NCNA, Chekiang Front, 3 November 1954. English language broadcast, in SCMP 922, 4 November 1954, p. 13.

49 *Ibid.* 1 November 1954, English language broadcast, in SCMP 920, 2 November 1954, p. 37.

50 *Ibid.* 3 November 1954, in SCMP 922, 4 November 1954, p. 13.

51 NCNA, 23 November 1954, in SCMP 934, 24 November 1954, p. 21.

52 *Ibid.* 3 December 1954, in SCMP 941, 4–6 December 1954, p. 2.

53 *Jen-min Jih-pao*, 5 December 1954, in SCMP 941, 4–6 December 1954, p. 6. Also in *People's China*, supplement, 16 December 1954.

54 Cf. 'The War Character of the U.S.-Chiang Kai-shek Treaty Cannot Be Concealed', *Jen-min Jih-pao*, 7 December 1954, in SCMP 943, 8 December 1954, pp. 1–4. The possibility of U.S. commitment to the offshore islands is briefly mentioned in a thorough textual analysis of the Treaty, in NCNA, 5 December 1954, SCMP 491, 4–6 December 1954.

55 George K. C. Yeh, Dulles OHC transcript of a tape-recorded interview conducted by Spencer Davis (1964), p. 15.

56 John R. Beal, *John Foster Dulles: 1888–1959* (New York: Harper, 1959), p. 335.

57 Dwight D. Eisenhower, *op. cit.* pp. 470–1.

58 Exchange of notes between John Foster Dulles and George K. C. Yeh, December 1954, *loc. cit.*

59 Dwight D. Eisenhower, *op. cit.* p. 473.

60 Chou En-lai, 'Statement on U.S.-Chiang Kai-shek Treaty', NCNA, 8 December 1954, p. 2. Cf. Chung-kuo jen-min chiao hsüeh hui, *Oppose U.S. Occupation of Taiwan and 'Two Chinas' Plot*, *loc. cit.* pp. 18–27.

61 *Daily Telegraph*, 16 December 1954.

62 Declaration of the Second National Committee of the Chinese People's Political Consultative Conference, 25 December 1954, in *Important Documents Concerning the Question of Taiwan*, *loc. cit.* pp. 174–5.

63 *New York Times*, 11 January 1955.

64 Chiang Kai-shek, 1955 New Year's Message, *New York Times*, 2 January 1955.

65 Washington *Post*, 11 January 1955, Cf. NCNA, Chekiang Front, 10 January 1955, in SCMP 965, 11 January 1955, p. 11.

66 NCNA, 3 January 1955.

67 South China *Morning Post*, 17 January 1955.

68 NCNA, 20 January 1955.

69 *New York Times*, 15 and 17 January 1955.

70 *New York Times*, 19 January 1955, and NCNA, Chekiang Front, 18 January 1955, in SCMP 971, 19 January 1955, p. 1.

71 *New York Times,* 20 January 1955.
72 Cf. Chou En-lai's statement on U.S. intervention in the Chinese people's liberation of Taiwan, 24 January 1955, NCNA, 24 January 1955, in SMCP 974, 22–6 January 1955, pp. 1–2.
73 Quoted in Dwight D. Eisenhower, *op. cit.* p. 467.
74 Robert Murphy, interview with author, 21 July 1970; Sherman Adams, interview with author, 28 September 1970. Admiral Burke believed, on the other hand, that the Administration should not have let the Tachens go, and certainly not under PRC pressure. Interview with author, 15 September 1970.
75 Dwight D. Eisenhower, *op. cit.* p. 469.
76 *Jen-min Jih-pao,* 16 February 1955, in SCMP 990, 17 February 1955, pp. 1–2. Cf. Liang Szu-yi, 'A Crime Against Humanity: The ruthless abduction of 20,000 inhabitants of the Tachens by U.S. forces and Chiang troops', *People's China,* 1 May 1955, pp. 8–10, and Red Cross Society of China, 'Disaster Strikes the Tachens', *People's China,* supplement, 1 May 1955.
77 *New York Times,* 25 February 1955, and NCNA, Chekiang Front, 26 February 1955, in SCMP 996, 27 February 1955, p. 7.
78 Mme Chiang Kai-shek pointed out that 'It would have been well-nigh impossible to keep on supplying our army there, with the Communists being so near, and for us, at the same time, to hold on to Quemoy and and Matsu. It was the question of logistics . . .' Dulles OHC transcript of a tape-recorded interview conducted by Spencer Davis (1966), p. 13.
79 Dwight D. Eisenhower, *op. cit.* p. 467.
80 George K. C. Yeh, Dulles OHC interview, *op. cit.* p. 21.
81 Washington *Post,* 25 January 1955.
82 Dwight D. Eisenhower, *op. cit.* appendix N, p. 608.
83 *New York Times,* 10 February 1955.
84 *Jen-min Jih-pao,* 29 January 1955, in *People's China,* 16 February 1955, p. 36.
85 *New York Times,* 10 February 1955.
86 *Ibid.* 7 February 1955.
87 For an examination of the complex legal and political issues surrounding the status of Taiwan, see William M. Bueler, 'Taiwan: A Problem of International Law or Politics', *The World Today,* June 1971, pp. 256–66.
88 *New York Times,* 8 February 1955. Curiously, Peking denounced the Committee's understanding as a subterfuge for Washington's retaining its control of Nationalist-held territories. NCNA, 16 February 1955.
89 Liu Ke-lin, 'A Treaty for Aggressive War', *People's China,* 1 January 1955, p. 16.
90 Dwight D. Eisenhower, *op. cit.* p. 472.
91 Arthur Radford, Dulles OHC transcript of a tape-recorded interview conducted by Philip A. Crowl (1965), p. 38.
92 *New York Times,* 12 April 1955.
93 *Ibid.* 30 January 1955.
94 *Ibid.* 4 February 1955.
95 New York *Herald Tribune,* 9 March 1955.
96 Dwight D. Eisenhower, Dulles OHC transcript of a tape-recorded interview conducted by Philip A. Crowl (1964), p. 21.
97 Chiang Kai-shek, Dulles OHC transcript of a tape-recorded interview conducted by Spencer Davis (1966), p. 14, and George K. C. Yeh, Dulles OHC interview, *op. cit.* p. 21.
98 Dwight D. Eisenhower, *Mandate for Change,* p. 476.

99 *Ibid.* p. 475.
100 Personal Memorandum prior to conversation with Eden, 24 February 1955, File IX, 'Bangkok Trip', Dulles Papers, *loc. cit.*
101 Dwight D. Eisenhower, *Mandate for Change,* p. 475.
102 *Ibid.* p. 477.
103 *New York Times,* 17 March 1955.
104 *Ibid.* 9 March 1955.
105 *Ibid.* 24 April 1955; New York *Herald Tribune,* 27 April 1955.
106 Dwight D. Eisenhower, *Mandate for Change,* p. 480; *New York Times,* 26 April 1955. Speculation at the time, restated by Senator Kennedy in his 1960 campaign, that the Administration had pressed for total evacuation of Quemoy and Matsu, was unfounded. Hinton mistakenly endorses this theory without offering any supporting evidence. Harold Hinton, *op. cit.* p. 263. Cf. Dwight D. Eisenhower, *Mandate for Change,* pp. 481, 611–12.
107 *Ibid.* appendix P, p. 611.
108 Washington *Post,* 26 March 1955; *New York Times,* 27 March 1955.
109 Report from Secretary Dulles to President Eisenhower, quoted in Dwight D. Eisenhower, *Mandate for Change,* p. 482.
110 John Foster Dulles, 3 March 1955 statement, in U.S. Information Service bulletin, London, 4 March 1955.
111 Letter to the author from former Assistant (subsequently Under) Secretary of State Livingston T. Merchant, 5 October 1970.
112 Personal Memorandum prior to conversation with Eden, *op. cit.*
113 New York *Herald Tribune,* 12 August 1954.
114 Washington *Post,* 8 November 1954.
115 NCNA, 13 October 1954.
116 *New York Times,* 16 December 1954.

Chapter 7

1 Anthony Eden, *Full Circle: The Memoirs of Anthony Eden* (London: Cassell, 1960), p. 311.
2 Cf. Hayward R. Alker and Bruce M. Russett, *World Politics in the General Assembly* (New Haven, Conn.: Yale University Press, 1965).
3 I am grateful to John Gittings for this important qualification.
4 NCNA, Bandung, 23 April 1955, in SCMP 1033, 23–5 April 1955, p. 1.
5 Cf. Chou En-lai, 'Report on the Present International Situation, China's Foreign Policy, and the Question of the Liberation of Taiwan', to the Third Session of the First National People's Congress, 28 June 1956, in Chung-kuo jen-min chiao hsüeh hui, *Oppose U.S. Occupation of Taiwan and 'Two Chinas' Plot* (*A Selection of Important Documents*) (Peking: Foreign Languages Press, 1958), pp. 146–8.
6 Wang Chih-shen, 'Continue Efforts to Strive for the Peaceful Liberation of Taiwan', *Shih-shih Shou-tse [Current Events],* 6 May 1957, in *Extracts from China Mainland Magazines* (Hong Kong: American Consulate General) [hereinafter abbreviated ECMM] 92, 29 July 1957, p. 5.
7 Chou En-lai, *op. cit.* pp. 43–5, and Political Report to the Second Plenary Session of the Second National Committee of the Chinese People's Political Consultative Conference, 30 January 1956, in CB 375, 2 February 1956, p. 9.

8 Cf. Kenneth T. Young, *Negotiating with the Chinese Communists: The United States Experience, 1953–1967* (New York: McGraw-Hill, for the Council on Foreign Relations, 1968).

9 New York *Herald Tribune*, 3 August 1955.

10 Anthony Eden, *op. cit.* p. 64.

11 John Foster Dulles, *War or Peace* (London: Harrap, 1950), p. 186. See also chapter 2, 'Know Your Enemy'.

12 *New York Times*, 24 April 1955.

13 *Ibid.* 1 August 1955.

14 *Ibid.* 11 January 1958.

15 Rachel F. Wall, 'East-West Relations', in *Survey of International Affairs, 1956–58* (London: Oxford University Press, for the Royal Institute of International Affairs, 1962), p. 339.

16 *Documents on International Affairs, 1957* (London: Oxford University Press, for the Royal Institute of International Affairs, 1961), p. 113.

17 *Quotations from Chairman Mao Tse-tung* (Peking: Foreign Languages Press, 1966), pp. 80–1.

18 Mao Tse-tung, 'On the Correct Handling of Contradictions Among the People', 27 February 1957, in *ibid.* pp. 67–8.

Chapter 8

1 *Quotations from Chairman Mao Tse-tung* (Peking: Foreign Languages Press, 1966), pp. 80–1; Chou En-lai's report on Chinese foreign policy to the Fifth Session of the National People's Congress, 10 February 1958, in BBC/FE 741, 13 February 1958, supplement.

2 Cf. Donald Zagoria, *The Sino-Soviet Conflict, 1956–61* (New York: Atheneum, 1967), chapter 5.

3 Joseph Alsop, 'Arguments at the Brink', New York *Herald Tribune*, 7 September 1958; cf. James Reston, 'War-Making Power', *New York Times*, 4 September 1958.

4 Radio Foochow, 18 December 1957 and 2 January 1958, Chinese language broadcasts, in BBC/FE, economic supplement 298, 2 January 1958. NCNA, 1 January 1958, Chinese language broadcast, in BBC/FE, economic supplement 299, 9 January 1958. This PRC build-up was confirmed on the basis of intelligence estimates by Assistant Secretary Robertson at secret hearings of the House Foreign Affairs Committee on 20 March, New York *Herald Tribune*, European edition, 22–3 March 1958.

5 Radio Taipei, 5 February 1958, Chinese language broadcast, in BBC/FE 740, 11 February 1958, p. 16.

6 Donald Zagoria, *op. cit.* pp. 189–94.

7 Thomas S. Gates, interview with author, 16 July 1970.

8 Neil McElroy, interview with author, 16 September 1970.

9 Radio Peking, 17 July 1958, Home Service transmitted live from Tienanmen Square, in BBC/FE 787, 24 July 1958, p. 11. Cf. 'Eisenhower Has Hoisted the Pirate's Skull and Cross-bones', in *Jen-min Jih-pao*, 21 July 1958, in SCMP 1819, 25 July 1958, pp. 30–3.

10 'U.S.-British Aggressive Cooperation in Looking For a Grave', *Jen-min Jih-pao*, 18 July 1958, in SCMP 1818, 24 July 1958, p. 1.

11 *Jen-min Jih-pao*, 20 July 1958, in NCNA, 21 July 1958.

12 Radio Taipei, 24 July and 21 July 1958, English language broadcasts, in BBC/FE 787, 24 July 1958, pp. 20–1.

13 NCNA, 24 July 1958.

14 Franz Schurmann, *Ideology and Organization in Communist China*, 2nd edition (Berkeley, Calif.: University of California Press, 1968), p. 480.

15 *Hung Ch'i*, August 1958, p. 14.

16 NCNA Foreign Service, 25 January 1958, Chinese language broadcast to Taiwan, in BBC/FE 737, 30 January 1958, p. 17.

17 Liu Shao-ch'i, Report to the Second Session, Eighth Chinese Communist Party Congress, NCNA, 26 May 1958. Cf. Yang Chung-kwang, 'U.S. Economic Crisis and Labor Movement in Capitalist Countries', *Shih-chieh Chih-shih*, 10 May 1958, in ECMM 137, 18 July 1958. The U.S. economic crisis was fully reported by the mainland press and radio. Cf. BBC/FE 759, 17 April 1958; 760, 22 April 1958; 761, 24 April 1958; 763, 1 May 1958.

18 *New York Times*, 7 September 1958.

19 *Ibid.* 14 September 1958.

20 *Ibid.* 14 September 1958.

21 *Ibid.* 13 September 1958.

22 *Ibid.* 22 October 1958.

23 Cf. Charles McClelland, 'Decisional Opportunity and Political Controversy: The Quemoy Case', *Journal of Conflict Resolution*, September 1962, p. 211.

24 Radio Peking, 28 February 1958, Chinese language broadcast, in BBC/FE 747, 6 March 1958, p. 8.

25 Radio Peking, 20 February 1958, Chinese language broadcast to Taiwan, in *ibid.* p. 9.

26 Radio Taipei, 27 February 1958, Chinese language broadcast, in BBC/FE 746, 4 March 1958, p. 13.

27 Alice Langley Hsieh, *Communist China's Strategy in the Nuclear Era* (Englewood Cliffs, N.J.: Prentice-Hall, 1962), p. 111.

28 NCNA, 10 March 1958, in BBC/FE 749, 13 March 1958, p. 3. Cf. NCNA, 10 April 1958, in BBC/FE 759, 17 April 1958, p. 2.

29 NCNA, 2 May 1958, in BBC/FE 765, 8 May 1958, p. 5.

30 *New York Times*, 13 April 1958. Cf. *Jen-min Jih-pao*, 18 April 1958, in NCNA, 18 April 1958.

31 London *Times*, 1 July 1958.

32 *New York Times*, 2 July 1958. A spokesman for the Chinese Foreign Ministry complained, 'If the United States can violate an agreement [to hold ambassadorial talks] for more than six months, why can't China demand to resume its implementation within fifteen days?' NCNA, 2 July 1958.

33 NCNA, 16 July 1958.

34 New York *Herald Tribune*, European edition, 11 July 1958.

35 NCNA, 3 August 1958, in SCMP 1827, 5 August 1958, pp. 25–26. Also in *Peking Review*, 12 August 1958, pp. 6–7.

36 Alice Langley Hsieh, *op. cit.* pp. 121–2, and Donald Zagoria, *op. cit.* pp. 201, 206.

37 New York *Herald Tribune*, 16 June 1958.

38 *Jen-min Jih-pao*, 8 August 1958, in SCMP 1832, 14 August 1958, p. 2.

39 *Ibid.* pp. 3, 4.

40 Cf. *Peking Review*, 6 September 1963.

41 General Tung Ch'i-wu, 'The People's Liberation Army Has No Match in the Whole World'; General Liu Shan-pen, 'Swift Expansion of Our

Air Force'; Teng Chao-hsiang, 'The People's Navy in a Leap Forward', *Wen Hui Pao*, 1 August 1958, in CB 514, 6 August 1958, pp. 8, 12, 11 respectively.

42 Full text in *New York Times*, 10 August 1958.

43 *Ta Kung Pao*, 17 August 1958, in NCNA, 18 August 1958. See also *Kuang-ming Jih-pao*, 17 August 1958, in *ibid.*

44 *New York Times*, 11 August 1958.

45 *Jen-min Jih-pao*, 15 August 1958, in NCNA, 17 August 1958. A lengthy analysis and commentary on the non-recognition memorandum appeared in *Jen-min Jih-pao*, 16 August 1958, in SCMP 1836, 20 August 1958, pp. 1–4.

46 Yu Chao-li, 'The Forces of Decay', *Hung Ch'i*, 16 August 1958, in SCMP 1837, 21 August 1958, pp. 42–7. Also in *Peking Review*, 19 August 1958, pp. 8–11. 'Yu Chao-li' is a pseudonym generally taken to represent CCP Politburo opinions on imperialism and anti-imperialist strategies. Literally, it means 'strength of millions', referring to the inferiority of weapons when opposed by the popular masses. Donald Zagoria, *op. cit.* p. 201.

47 Cf. the interpretation offered by Alice Langley Hsieh, *op. cit.* p. 121, and Donald Zagoria, *op. cit.* pp. 209–10.

48 *New York Times*, 21 September 1958. NCNA, Fukien Front, 24 and 25 August 1958, in SCMP 1842, 26 August 1958, pp. 32–3.

49 China News Service, Fukien Front, 28 August 1958, in SCMP 1844, 30 August 1958, p. 23.

50 Text of letter in DSB, 8 September 1958, p. 379.

51 *New York Times*, 28 August 1958.

52 *Pravda*, 31 August 1958, in CDSP, 10 October 1958, p. 17.

53 *New York Times*, 28, 30 and 31 August and 4 September 1958.

54 Defense Secretary McElroy asserted that 'Our whole program of military support of the Taiwanese has been to maintain an effective defense. This I think we've done.' Interview with author, 16 September 1970.

55 *Ibid.* 5 September 1958; also, DSB, 22 September 1958, pp. 445–6.

56 *New York Times*, 15 September 1958, and Washington *Post*, 18 September 1958. Cf. Hanson Baldwin, 'Quemoy's Future Dim', *New York Times*, 19 September 1958.

57 Cf. Kenneth Young, *Negotiating with the Chinese Communists: The United States Experience, 1953–1967* (New York: McGraw-Hill, 1968), p. 177; Tang Tsou, *The Embroilment over Quemoy*, International Study Paper No. 2 (Salt Lake City, Utah: University of Utah Press, 1959), pp. 31–2.

58 *Jen-min Jih-pao*, 30 September 1958, in SCMP 1868, 1 October 1958, p. 35. Cf. Statement of PRC Ministry of National Defence, 29 September 1958, in *Peking Review*, 7 October 1958, pp. 12–13.

59 *New York Times*, 25 and 29 September 1958.

60 Neil McElroy, interview with author, 16 September 1970. Admiral Radford argues in a similar vein that 'the only reason they [the Chinese Communists] have never tried to take (the offshore islands) is they have not been ready to take them. By the time they were ready, or thought they were ready to take them, we had increased the power of the Chinese [Nationalist] forces to the extent that they couldn't do it without heavy losses. One of the factors being air power. You know, the Communists had built many air fields in Fukien province. By that

time, we had given the Nationalists jet fighters. In dog fights the Nationalist pilots really trimmed the Chinese Communist fighters.' Arthur Radford, Dulles OHC transcript of a tape-recorded interview conducted by Philip A. Crowl (1965), p. 43.

61 Admiral Arleigh Burke, Dulles OHC transcript of a tape-recorded interview conducted by Richard D. Challener (1966), p. 27.

62 Walter Lippmann, 'A Mediator is Needed', New York *Herald Tribune,* European edition, 26 September 1958.

63 Declaration of the Government of the People's Republic of China on China's Territorial Sea, 4 September 1958, in Chung-kuo jen-min chiao hsüeh hui, *Oppose U.S. Military Provocation in the Taiwan Straits Area: A Selection of Important Documents* (Peking: Foreign Languages Press, 1958), pp. 14–15.

64 NCNA, 6 September 1958, in SCMP 1851, 11 September 1958, pp. 1–3.

65 Kenneth Young, *op. cit.* p. 153.

66 Department of State, 'Summary of efforts by the United States to reach an agreement with the Chinese Communists on the renunciation of force in the Taiwan area', 13 September 1958, in *New York Times,* 14 September 1958.

67 *China Reconstructs,* November 1958, p. 1. Also Chung-kuo jen-min chiao hsüeh hui, *op. cit.* pp. 7–8.

68 NCNA, 14 September 1958.

69 *New York Times,* 9 September 1958. For the full text of Khrushchev's 7th September letter to Eisenhower, see Paul E. Zinner (ed.), *Documents on American Foreign Relations,* 1958 (New York: Harper, for the Council on Foreign Relations, 1959), pp. 443–52.

70 DSB, 29 September 1958, p. 499.

71 *New York Times,* 20 September 1958.

72 DSB, 6 October 1958, pp. 530–1.

73 *Pravda,* 6 October 1958, in CDSP 10.40, p. 1.

74 *New York Times,* 14 September 1958. Secretary of the Air Force Douglas announced on 27 September that the Administration would use nuclear weapons in the defence of Quemoy if necessary. *New York Times,* 28 September 1958.

75 *Ibid.* 19 September 1958.

76 DSB, 29 September 1958, pp. 483–4.

77 *New York Times,* 20 September 1958.

78 *Ibid.* 30 September 1958.

79 Memorandum Number 3, 13 October 1958, pp. 4–5, File ix, 'Rome-Taipei Trip', Dulles Papers, John Foster Dulles Library of Diplomatic History, Princeton University Library.

80 Department of State Press Release 574, 30 September 1958.

81 Memorandum Number 3, 13 October 1958, *op. cit.* pp. 3–4.

82 *Ibid.* p. 6.

83 *New York Times,* October 1958.

84 *Ibid.* 8 October 1958.

85 NCNA, 6 October 1958, in SCMP 1871, 9 October 1958, p. 45.

86 P'eng Teh-huai, 'Message to All Compatriots, Military and Civilian, in Taiwan, Penghu, Quemoy and Matsu!' 6 October 1958, in SCMP 1871, 8 October 1958, p. 45.

87 Order of PRC Ministry of National Defense to Fukien Front, 13 October 1958, in *Peking Review,* 14 October 1958, supplement.

88 Admiral Arleigh Burke, Address before Sigma Delta Chi Journalism Fraternity, San Diego, Calif., 22 November 1958, in *Navy Public Statements* (Washington, D.C.: Department of the Navy, January, 1959), p. 21.

89 'Chinese Strategy in the Taiwan Strait', *New Times* 46 (Moscow, November 1958), pp. 8–11, quoted in Alice Langley Hsieh, *op. cit.*, p. 128.

90 Department of State Press Release 634, 23 October 1958. Cf. 'On the Chiang Kai-shek–Dulles Talks', *Jen-min Jih-pao*, 30 October 1958, in *Peking Review*, 4 November 1958, pp. 9–11.

91 John Foster Dulles, Personal Memorandum for meeting with Chiang Kai-shek, 22 October 1958, File IX, 'Rome-Taipei Trip', Dulles Papers, *loc. cit.*

92 Statement by Secretary of State John Foster Dulles, White House Press Release, 24 October 1958.

93 Walter S. Robertson, letter to Elmo Roper, 31 October 1958, General File 802, Dwight D. Eisenhower Library.

94 *New York Times,* 1 November 1958.

95 *Ibid.* 2, 13 and 14 November 1958.

96 Chiang Kai-shek revealed in 1966 that 'today, about the same number of troops are there [on the offshore islands] as there were at the time of the bombardment in 1958'. Generalissimo and Mme. Chiang Kai-shek, Dulles OHC transcript of a tape-recorded interview conducted by Spencer Davis (1966), p. 25.

97 Washington *Post,* 3 September 1958, and New York *Herald Tribune,* 11 September 1958.

98 Dwight D. Eisenhower, *The White House Years: Waging Peace, 1956–1961* (Garden City, New York: Doubleday, 1962), p. 211.

99 *Ibid.* appendix O, p. 693.

100 *Peking Review,* 6 September 1963, quoted in Coral Bell, 'The Foreign Policy of China', in F. S. Northedge (ed.), *The Foreign Policies of the Powers* (London: Faber, 1968), p. 126.

101 Cf. Tang Tsou, *op. cit.*

102 Charles McClelland, *op. cit.* p. 203.

103 *New York Times,* 23 August 1958.

104 Dwight D. Eisenhower, *op. cit.* p. 296.

105 *Ibid.* p. 293.

106 Cf. V. D. Sokolovsky (ed.), *Military Strategy: Soviet Doctrine and Concepts* (New York: Praeger, 1963), Chapter 4.

107 Dwight D. Eisenhower, *op. cit.* p. 295.

108 Charles McClelland, *op. cit.* p. 209, footnote 3; Tang Tsou, *op. cit.* pp. 15–22.

109 Cf. the revealing Cultural Revolutionary leader, 'From the Defeat of P'eng Teh-huai to the Bankruptcy of China's Khrushchev', *Jen-min Jih-pao,* 15 August 1967, in SCMP, 16 August 1967.

Chapter 9

1 Thomas Schelling points out that 'When communication fails, it is not easy to decide whether the transmitter is too weak for the receiver or the receiver too weak for the transmitter, whether the sender speaks the receiver's language badly or the receiver misunderstands the sender's.

Between the two of us, Americans and Communist China, we appear to have suffered at least one communication failure in each direction in 1950.' *Arms and Influence* (New Haven, Conn.: Yale University Press, 1966), p. 55. As I have made clear in chapter 3, however, there were several communication failures in each direction in 1950.

2 Dwight D. Eisenhower, *The White House Years: Waging Peace, 1956–1961* (Garden City, N.Y.: Doubleday, 1965), p. 295.

3 Cf. J. H. Kalicki, 'China, America and Arms Control', *The World Today*, April 1970 and 'Nixon's Asia', *Pacific Community*, October 1972.

4 Quoted in *U.S. News and World Report*, 31 October 1958, p. 80.

5 Robert Jervis argues that decision-makers tend to discount signals because stakes are too high and/or because the signals are inherently incredible and/or because of emotional/irrational affect. On the other hand, they tend to believe signals when they have very little additional information to help predict their opponents' behavior, when they are duped by the enemy, or because of a mutual recognition that future credibility depends on reliable signalling. *The Logic of Images in International Relations* (Princeton: Princeton University Press, 1970), pp. 95–97. His theory is by and large confirmed by the Korean crises, in the former instance, and by the Taiwan Straits crises, in the latter.

6 Cf. Lin Piao, *Long Live the Victory of the People's War!* (Peking: Foreign Languages Press, 1965).

7 Mao Tse-tung, *Selected Works*, Vol. IV (Peking: Foreign Languages Press, 1965), p. 99.

8 John Foster Dulles, Memorandum 3, 13 October 1958, File IX, 'Rome-Taipei Trip – 10/17/58–10/24/58', Dulles Papers, John Foster Dulles Library of Diplomatic History, Princeton University Library.

The author has made every effort to secure permission to draw upon the various sources he has used in writing this book, but apologies if any material has been used without such permission.

BIBLIOGRAPHICAL NOTE

This bibliography is divided into five sections: (1) memoirs, collected writings and papers; (2) documents, government publications, and signed Chinese articles; (3) interviews and correspondence; (4) radio transcripts and newspapers; and (5) books and articles.

Section 1 is a list of publications and materials written and collected by key decision-makers and by persons in contact with and/or with influence over them. They often contain excerpts from, commentaries on, and references to documents and correspondence of special relevance to Sino-American relations.

Section 2 is a list of official materials. I have chosen to include signed Chinese articles because by and large they represent PRC official thinking on Sino-American affairs. These articles appear in translation, principally in *People's China* and its successor *Peking Review*, New China News Agency press releases and the publications of the US Consulate-General in Hong Kong: *Current Background* [*CB*], *Extracts from China Mainland Magazines* [*ECMM*], and *Survey of the China Mainland Press* [*SCMP*]. Signed Western newspaper articles, which are of course unofficial, have been cited in the endnote section preceding this bibliography.

In Section 3, there is a list of pertinent interviews conducted for the oral history projects of the Dulles Library of Diplomatic History in Princeton University and of the Dwight D. Eisenhower Memorial Library in Abilene, Kansas. It also lists the interviews conducted by the author (all of which were tape-recorded and transcribed except those with C. B. Marshall and Admiral Radford). Most of the correspondence which I have cited is part of the personal papers of Secretary Dulles and President Eisenhower, or of the Hoover Institution Archives.

In Section 4 appears a brief list of primary sources used in the Chatham House Press Library, namely the BBC radio transcription series and the newspapers whose transcripts and articles are cited specifically (when used) in the endnote section. Finally, Section 5 comprises the secondary sources, beyond those listed in the preceding sections, either cited in or directly relevant to this study.

BIBLIOGRAPHY

1. Memoirs, collected writings, and papers

Acheson, Dean. *Present at the Creation: My Years at the State Department.* (New York: Norton, 1969).

Adams, Sherman. *First Hand Report: The Story of the Eisenhower Administration* (New York: Harper, 1961).

Cooke, Admiral Charles M. Collection, Archives of the Hoover Institution on War, Revolution and Peace, Stanford University, Stanford, Calif.

Cordier, Andrew W. and Wilder Foote (eds.). *Public Papers of the Secretaries-General of the United Nations,* vol. 1: *Trygve Lie (1946–1953)* (New York: Columbia University Press, 1968).

Dulles, John Foster. Papers, Princeton University Library, Princeton, New Jersey.

Eden, Anthony. *Full Circle: The Memoirs of Anthony Eden* (London: Cassell, 1960).

Eisenhower, Dwight D. Papers, Dwight D. Eisenhower Memorial Library, Abilene, Kansas.

The White House Years: Mandate for Change, 1953–1956 (Garden City, New York: Doubleday, 1963).

The White House Years: Waging Peace, 1956–1961 (Garden City, New York: Doubleday, 1965).

Ély, Paul. *Mémoires: L'Indochine dans la tourmente* (Paris: Plon, 1964).

Giap, Vo Nguyen. *People's War, People's Army: The Viet Cong Insurrection Manual for Under-developed Countries.* Foreword by Roger Hilsman; profile of Giap by Bernard B. Fall (New York: Praeger, 1962).

Hornbeck, Stanley K. Papers, Archives of the Hoover Institution on War, Revolution and Peace, Stanford University, Stanford, Calif.

Hull, Cordell. *The Memoirs of Cordell Hull* (New York: Macmillan, 1948).

Liu Shao-ch'i. *Collected Works* (Kowloon, Hong Kong: Union Research Institute, 1968–present).

On Internationalism and Nationalism (Peking: Foreign Languages Press, 1949).

MacArthur, Douglas. *Reminiscences* (New York: McGraw-Hill, 1964).

Mao Tse-tung. *On Guerrilla Warfare,* ed. and tr. by Samuel B. Griffith (New York: Praeger, 1961).

Selected Works (Peking: Foreign Languages Press, 1965), 4 volumes.

Murphy, Robert. *Diplomat Among Warriors* (New York: Doubleday, 1964).

Navarre, Henri. *Agonie de l'Indochine, 1953–1954* (Paris: Plon, 1956).

Nixon, Richard M. *Six Crises* (New York: Doubleday, 1962).

Panikkar, K. M. *In Two Chinas* (London: Allen and Unwin, 1955).

The Pentagon Papers: The Defense Department History of United States

Decision Making on Vietnam, Senator Gravel edition (Boston: Beacon Press, 1972), vol. i.

Quotations from Chairman Mao Tse-tung (Peking: Foreign Languages Press, 1966).

Rankin, Karl Lott. *China Assignment* (Seattle: University of Washington Press, 1964).

Ridgway, Matthew B. *Soldier: The Memoirs of Matthew B. Ridgway, as told to Harold H. Martin* (New York: Harper, 1956).

Talbott, Strobe (ed.). *Khrushchev Remembers* (Boston: Little, Brown and Co., 1970).

Truman, Harry S. *Years of Trial and Hope* (London: Hodder & Stoughton, 1955).

2. Documents, government publications, and signed Chinese articles

Acheson, Dean. 'Crisis in Asia: An Examination of U.S. Policy', Department of State *Bulletin,* 23 January 1950.

Ah Ying. 'Hero of Taiwan's Restoration', *China Reconstructs,* November 1955.

Background Information Relating to Southeast Asia and Vietnam, US Senate, 89th congress, 2nd Session, Committee on Foreign Relations (Washington, D.C.: Government Printing Office, 1966).

Background Materials – Limited Circulation (Hong Kong: US Consulate General, 1953).

'Basic Differences between the Proletarian and Bourgeois Military Lines', *Peking Review,* 24 November 1967.

Bernstein, Barton J. and Allen J. Matusow (eds.). *The Truman Administration: A Documentary History* (New York: Harper, 1966).

Burke, Admiral Arleigh. Address before Sigma Delta Chi Journalism Fraternity, San Diego, Calif., 22 November 1958 in *Navy Public Statements* (Washington, D.C.: Department of the Navy, January 1959), pp. 17–24.

Carlyle, Margaret (ed.). *Documents on International Affairs, 1949–1950* (London: Oxford University Press, for the Royal Institute of International Affairs, 1953).

Chang Min-yang. 'Use Two Tactics of Revolution to Oppose Two Tactics of Counter-Revolution – Notes on Study of the Selected Works of Mao Tse-tung, Vol. iv', *Shih-chieh Chih-shih* 20 (1960) in SCMM 239 (1960).

Chao Chun. 'Dulles' Bluster About Taiwan Futile', *Ta Kung Pao,* 18 March 1955, in SCMP 1011, 19–20 March 1955.

Chen Han-seng. 'Taiwan – China's Largest Island', *China Reconstructs,* January 1955.

Chen Po-ta. 'Under the Banner of Mao Tse-tung', 16 July 1958, in ECMM 138, 11 August 1958.

Chen Ti-chiang. 'Cairo Declaration Is Binding International Treaty', *Jen-min Jih-pao,* 8 February 1955, in SCMP 984, 9 February 1955.

'Chiang and U.S. – Accomplices in Piracy', *People's China,* 16 November 1954.

'United Nations Should Punish U.S. Aggression Against China', *Ta Kung Pao,* 15 November 1954, in SCMP 927, 13–15 November 1954.

Ch'en Yi. 'The International Situation and our Foreign Policy', NCNA, 23 September 1956, in *Current Background,* 6 October 1956.

'The Years of Struggle for World Peace and Progress', in *Ten Glorious Years* (Peking: Foreign Languages Press, 1960).

Cheng Chih-jang. 'U.S. Aggression Against Taiwan Is Violation of International Law', *Jen-min Jih-pao*, 27 September 1954, in SCMP 897, 28 September 1954.

Cheng-ch'ü Ch'ih-chiu Ho-ping, Cheng-ch'ü Jen-min Min-chu [For a Lasting Peace, For a People's Democracy] Peking, Cominform weekly.

Chi Chao-ting. 'The Basic Issue in the Taiwan Straits Area', *China Reconstructs*, December 1958.

Chi Lung. 'The New Design of American Foreign Policy', *Shih-chieh Chih-shih* [World Culture], 20 January 1957, in ECMM 75, 25 March 1957.

'Our Peaceful Foreign Policy and Firm Stand', *Shih-chieh Chih-shih*, 5 March 1958, in ECMM 126, 28 April 1958.

'U.S. Strategy Is in a Blind Alley', *Shih-chieh Chih-shih* 23, 5 December 1957, in ECMM 121, 3 March 1958.

Chiang Yuan-chun. 'Chiang Kai-shek Must Not Attend International Conference', *Jen-min Jih-pao*, 20 February 1955, in SCMP 992, 20–21 February 1955.

'Chinese People Will Not Bow to War Threats', *Jen-min Jih-pao*, 8 February 1955, in SCMP 984, 9 February 1955.

'Churchill's Double-Dealing Exposed', *Jen-min Jih-pao*, 4 February 1955, in SCMP 982, 5–7 February 1955.

'Dulles Has Miscalculated', *Jen-min Jih-pao*, 21 February 1955, in SCMP 993, 22 February 1955.

'Dulles Wants Others to Fight for U.S. Over Taiwan', *Jen-min Jih-pao*, 7 April 1955, in SCMP 1025, 8–10 April 1955.

'Dulles' War Clamor to Extend Aggression', *Jen-min Jih-pao*, 5 March 1955, in SCMP 1001, 6 March 1955.

'U.S.-Sponsored Bangkok Conference', *Jen-min Jih-pao*, 13 January 1955, in SCMP 968, 14 January 1955.

'U.S. Trying to Coerce U.N. to Interfere', *Jen-min Jih-pao* 13 February 1955, in SCMP 987, 12–14 February 1955.

Chieh-fang Chun-hua Pao [People's Liberation Army Pictorial] (Shanghai: Political Department, Central People's Government Revolutionary Military Council, monthly).

Chien Chun-jiu. 'A Great Alliance of Friendship and Peace', *People's China*, 16 February 1954.

Chin Yuan-hsun. 'American "Democracy" and "Freedom" As I See Them', *Hsueh Hsi*, 3 September 1957, in ECMM 3, 16 December 1957.

China Reconstructs (Peking: China Welfare Institute, bimonthly 1952–4, monthly from 1955).

China Yearbook (Taipei: China Publishing Company, annually from 1951).

Chou En-lai. 'China Protests', *People's China*, 16 September 1950.

'Chou En-lai on Truman's Statement', *People's China*, 16 July 1950.

'Chou En-lai's 2nd Message to U.N.', *People's China*, 16 September 1950.

'8-Point Statement Regarding Peace Treaty with Japan', NCNA, 4 December 1950, in SCMP, 5 December 1950.

'Fight for the Consolidation and Development of the Chinese People's Victory', Report to cadres convened by the Chinese People's Political Consultative Conference to commemorate the first anniversary of the founding of the People's Republic of China, 30 September 1950, in *Current Background* 12, 5 October 1950.

'The First Year of People's China', *People's China*, 16 October 1950.

'The Great Decade', *Jen-min Jih-pao,* 6 October 1959, in *Current Background* 598, 15 October 1959.

'The Present International Situation and China's Foreign Policy', Report to the Fifth Session of the First National People's Congress on 10 February 1958, NCNA 11 February 1958, in *Current Background* 492, 14 February 1958.

'The Present International Situation, China's Foreign Policy, and the Question of the Liberation of Taiwan', Report to the Third Session of the First National People's Congress, NCNA, 28 June 1956, in *Current Background* 395, 5 July 1956.

'Report on Asian-African Conference' to the Standing Committee of the National People's Congress, 13 May 1955, in *Current Background* 328, 17 May 1955.

'Report on the Work of the Government', 23 September 1954, in *People's China,* 16 October 1954.

'Report on the Work of the Government' to the First Session of the Second National People's Congress, NCNA, 18 April 1959, in *Current Background* 559, 23 April 1959.

'Report on the World Situation, the Tour of Europe, and Southeast Asia 1957' to the Third Plenary Session of the Second National Committee of the Chinese People's Political Consultative Conference, NCNA, 5 March 1957, in *Current Background* 439, 8 March 1957.

'Situation in the Taiwan Straits Area', NCNA, 6 September 1958, in SCMP, 11 September 1958.

'Statement on Acheson's Speech', *People's China,* 1 April 1950.

'Statement on U.S.-Chiang Kai-shek Treaty', 8 December 1954, *People's China,* 16 December 1954.

'U.S. Intervention in Liberation of Taiwan', 24 January 1955, *People's China,* supplement, 16 February 1955.

Chou Tung. 'Marshall Plan for Asia', *Ta Kung Pao,* 6 January 1955, in SCMP 963, 6–7 January 1955.

'A Chronicle of Principal Events Relating to the Indo-China Question', *Shih-chieh Chih-shih,* supplement, NCNA, 23 April 1954, in *Current Background* 285, 5 May 1954.

Chu Jung-fu. 'Foreign Relations of New China During the Past Five Years', *Shih-chieh Chih-shih,* 5 October 1954, in *Current Background* 307, 6 December 1954.

'U.S. Plot Against Negotiated Peace', NCNA, 20 April 1954, in SCMP 792, 21–2 April 1954.

Chuang Chia-nung. 'U.S. Penetration in Taiwan', *China Reconstructs,* August 1957.

Chung-hua jen-min kung-ho t'iao-yueh chi, Treaty Series of the Chinese People's Republic.

Chung-kuo jen-min chiao hsüeh hui [The Chinese People's Institute of Foreign Affairs], *Oppose U.S. Military Provocations in the Taiwan Straits Area: A Selection of Important Documents* (Peking: Foreign Languages Press, 1958).

Oppose U.S. Occupation of Taiwan and 'Two Chinas' Plot: A Selection of Important Documents (Peking: Foreign Languages Press, 1958).

Two Tactics, One Aim: An Exposure of the Peace Tricks of U.S. Imperialism (Peking: Foreign Languages Press, 1960).

Communiqué on Meeting Between Mao Tse-tung and N. S. Khrushchev, 3 August 1958, in *Peking Review,* 12 August 1958.

Corps for Criticizing Ch'en of the Red Guards of the Second Foreign Languages Institute of Peking under the Congress of Red Guards, *Collection of Ch'en Yi's Speeches* (Peking, 1967), in *Current Background* 636, 9 December 1968.

Curl, Peter V. (ed.). *Documents on American Foreign Relations 1953–1954* (New York: Harper, for the Council on Foreign Relations 1954, 1955).

Current Background [CB] (Hong Kong: U.S. Consulate General).

Current Digest of the Soviet Press [CDSP] (Ann Arbor: University of Michigan Press).

Daniels, Robert V. (ed.). *A Documentary History of Communism* (New York: Vintage, 1962).

Dennett, Raymond and Robert K. Turner (eds.). *Documents on American Foreign Relations, January 1–December 1, 1950* (Princeton: Princeton University Press, for the World Peace Foundation, 1951).

The Draft Constitution of the People's Republic of China, NCNA, 15 June 1954, in *Current Background* 286, 17 June 1954.

Dulles, John Foster. 'The Communist Threat in the Taiwan Area', 4 September 1958 Statement (Washington, D.C.: Department of State Publication 6708, Far Eastern Series No. 76, September 1958).

'The Evolution of Foreign Policy', Department of State *Bulletin,* 25 January 1954, pp. 107–8.

Memorandum 3, 13 October 1958, File IX, 'Rome-Taipei Trip – 10/17/58 – 10/24/58', Dulles Papers.

'Memorandum on Indochina', 15 July 1954, Official File 152, Dwight D. Eisenhower Library.

'A Militaristic Experiment', Department of State *Bulletin,* 10 July 1950, p. 49.

'Our Foreign Policies in Asia', Department of State *Bulletin,* 28 February 1955, pp. 237–328.

'Our Policies Toward Communism in China', Department of State *Bulletin,* 15 July 1957, pp. 91, 95.

Paper used in conversation with Prime Minister Eden, 24 February 1955, in File IX, 'Bangkok Trip', Dulles Papers.

Eden, Anthony. 'Indo-China: Attitude of Her Majesty's Government', Cmnd. 2834, April 1954.

Extracts from China Mainland Magazines [ECMM] (Hong Kong: U.S. Consulate General).

Fan Po-ch'uan. 'American Aggression Against China', NCNA, 22 November 1950, in *Current Background* 33, 30 November 1950.

Fang, C. C. 'Into the Boots of Japanese Imperialism', *People's China,* 1 December 1950.

Feng Pin-fu. 'Resolutely Smash the "Two China" Plot', *Shih-chieh Chih-shih,* 3 March 1958, in ECMM 127, 5 May 1958.

Folliot, Denise (ed.). *Documents on International Affairs, 1955* (London: Oxford University Press, for the Royal Institute of International Affairs, 1957).

Frankland, Noble (ed.). *Documents on International Affairs, 1955* (London: Oxford University Press, for the Royal Institute of International Affairs, 1958).

Gates, Thomas S. Jnr. Address to Latin American World Affairs Council, 27 October 1958, in *Navy Public Statements* (Washington, D.C.: Department of the Navy, January 1959), pp. 1–5.

Gettleman, Marvin E. (ed.). *Vietnam: History, Documents, and Opinions on a Major World Crisis* (Harmondsworth, Mddx.: Penguin, 1966).

Highlights of the Chinese Communist Press (Hong Kong: U.S. Consulate General, 1952–3).

Ho Cheng. 'Taiwan Must Be Liberated', *People's China*, 1 September 1954.

Hsiao P'ing and Ch'i Min. 'Strengthening the Sino-Soviet Alliance Is Our Obligation', *Shih-chieh Chih-shih*, 5 February 1958, in ECMM 128, 12 May 1958.

Hsiao Yu. 'Churchill Assumes Disgraceful Role', *Kuang-ming Jih-pao*, 4 February 1955, in SCMP 982, 5–7 February 1955.

Hsieh Fan. 'Anglo-U.S. Conflict in Current World Situation', *Shih-chieh Chih-shih*, 20 May 1958, in ECMM 133, 23 June 1958.

Hsin-hua pan-yueh k'an [New China Semimonthly]. Peking, 1949–55.

Hsueh Hsi [Study]. Peking, monthly.

Hua Ch'i. 'Historical Facts of American Encroachment upon Taiwan during Past Hundred Years', *Ta Kung Pao*, 3 August 1954, in SCMP 866, 11 August 1954.

Huang Shao-hung. 'Warning to Followers of Chiang Kai-shek', *Ta Kung Pao*, 14 September 1954, in SCMP 889, 16 September 1954.

Hummell memorandum to John Foster Dulles, November 1950, File ix, 'Korea-U.N.', Dulles Papers.

Hung Ch'i [Red Flag] (Peking: Central Committee of the Chinese Communist Party, fortnightly from 1958).

Important Documents Concerning the Question of Taiwan (Peking: Foreign Languages Press, 1955).

Jen-min Jih-pao [People's Daily], Peking.

Jen-min Shou-ts'e 1952 [People's Handbook, 1952], Tientsin.

Joint Declaration of All Democratic Parties and People's Organizations of the People's Republic of China, *People's China*, supplement, 1 September 1954.

K'e Fu. 'An Interview With Wei Li-huang and His Wife', *Wen Hui Pao*, 30 March 1955, in SCMP 1020, 31 March – 1 April 1955.

Kiang Nan. 'Dulles Renews Slander Against China', NCNA, 13 November 1954, in SCMP 927, 13–15 November 1954.

'Gulf between U.S. Words and Deeds', NCNA, 28 March 1954, in SCMP 776, 27–9 March 1954.

'No Reason For Delay in U.N. Discussion of Taiwan', NCNA, 1 November 1954, in SCMP 920, 2 November 1954.

'People Won't Tolerate Warmongers', NCNA, 6 January 1955, in SCMP 963, 6–7 January 1955.

'Radford's Bag of Tricks in His Far East Tour', NCNA, 4 January 1955, in SCMP 961, 5 January 1955.

'U.S. Provocations Aimed at Keeping Tension', NCNA, 3 August 1954, in SCMP 861, 3–4 August 1954.

'U.S. Sabotage of Geneva Conference', NCNA, 15 April 1954.

'U.S. Seventh Fleet Must Withdraw from Taiwan Strait', NCNA, 9 October 1954, in SCMP 905, 11 October 1954.

'U.S. Tries to Stir Up War Against China', NCNA, 30 July 1954, in SCMP 860, 31 July–2 August 1954.

King, Gillian (ed.). *Documents on International Affairs, 1958* (London: Oxford University Press, for the Royal Institute of International Affairs, 1962).

Kuang-ming Jih-pao [The Enlightenment Daily], Peking.

Kung Pu-sheng. 'A Conspiracy Against the Chinese People', *International Affairs* (Moscow: January 1958) in Chung-kuo jen-min chiao hsüeh hui, *Oppose U.S. Occupation of Taiwan and 'Two Chinas' Plot: A*

Selection of Important Documents (Peking: Foreign Languages Press, 1958).

Kuo Mo-jo. 'Asia Without Nuclear Weapons', *Peking Review*, 15 April 1958.

'Five Wonderful Years', *People's China*, 16 September 1954.

Li Chu-chen. 'Appeal to Taiwan Industrialists and Businessmen', *Jen-min Jih-pao*, 14 September 1954, in SCMP 888, 15 September 1954.

Li Chung-ching. 'False Views on Taiwan', *Jen-min Jih-pao*, 23 September 1954, in SCMP 895, 24 September 1954.

Li Kao. 'U.S. Gloom Over Geneva Conference Analyzed', NCNA, 10 March 1954, in SCMP 764, 11 March 1954.

Liang Szu-yi. 'A Crime Against Humanity: The ruthless abduction of 20,000 inhabitants of the Tachens by U.S. forces and Chiang troops', *People's China*, 1 May 1955.

Lin Chu. 'Misery on Taiwan', *People's China*, 16 February 1955.

Lin Hai. 'The East Wind Prevails Over the West Wind', *Peking Review*, 18 March 1958.

Lin Piao. 'Hold High the Red Banner of the Party's General Line and Chairman Mao Tse-tung's Military Thought and Advance in Big Strides', NCNA, 29 September 1959, in *Current Background* 596, 7 October 1959.

'The Victory of the Chinese People's Revolutionary War Is a Victory for the Thought of Mao Tse-tung', *Hung Ch'i* 19 (1960), in SCMM 321 (1960).

Long Live the Victory of the People's War! (Peking: Foreign Languages Press, 1965).

Lin Ta-kuang. 'U.S. Espionage and Subversion Against China – The Damning Record', *People's China*, 1 February 1955.

Liu Chang-sheng. 'On the Question of War and Peace', *Peking Review*, 26 April 1960.

Liu Ke-lin. 'A Treaty for Aggressive War', *People's China*, 1 January 1955.

Liu Li-shen. 'A Student Back from America', *China Reconstructs*, August 1956.

Liu Shan-pen. 'Swift Expansion of our Air Force', *Wen Hui Pao*, 1 August 1958, in *Current Background* 514, 6 August 1958.

Liu Shao-ch'i. *On Internationalism and Nationalism* (Peking: Foreign Languages Press, 1949).

'Political Report' to the Eighth National Chinese Communist Party Congress, NCNA, 16 September 1956, in *Current Background* 412, 28 September 1956.

'Report on the work of the Central Committee of the Communist Party of China' to the Second Session of the Eighth National Congress, *Peking Review*, 3 June 1958.

Liu Tse-yung. 'A Major Step To Protect China's Sovereign Rights', *Peking Review*, 16 September 1958.

'Mao Tse-tung Memorandum', *Congressional Record*, 29 April 1954.

Mei Ju-ao. 'The Aggressor and the Law', *People's China*, 1 March 1955.

Meng Yung-chen. 'China Ahead of U.S.A. in Wheat', *Peking Review*, 12 August 1958.

'Nine Years of Great Strides Forward', *Peking Review*, 30 September 1958.

'On the U.S. Presidential Election', *Shih-chieh Chih-shih*, 20 October 1956, in ECMM 61, 17 December 1956.

Pao-wei Ho-p'ing [Safeguarding Peace] (Peking: China Peace Committee, monthly).

252 *Bibliography*

Peking Review (Peking: Foreign Languages Press, weekly from March 1958).

Peng Lin. 'U.S. Interference in Taiwan is Perfidy', *Kuang-ming Jih-pao*, 25 August 1954, in SCMP 877, 26 August 1954.

P'eng Teh-huai. 'The Chinese People's Liberation Army', Speech to the Chinese Communist Party Eighth National Congress, NCNA, 19 September 1956, in *Current Background* 422, 18 October 1956.

'The Chinese People's Volunteers Are an Invincible Force', NCNA, 31 July 1951, in *Current Background* 208, 10 September 1952.

'Message to Compatriots in Taiwan', NCNA, 6 October 1958, in SCMP 1871, 7 October 1958.

'Report on the Work of Resisting U.S. Aggression and Aiding Korea', to the Central People's Government Council at the Twenty-Fourth Meeting, NCNA, 12 September 1953, in SCMP 649, 12–14 September 1953.

People's China (Peking: Foreign Languages Press, fortnightly).

PLA General Political Department, *Kung-tso T'ung-hsün* [Bulletin of Activities] 17, 25 April 1961, in J. Chester Cheng (ed.), *The Politics of the Chinese Red Army* (Stanford, Calif.: Hoover Institution, 1966).

PRC Government, 'Declaration on China's Territorial Sea', in *Peking Review*, 9 September 1958.

'Statement Supporting Soviet Proposal for an Emergency Special U.N. General Assembly Session', 8 August 1958, in *Peking Review*, 12 August 1958.

PRC Ministry of Foreign Affairs, 'Statement on Sino-American Talks', 12 April 1958, in *Peking Review*, 22 April 1958.

Po I-po. 'Three Years of Achievement of the People's Republic of China', *Cheng-chü Ch'ih-chiu Ho-ping, Cheng-ch'ü Jen-min Min-chu* [*For a Lasting Peace, For a People's Democracy*], in NCNA, 1 October 1962.

Powell, Ralph L. 'Politico-Military Relationships in Communist China' (Washington, D.C.: Department of State, Bureau of Intelligence and Research, 1963).

Raskin, Marcus G. and Bernard B. Fall (eds.). *The Viet-Nam Reader: Articles and Documents on American Foreign Policy and the Viet-Nam Crisis* (New York: Vintage, 1965).

Red Cross Society of China, 'Disaster Strikes the Tachens', *People's China*, supplement, 1 May 1955.

Red Flag Revolutionary Rebel Corps, Peking Foreign Language Institute and Capital's Congress of Red Guards, 'Topple Ch'en Yi, Liberate the Foreign Affairs System', etc., *Wen-ko Feng-yun* [Cultural Revolution Storm] 4 (Peking, 1967), in SCMM 635, 2 December 1968.

Review of the Formosa Press (Taipei: U.S. Consulate General, 1952).

'Selected Edition of Liu Shao-ch'i's Counter-Revolutionary Crimes' in SCMM 651–3, 22 and 28 April 1969, 5 May 1969.

Shanley, Bernard M. (Special Counsel to the President). Correspondence with Representative Paul C. Jones of Missouri, 3–25 May 1954, Official File 862, Dwight D. Eisenhower Library.

Shao Li-tzu. 'Better Late Than Never', *Ta Kung Pao*, 13 September 1954, in SCMP 888, 15 September 1954.

Shih-chieh Chih-shih [World Culture], semimonthly.

Shih-chieh Chih-shih Shou-ts'e [World Affairs Handbook], annual.

Shih-chieh Ch'ing-nien [World Youth].

Shih-shih Shou-ts'e [Current Events] (Peking Popular Reading Matters Publishing House, semimonthly).

Siao, Emi. 'New China – A Great Power for World Peace', *People's China*, 1 April 1954.

Soong Ching-ling [Madame Sun Yat-sen]. 'The First Five Years', *China Reconstructs*, January 1955.

'Five Years Ago – and Now', *China Reconstructs*, January 1957.

'Friendship of the Peoples and Peace', *China Reconstructs*, January 1954.

'A New Force for Peace', *China Reconstructs*, October 1955.

'A Proof that Peace Can Win', *China Reconstructs*, September–October 1954.

'The Socialist Camp in the Present World Situation', *Jen-min Jih-pao*, 7 November 1958, in NCNA, 8 November 1958.

Stump, Admiral Felix B. 'Communism versus The Freedom in the Pacific', Address before Navy League, Washington, D.C., 24 October 1958, in *Navy Public Statements* (Washington, D.C.: Department of the Navy, January 1959), pp. 25–30.

Su Yü. 'The Liberation of Taiwan in Sight', *People's China*, 16 February 1950.

Sung Li. 'From Suez to Lebanon', *Peking Review*, 12 August 1958.

Survey of China Mainland Magazines [SCMM] (Hong Kong: US Consulate General).

Survey of the China Mainland Press [SCMP] (Hong Kong: US Consulate General).

Szu Li. 'Restore Peace in Indo-China', *People's China*, 1 April 1954.

Ta Kung Pao [The Impartial Daily], Hong Kong, Peking, Shanghai, and Tientsin.

Tan Wen-jai. 'U.S. Atomic War Scheming Denounced', *Jen-min Jih-pao*, 16 January 1955, in SCMP 969, 15–17 January 1955.

Teng Chao-hsiang. 'The People's Navy in a Leap Forward', *Wen Hui Pao*, 1 August 1958, in *Current Background* 514, 6 August 1958.

Thirty-Three Leading Counter-revolutionary Revisionists (Canton Area Workers' Revolutionary Committee: Printing System Committee, March 1968), in *Current Background* 874, 17 March 1969.

Truman, Harry S. 'United States Policy Toward Formosa', Department of State *Bulletin*, 16 January 1950.

Tsai Ying-p'ing. 'The Road to Final Victory', *People's China*, 16 February 1950.

Tsui Chi. 'Aggressors Must Not Be Encouraged', *Jen-min Jih-pao*, 15 March 1955, in SCMP 1008, 16 March 1955.

Tsui Ch'in and T'an Wen-jui. 'Comment on the Present Foreign Policy of the United States', *Shih-chieh Chih-shih* 6 (1960), in SCMM 213 (1960).

Tung Ch'i-wu. 'The People's Liberation Army Has No Match in the Whole World', *Wen Hui Pao*, 1 August 1958, in *Current Background* 514, 6 August 1958.

Tung Feng. 'The Bandung Spirit Thrives', *Peking Review*, 29 April 1958.

United Nations General Assembly, *Official Records*.

United Nations Secretariat, Department of Public Information, *Korea and the United Nations* (New York: United Nations, October 1950).

'How the United Nations Met the Challenge of Korea' (New York: United Nations, 1953).

United Nations Security Council, *Official Records*.

US Air Force Historical Study Number 72, *United States Air Force Operations in the Korean Conflict, 1 November 1950–30 June 1953* (Washington, D.C.: USAF Historical Division, 1955).

US Congress, *Congressional Record* (Washington, D.C.: Government Printing Office, daily during Congressional sessions).

US Department of the Army, *Communist China: Ruthless Enemy or Paper Tiger? A Bibliographic Survey* (Washington, D.C.: Department of the Army, 1962).

Office of Military History, *Korea 1950* (Washington, D.C.: Government Printing Office, 1951).

US Department of State, *American Foreign Policy, 1950–1955* (Washington, D.C.: Department of State Publication 6446, General Foreign Policy Series 117, 1957).

American Foreign Policy, Current Documents, 1958 (Washington, D.C.: Department of State Publication 7322, 1962).

The Department of State Bulletin [DSB] (Washington, D.C.: Government Printing Office, weekly).

Events Prior to the Attack on June 25, 1950: The Conflict in Korea (Washington, D.C.: Government Printing Office, 1951).

The Fight Against Aggression in Korea (Washington, D.C.: Government Printing Office, 1950).

Foreign Ministers Meeting: Berlin Discussions, January 25th–February 18th, 1954 (Washington, D.C.: Department of State Publication 5399, 1954).

A Historical Summary of United States – Korean Relations (Washington, D.C.: Government Printing Office, 1962).

Indochina: The War in Viet-Nam, Cambodia, and Laos (Washington, D.C.: Department of State Publication 5092, Far Eastern Series 58, 1953).

International Defense Commitments of the United States (Washington, D.C.: Government Printing Office, September 1966).

North Korea: A Case Study in the Techniques of Violence (Washington, D.C.: Government Printing Office, 1961).

The Record on Korean Unification (Washington, D.C.: Government Printing Office, 1960).

The Republic of China (Washington, D.C.: Department of State Publication 6844, Far Eastern Series 81, October 1959).

Strengthening the Forces of Freedom: Selected Speeches and Statements of Secretary of State Acheson, February 1949–April 1950 (Washington, D.C.: Government Printing Office, 1950).

US Policy in the Korean Conflict, July 1950–February 1951 (Washington, D.C.: Government Printing Office, 1951).

US Policy in the Korean Crisis (Washington, D.C.: Government Printing Office, 1950).

United States Relations With China (Washington, D.C.: Department of State Publication 3573, Far Eastern Series 30, 1949).

Bureau of Intelligence and Research, *Chinese Communist World Outlook, A Handbook of Chinese Communist Statements: The Public Record of a Militant Ideology* (Washington, D.C.: Department of State Publication 7379, 1962).

US House of Representatives, Committee on Appropriations, *Department of State, Justice, and Commerce Appropriations for 1955,* Hearings, 83rd Congress, 2nd Session.

Committee on Foreign Affairs, *Special Study Mission to Southeast Asia and the Pacific:* Report by Hon. Walter H. Judd, Minnesota, Chairman; Hon. Marguerite Stitt Church, Illinois; Hon. E. Ross Adair, Indiana;

Hon. Clement J. Zablocki, Wisconsin. 83rd Congress, 2d Session, 29 January 1954.

US Senate, Committees on Armed Services and Foreign Relations, 82nd Congress, 1st Session, *Hearings to Conduct an Inquiry into the Military Situation in the Far East and the Facts Surrounding the Relief of General of the Army Douglas MacArthur from his Assignments in That Area* (Washington, D.C.: Government Printing Office, 1951).

Committee on Foreign Relations, *Indochina:* Report of Senator Mike Mansfield on a Study Mission to the Associated States of Indochina – Vietnam, Cambodia, Laos. 83rd Congress, 1st Session, 27 October 1953.

The United States and the Korean Problem (Washington, D.C.: Government Printing Office, 1953).

Subcommittee on the Far East of the Committee on Foreign Relations, *The Far East and South Asia:* Report of Senator H. Alexander Smith, Chairman, on a Study Mission to the Far East. 83rd Congress, 2nd Session, 25 January 1954.

Vital Speeches of the Day (New York: City News Publishing House, daily).

Wang Chih-shen. 'Continue Efforts to Strive for the Peaceful Liberation of Taiwan', *Shih-shih Shou-ts'e* 9, 6 May 1957, in ECMM 92, 29 July 1957.

Wang Ching-yao. 'Another Great Victory for the World Forces of Peace', *Shih-shih Shou-ts'e,* 10 August 1955, in ECMM 3, 29 August 1955.

Wang Yun-sheng. 'Taiwan Was and Is Chinese', *People's China,* 16 October 1954.

' "Two Chinas" Fraud Serves War', *Ta Kung Pao,* 29 January 1955, in SCMP 977, 29–31 January 1955.

Wen Hui Pao [*The Cultural Contact Daily*], Shanghai and Hong Kong.

Willoughby, Major General Charles A. Prepared Statement to Senate Foreign Relations Committee, 'The Communist Threat in the Far East', in 'Review of Foreign Policy, 1958', *Hearings,* 85th Congress, 2d Session, 3 April 1958, Part 2, pp. 467–503.

Wu Chuan. 'Asia Opposes Military Blocs', NCNA, 16 August 1954, in SCMP 780, 18–19 August 1954.

'Dulles is Dragging France Down a Hopeless Road', NCNA, 18 April 1954, in SCMP 790, 19 April 1954.

'U.S.-Chiang Kai-shek "Treaty" Does Not Affect Taiwan's Status', *Jen-min Jih-pao,* 4 December 1954, in SCMP 941, 4–6 December 1954.

'U.S. SEATO Schemes Must Be Smashed', NCNA, 6 August 1954, in SCMP 864, 7–9 August 1954.

Wu Min. 'U.S. Efforts For SEATO War Bloc', NCNA, 16 August 1954, in SCMP 870, 18–19 August 1954.

Yang Chung-kwang. 'U.S. Economic Crisis and Labor Movement in Capitalist Countries', *Shih-chieh Chih-shih,* 10 May 1958, in ECMM 137, 18 July 1958.

Yang Kan-ling. 'Why Is U.S. Imperialism a Paper Tiger?', *Peking Review,* 9 December 1958.

Yang Yung. 'Report on the Work of the Chinese People's Volunteers During the Eight Years of Resistance to U.S. Aggression and Aid to Korea', speech to an enlarged joint session of the Standing Committee, National People's Congress, and the National Committee of the Chinese

People's Political Consultative Conference, NCNA, 30 October 1958, in *Current Background* 535, 11 November 1958.

Yeh Ching-yao. 'I Left Taiwan', *China Reconstructs,* June 1957.

Yeh Mang. 'The Criminal Act of American Imperialist Aggression in Taiwan', *Shih-chieh Chih-shih,* 7 July 1950.

Yeh Sheng. 'Recent U.S. Activities in Taiwan', *Shih-chieh Chih-shih,* 20 July 1955, in ECMM 9, 10 October 1955.

Ying Tao. 'The "Two Chinas" Hoax', *Peking Review,* 11 March 1958.

Yu Chao-li. 'The Forces of the New Are Bound to Defeat the Forces of Decay', *Hung Ch'i,* 16 August 1958, NCNA, 15 August 1958, in SCMP 1837, 21 August 1958.

'The Tales of Dulles and the Truth About China', *Hung Ch'i,* 16 February 1959, in ECMM 160, 9 March 1959.

Yu Kan. 'Great Achievements of the People's Republic of China in Past Three Years', *Current Affairs Manual* 17 reprinted in Canton *Nanfang Jih-pao* [Southern Daily], 23 September 1952, in *Current Background* 218, 5 November 1952.

Zinner, Paul E. (ed.). *Documents on American Foreign Relations, 1955* (New York: Harper, for the Council on Foreign Relations, 1956).

Documents on American Foreign Relations, 1958 (New York: Harper, for Council on Foreign Relations, 1959).

3. Interviews and correspondence

'Mr. Acheson Answers Some Questions', interview with Gaddis Smith, 24 September 1969, in *New York Times Book Review,* 12 October 1969.

Adams, Sherman, Dulles Oral History Collection [OHC] interview conducted by Richard D. Challener, in Lincoln, N.H., 15 August 1954.

Interview with author, in Lincoln, N. H., 28 September 1970.

Letter to Rep. Paul J. Kilday, 31 January 1955, Official File 101-M, Dwight D. Eisenhower Library.

Anderson, Dillon. Dulles OHC interview conducted by Richard D. Challener, in Houston, Texas, 13 June 1966.

Memorandum to Sherman Adams with reference to Robert Bowie, 18 January 1956, Official File 8, Dwight D. Eisenhower Library.

Bowie, Robert R. Dulles OHC interview conducted by Richard D. Challener, in Washington, D.C., 11 January 1966.

Burke, Admiral Arleigh A. Dulles OHC interview conducted by Richard D. Challener, in Washington, D.C. 11 January 1966.

Interview with author, in Washington, D.C., 15 September 1970.

Chiang Kai-shek, Generalissimo and Madame. Dulles OHC interview conducted by Spencer Davis, in Taipei, Taiwan, 24 September 1966.

Chou En-lai, interview conducted by Felix Greene, *Far East Reporter* (San Francisco, Calif.: City Lights Books, 1960).

Chung Il Kwon. Dulles OHC interview conducted by Spencer Davis, in Seoul, Korea, 29 September 1964.

Crowe, Ambassador Philip K. Dulles OHC interview conducted by Richard D. Challener, in Woodstock, Vt., 4 October 1965.

Donovan, Robert J. Dulles OHC interview conducted by Richard D. Challener, in Washington, D.C., 12 January 1966.

Drummond, Roscoe. Dulles OHC interview conducted by Richard D. Challener, in Washington, D.C., 13 January 1966.

Dulles, Eleanor Lansing. Interview with author, in Washington, D.C., 16 September 1970.

Eisenhower, Dwight D. Correspondence with Representative Walter H. Judd, 6 May–14 July 1955, Official File 59, Dwight D. Eisenhower Library.

Dulles OHC interview conducted by Philip A. Crowl, in Gettysburg, Pa., 28 July 1964.

Folliard, Edward T. Eisenhower Oral History Project [OHP] interview conducted by John Luter, in Washington, D.C., 7 September 1967.

Gates, Thomas S. Interview with author, in New York City, 16 July 1970.

Gray, Gordon. Dulles OHC interview conducted by Richard D. Challener, in Washington, D.C., 4 March 1966.

Interview with author, in Washington, D.C. 16 September 1970.

Gross, Representative H. R. Correspondence with Gerald D. Morgan, Administrative Assistant to the President, 24 January–18 February 1955, General File 803, Dwight D. Eisenhower Library.

Hagerty, James. Interview with author, in New York City, 21 July 1970.

Hunt, H. L. Correspondence with General Wilton B. Persons, Deputy Assistant to the President, 22 April–9 May 1955, General File 803, Dwight D. Eisenhower Library.

Jenner, Senator William E. Press release and correspondence with Assistant Secretary of State Walter Robertson, 11–20 October 1954, Official File 168, Dwight D. Eisenhower Library.

Johnson, U. Alexis. Dulles OHC interview conducted by Philip A. Crowl, in Washington, D.C., 28 May 1968.

Judd, Walter H. Dulles OHC interview conducted by Philip A. Crowl, in Washington, D.C., 11 December 1965.

LeMay, General Curtis E. Dulles OHC interview conducted by Gordon A. Craig, in Chatsworth, Calif., 28 April 1966.

Lovett, Robert. Interview with author, in New York City, 27 July 1970.

McElroy, Neil. Dulles OHC interview conducted by Philip A. Crowl, in Cincinnati, Ohio, 6 May 1964.

Eisenhower OHP interview conducted by Ed Edwin, in Cincinnati, Ohio, 8 and 9 May 1967.

Interview with author, in Washington, D.C., 16 September 1970.

Mansfield, Mike. Dulles OHC interview conducted by Richard D. Challener, in Washington, D.C., 10 May 1966.

Marshall, Charles Burton. Interview with author, in Washington, D.C., 16 September 1970.

Merchant, Livingston. Dulles OHC interview by Philip A. Crowl, in Washington, D.C., 13 March–17 April 1965.

Letter to the author, 5 October 1970.

Murphy, Robert D. Interview with author, in New York City, 21 July 1970.

Nixon, Richard. Dulles OHC interview conducted by Richard D. Challener, in New York City, 5 March 1965.

Park, Too-chin. Dulles OHC interview conducted by Spencer Davis, in Seoul, Korea, 28 September 1965.

Radford, Admiral Arthur W. Dulles OHC interview conducted by Philip A. Crowl, Washington, D.C., 8 May 1965.

Interview with author, in Washington, D.C., 15 September 1970.

Ridgway, General Matthew B. Dulles OHC interview conducted by Philip A. Crowl, in Pittsburgh, Pa., 1 May 1964.

Interview with author, in Pittsburgh, Pa., 10 August 1970.

Stump, Admiral Felix S. Dulles OHC interview conducted by Richard D. Challener, in Valley Forge, Pa., 29 October 1964.

Twining, General Nathan. Dulles OHC interview conducted by Philip A. Crowl, in Washington, D.C., 1965.

Yeh, George K.C. Dulles OHC interview conducted by Spencer Davis, in Taipei, Taiwan, 23 September 1964.

4. Radio transcripts and newspapers

British Broadcasting Corporation, *Summary of World Broadcasts* – Part V: The Far East (Reading, Berks.: BBC Monitoring Service) [BBC/FE].

Press Library, Royal Institute of International Affairs, London:
China Digest
Christian Science Monitor
Daily Telegraph
Free China Information Bulletin
Il Popolo
Le Monde
London Times
Manchester Guardian
New China News Agency [NCNA], Peking (unless otherwise indicated in endnotes)
New Delhi Statesman
New York Herald Tribune
New York Times
South China Morning Post
United States Information Bulletin, London
Washington Post

5. Books and articles (See also Section 1, above.)

Acheson, Dean. 'The Bases of a Foreign Program', *New York Times Magazine*, 6 January 1957.
'Foreign Policy and Presidential Moralism', *The Reporter*, 2 May 1957.
'The Illusion of Disengagement', *Foreign Affairs*, April 1958.
' "Instant Retaliation": The Debate Continued', *New York Times Magazine*, 28 March 1954.
'Legislative-Executive Relations', *Yale Review*, Summer 1956.
Power and Diplomacy (Cambridge, Mass.: Harvard University Press, 1958).
'The Premises of American Policy', *Orbis*, Fall 1959.

Alsop, Stewart. 'The Story Behind Quemoy: How We Drifted Close to War', *Saturday Evening Post*, 13 December 1958.

Appleman, Roy E. *South to the Naktong, North to the Yalu (June–November 1950), US Army in the Korean War* (Washington, D.C.: Government Printing Office, 1960).

Bachrach, Peter and Morton Baratz. 'Decisions and Non-Decisions: An Analytical Framework', *American Political Science Review*, September 1963.

Baker, George W. and Dwight W. Chapman (eds.). *Man and Society in Disaster* (New York: Basic Books, 1962).

Barber, Hollis W. *The United States in World Affairs, 1955* (New York: Harper, for the Council on Foreign Relations, 1957).

Barnett, A. Doak. *Communist China and Asia: A Challenge to American Policy* (New York: Random House, 1960).

Barnett, Robert W. *Quemoy: The Use and Consequence of Nuclear Deter-*

rence (Cambridge, Mass.: Harvard Center for International Affairs, March 1960).

Barraclough, Geoffrey. *Survey of International Affairs, 1956–1958* (London: Oxford University Press, for the Royal Institute of International Affairs, 1962).

Barraclough, Geoffrey and Rachel F. Wall. *Survey of International Affairs, 1955–1956* (London: Oxford University Press, for the Royal Institute of International Affairs, 1960).

Bator, Victor. *Vietnam, A Diplomatic Tragedy* (Dobbs Ferry, N.Y.: Oceana Press, 1965).

Beal, John Robinson. *John Foster Dulles: 1888–1959* (New York: Harper, 1959).

Bell, Coral. *The Conventions of Crisis: A Study in Diplomatic Management* (London: Oxford University Press, 1971).

'The Diplomacy of Mr. Dulles', *International Journal*, Winter 1964–5.

'The Foreign Policy of China', in F. S. Northedge (ed.), *The Foreign Policies of the Powers* (London: Faber, 1968).

Negotiation from Strength: A Study in the Politics of Power (London: Chatto & Windus, 1962).

Survey of International Affairs, 1954 (London: Oxford University Press, for the Royal Institute of International Affairs, 1957).

Beloff, Max. *Soviet Policy in the Far East, 1944–1951* (London: Oxford University Press, 1953).

Berger, Carl. *The Korea Knot: A Military-Political History* (Philadelphia: University of Pennsylvania Press, 1957).

Black, Cyril and Thomas Thornton (eds.). *Communism and Revolution: The Strategic Uses of Political Violence* (Princeton: Princeton University Press, 1964).

Blum, Robert. *The United States and China in World Affairs*, ed. by A. Doak Barnett (New York: McGraw-Hill, for the Council on Foreign Relations, 1966).

Bobrow, Davis D. 'The Chinese Communist Conflict System', *Orbis*, Winter 1966.

'Peking's Military Calculus', *World Politics*, January 1964.

Boulding, Kenneth. *Conflict and Defense: A General Theory* (New York: Harper, 1962).

The Image: Knowledge in Life and Society (Ann Arbor: University of Michigan Press, 1958).

Brandt, Conrad, Benjamin Schwartz and John K. Fairbank (eds.). *A Documentary History of Chinese Communism* (Cambridge, Mass.: Harvard University Press, 1953).

Brimmel, J. H. *Communism in Southeast Asia: A Political Analysis* (New York: Institute of Pacific Relations, 1958).

Brodie, Bernard. *Strategy in the Missile Age* (Princeton: Princeton University Press, 1965).

Brown, Seyom. *The Faces of Power: Constancy and Change in United States Foreign Policy from Truman to Johnson* (New York: Columbia University Press, 1968).

Bueler, William M. 'Taiwan: A Problem of International Law or Politics?', *The World Today*, June 1971.

Bundy, McGeorge (ed.). *The Pattern of Responsibility, from the Record of Secretary of State Dean Acheson* (Boston: Houghton Mifflin, 1952).

Cagle, Malcolm W. and Frank A. Manson. *The Sea War in Korea* (Annapolis, Maryland: United States Naval Institute, 1957).

Calvocoressi, Peter *et al. Survey of International Affairs, 1949–1950* (London: Oxford University Press, for the Royal Institute of International Affairs, 1953).

Chang Tao-li. *Why China Helps Korea* (Bombay: People's Publishing House, 1951).

Chen, Theodore Shi-en and Wen-hui C. Chen. 'The "Three-Anti" and "Five-Anti" Movements in Communist China', *Pacific Affairs*, March 1953.

Chiang I-shan. 'The Military Affairs of Communist China', in *Communist China 1949–1959* (Kowloon, Hong Hong: Union Research Institute, 1961), vol. I.

Chin Szu-k'ai. 'Communist China's Relations With the Soviet Union 1949–1957', Communist China Problem Research Series (Kowloon, Hong Kong: Union Research Institute, 1961).

'Foreign Relations', in *Communist China* 1949–1959 (Kowloon, Hong Kong: Union Research Institute, 1961), vol. II.

Chinese Association for the United Nations. *The Sino-American Treaty of Mutual Defense* (Taipei: Sino-American Publishing Company, 1955).

Clubb, O. Edmund. 'Chiang's Shadow Over Warsaw', *Reporter*, 2 October 1958.

'Chinese Communist Strategy in Foreign Relations', in H. Arthur Steiner (ed.), *Report on China*, Annals of The American Academy of Political Science (Philadelphia, Pa.: American Academy of Political and Social Science, 1951).

'Sino-American Relations and the Future of Formosa', in *Political Science Quarterly*, March 1965.

Clubb, Oliver E., Jnr. *The United States and the Sino-Soviet Bloc in Southeast Asia* (Washington, D.C.: Brookings, 1962).

Cooke, Admiral Charles M. 'Quemoy: The Immediate Threat to Peace', *Collier's*, 14 October 1955.

Coser, Lewis A. *The Functions of Social Conflict* (Glencoe, Ill.: Free Press, 1956).

Council on Foreign Relations. *The United States in World Affairs* (New York: Harper, annual).

Current Questions and Answers About Taiwan (Taipei: China Culture Publishing Foundation, 1955).

Dallin, David J. *Soviet Foreign Policy After Stalin* (Philadelphia: Lippincott, 1961).

Davis, Forrest and Robert A. Hunter. *The Red China Lobby* (New York: Fleet Publishing Corporation, 1963).

Davison, W. Phillips. *The Berlin Blockade* (Princeton: Princeton University Press, 1958).

Deitchman, Seymour J. *Limited War and American Defense Policy* (Cambridge, Mass.: MIT Press, 1964).

De Rivera, Joseph. *The Psychological Dimension of Foreign Policy* (Columbus, Ohio: Merrill, 1968).

Deutsch, Karl W. *The Nerves of Government: Models of Political Communications and Control* (New York: Free Press, 1966).

Dinerstein, Herbert S. *War and the Soviet Union: Nuclear Weapons and the Revolution in Soviet Military and Political Thinking*, revised edition (New York: Praeger, 1962).

Donelan, Michael. *The Ideas of American Foreign Policy* (London: Chapman & Hall, 1963).

Donovan, Robert J. *Eisenhower: The Inside Story* (New York: Harper, 1956).

Drummond, Roscoe and Gaston Coblentz. *Duel at the Brink: John Foster Dulles' Command of American Power* (London: Weidenfeld and Nicolson, 1961).

Dulles, Eleanor Lansing. *John Foster Dulles: The Last Year* (New York: Harcourt, Brace, 1963).

'Time and Decisions', *Foreign Policy Commitments: The Forensic Quarterly* (August 1969).

Dulles, Foster R. *American Foreign Policy Towards Communist China, 1949–1969* (New York: Crowell, 1972).

Dulles, John Foster. 'Challenge and Response in United States Policy', *Foreign Affairs*, October 1959.

'A Policy of Boldness', *Life*, 19 May 1952.

'Policy for Security and Peace', *Foreign Affairs*, April 1954.

War or Peace (London: Harrap, 1950).

War, Peace and Change (London: Macmillan, 1939).

Eckstein, Alexander. *Communist China's Economic Growth and Foreign Trade: Implications for U.S. Policy* (New York: McGraw-Hill, for the Council on Foreign Relations, 1966).

Eden, Sir Anthony. *Towards Peace in Indo-China* (London: Oxford University Press, for the Royal Institute of International Affairs, 1966).

Etzioni, Amitai. 'On Self-Encapsulating Conflicts', *Journal of Conflict Resolution*, September 1964.

Fairbank, John K. *China: The People's Middle Kingdom and the U.S.A.* (London: Oxford University Press, 1967).

'China's Foreign Policy in Historical Perspective', *Foreign Affairs*, April 1969.

The United States and China, revised edition (New York: Viking, 1958).

Fall, Bernard B. 'La politique américaine au Viet-Nam,' *Chronique de Politique Etrangère*, July 1955.

The Two Viet-Nams: A Political and Military Analysis (New York: Praeger, 1963).

Street Without Joy: Insurgency in Indochina 1946–1963 (Harrisburg, Pa.: Stackpole, 1963).

Farrell, John C. and Asa P. Smith (eds.). *Image and Reality in World Politics* (New York: Columbia University Press, 1968).

Festinger, Leon. *Conflict, Decision, and Dissonance* (Stanford, Calif.: Stanford University Press – Stanford Studies in Psychology: 3, 1964).

A Theory of Cognitive Dissonance (Evanston, Ill.: Row, Peterson, 1957).

Fielder, Peter C. 'The Pattern of Super-Power Crises', *International Relations* (London), April 1969.

Fifield, Russell M. *The Diplomacy of Southeast Asia, 1945–1958* (New York: Archon Shoestring, 1968).

Southeast Asia in United States Policy (New York: Praeger, 1963).

Futrell, Robert F. *The United States Air Force in Korea, 1950–3* (New York: Duell, Sloan and Pearce, 1961).

George, Alexander C. 'American Policy-Making and North Korean Aggression', *World Politics*, January 1955.

The Chinese Communist Army in Action (Cambridge, Mass.: Harvard University Press, 1965).

'Presidential Use of Force: The Korean War and the Cuban Missile Crisis' (Santa Monica, Calif.: The RAND Corporation, July 1967).

George, Alexander C., David K. Hall and William E. Simons. *The Limits of Coercive Diplomacy* (Boston: Little, Brown, 1971).

Gerson, Louis L. *John Foster Dulles, The American Secretaries of State and Their Diplomacy,* vol. xvii (New York: Cooper Square, 1967).

Gittings, John. *The Role of the Chinese Army* (London: Oxford University Press, 1967).

Goodrich, Leland M. 'Korea: Collective Measures against Aggression', *International Conciliation,* October 1953.

Korea: A Study of U.S. Policy in the United Nations (New York: Carnegie Endowment, 1956).

Goold-Adams, Richard. *John Foster Dulles, A Reappraisal* (New York: Appleton-Century-Crofts, 1962).

Graebner, Norman A. *The New Isolationism: A Study in Politics and Foreign Policy Since 1950* (New York: Ronald, 1956).

(ed.). *An Uncertain Tradition: American Secretaries of State in the Twentieth Century* (New York: McGraw-Hill, 1961).

Greene, Fred. *U.S. Policy and the Security of Asia* (New York: McGraw-Hill, 1968).

Griffith, General Samuel B., ii. *The Chinese People's Liberation Army* (London: Weidenfeld & Nicolson, 1968).

Peking and People's War (London: Pall Mall, 1966).

(ed.). *Mao Tse-tung on Guerrilla Warfare* (New York: Praeger, 1961).

Sun Tzu: The Art of War (Oxford: Clarendon Press, 1963).

Guhin, Michael A. *John Foster Dulles: A Statesman and His Times* (New York: Columbia University Press, 1972).

'The United States and the Chinese People's Republic: The Non-Recognition Policy Reviewed', *International Affairs,* January 1969.

Gurtov, Melvin. *The First Vietnam Crisis: Chinese Communist Strategy and United States Involvement, 1953–1954* (New York: Columbia University Press, 1967).

Guttman, Allen (ed.). *Korea and the Theory of Limited War* (Boston: Heath, 1967).

Halle, Louis J., Jnr. *American Foreign Policy* (London: Allen and Unwin, 1958).

The Cold War as History (London: Chatto & Windus, 1967).

Halperin, Morton H. *Contemporary Military Strategy* (London: Faber, 1968).

Limited War in the Nuclear Age (New York: Wiley, 1963).

Hammer, Ellen J. *The Struggle for Indochina* (Stanford: Stanford University Press, 1954).

Hammond, Paul. 'NSC-68: Prologue to Rearmament', in Warner Schilling, Paul Hammond and Glenn Snyder, *Strategy, Politics and Defense Budgets* (New York: Columbia University Press, 1962).

Han Jih-wu. *Taiwan Today,* revised edition (Taipei: Hwa Kuo Publishing Co., 1956).

Harris, Richard. *America and East Asia – A New 30 Years' War?* (London: Times Newspapers, 1968).

Hermann, Charles F. *Crises in Foreign Policy* (New York: Bobbs-Merrill, 1969).

Higgins, Trumbull. *Korea and the Fall of MacArthur, A Précis in Limited War* (New York: Oxford University Press, 1960).

Hinton, Harold C. *China's Relations with Burma and Vietnam: A Brief Survey* (New York: Institute of Pacific Relations, 1958).

Communist China in World Politics (London: Macmillan, 1966).

Hsieh, Alice Langley. *Communist China's Strategy in the Nuclear Era* (Englewood Cliffs, N.J.: Prentice-Hall, 1962).

Huck, Arthur. *The Security of China: Chinese Approaches to Problems of War and Strategy* (London: Chatto & Windus, for the Institute for Strategic Studies, 1970).

Hudson, G. F. *Fifty Years of Communism* (London: Watts, 1968).

'The Final Declaration of the Geneva Conference on Indo-China', *Far Eastern Affairs*, Number Four, St Antony's Papers, Number 20 (London: Oxford University Press, 1967).

The Hard and Bitter Peace: World Politics since 1945 (London: Pall Mall, 1966).

'Why We Must Defend Formosa', *Commentary*, April 1955.

Hudson, G. F., Richard Lowenthal and Roderick MacFarquhar, *The Sino-Soviet Dispute* (London: The China Quarterly, 1961).

Hughes, Emmet John. *The Ordeal of Power: A Political Memoir of the Eisenhower Years* (New York: Dell, 1964).

Iriye, Akira (ed.). *U.S. Policy Toward China* (Boston, Mass.: Little, Brown, 1968).

Jervis, Robert. *The Logic of Images in International Relations* (Princeton: Princeton University Press, 1970).

Joy, Adm. C. Turner. *How Communists Negotiate* (New York: Macmillan, 1955).

Kahn, Herman. *On Escalation* (New York: Praeger, 1965).

Kahn, Herman and Anthony J. Wiener (eds.). *Crisis and Arms Control* (Harmon-on-Hudson, New York: Hudson Institute, 1962).

Kalicki, Jan H. 'China, America and Arms Control', *The World Today*, April 1970.

'Nixon's Asia', *Pacific Community*, October 1972.

'Sino-American Relations After Cambodia', *The World Today*, September 1970.

'Sino-American Relations Despite Indochina,' *The World Today*, November 1971.

Kelman, Herbert C. (ed.). *International Behavior: A Social-Psychological Analysis* (New York: Holt, Rinehart & Winston, for the Society for the Psychological Study of Social Issues, 1965).

Kennan, George F. *American Diplomacy, 1900–1950* (New York: New American Library, 1951).

Kintner, William, David C. Schwartz *et al. A Study on Crisis Management* (Philadelphia, Pa.: University of Pennsylvania Foreign Policy Research Institute, 1965).

Kissinger, Henry A. *American Foreign Policy* (New York: Norton, 1969).

Nuclear Weapons and Foreign Policy (New York: Doubleday, 1957).

Knebel, Fletcher. 'We Nearly Went to War Three Times', *Look*, 8 February 1955.

Knorr, Klaus. *On the Uses of Military Power in the Nuclear Age* (Princeton, N.J.: Princeton University Press, 1966).

Knorr, Klaus and Sidney Verba (eds.). *The International System: Theoretical Essays* (Princeton: Princeton University Press, 1961).

Kundra, J. C. *Indian Foreign Policy, 1947–1954* (Gronigen, Netherlands: Walters, 1955).

Lacouture, Jean and Philippe Devillers. *La fin d'une guerre: Indochine 1954* (Paris: Editions du Seuil, 1960).

Lall, Arthur. *How Communist China Negotiates* (New York: Columbia University Press, 1968).

Lancaster, Donald. *The Emancipation of French Indochina* (London: Oxford University Press, for the Royal Institute of International Affairs, 1961).

Lanzetta, John T. 'Group Behavior Under Stress', in J. David Singer (ed.), *Human Behavior and International Relations: Contributions from the Social-Psychological Sciences* (Chicago: Rand McNally, 1965).

Larson, Arthur. *Eisenhower: The President Nobody Knew* (London: Leslie Frewin, 1969).

Leckie, Robert. *Conflict, The History of the Korean War, 1950–1953* (New York: Putnam's, 1962).

Lichterman, Martin. 'To the Yalu and Back', in Harold Stein (ed.), *American Civil-Military Decisions: A Book of Case Studies* (Birmingham: University of Alabama Press, for the Twentieth Century Fund, 1963).

Lie, Trygve. *In the Cause of Peace* (New York: Macmillan, 1954).

Luard, Evan (ed.). *The Cold War: A Reappraisal* (New York: Praeger, 1964).

Lubell, Samuel. *The Revolt of the Moderates* (New York: Harper, 1956).

Lyon, Peter. *War and Peace in South-east Asia* (London: Oxford University Press, for the Royal Institute of International Affairs, 1969).

MacFarquhar, Roderick (ed.). *Sino-American Relations, 1949–1971* (New York: Praeger, 1972).

McClelland, Charles A. 'Action Structures and Communication in Two International Crises: Quemoy and Berlin', *Background*, February 1964.

   'The Acute International Crisis', *World Politics*, October 1961.

   'Decisional Opportunity and Political Controversy: The Quemoy Case', *Journal of Conflict Resolution*, September 1962.

   'Systems and History in Internation Relations', *General Systems Yearbook* (1958).

McLellan, David S. 'Dean Acheson and the Korean War', *Political Science Quarterly*, March 1968.

   'The Role of Political Style: A Study of Dean Acheson', in Roger Hilsman and Robert Good, *Foreign Policy in the Sixties: The Issues and the Instruments* (Baltimore, Md.: Johns Hopkins University Press, 1968).

McNeill, Elton B. *The Nature of Human Conflict* (Englewood Cliffs, N.J.: Prentice-Hall, 1965).

Miller, John, Jnr., Major Owen J. Carroll and Margaret E. Tackley. *Korea, 1951–1953* (Washington, D.C.: Office of the Chief of Military History, Department of the Army, 1956).

Montross, Lynn and Nicholas A. Canzona. 'The Chosun Reservoir Campaign', in *U.S. Marine Operations in Korea, 1950–1953*, vol. III (Washington, D.C.: Historical Branch, U.S. Marine Corps, 1957).

Niksch, Larry A. *The Korean Armistice Negotiations* (Washington, D.C.: Library of Congress Legislative Reference Service, 20 February 1967).

North, Robert C. *The Foreign Relations of China* (Belmont, Calif.: Dickenson, 1969).

Northedge, F. S. (ed.). *The Foreign Policies of the Powers* (London: Faber, 1968).

   'The Nature of Foreign Policy', *The Foreign Policies of the Powers* (London: Faber, 1968).

Osanka, Franklin M. (ed.). *Modern Guerrilla Warfare: Fighting Communist Guerrilla Movements, 1941–1961* (New York: Free Press, 1964).

Osgood, Charles E. *An Alternative to War or Surrender* (Urbana: University of Illinois Press, 1962).

Osgood, Robert E. *Limited War: The Challenge to American Strategy* (Chicago: University of Chicago Press, 1957).

Paige, Glenn. *The Korean Decision: June 24–30, 1950* (New York: Free Press, 1968).

Rees, David. *Korea: The Limited War* (London: Macmillan, 1964).

Roberts, Chalmers. 'Caught in a Trap of our Own Making', *The Reporter*, 2nd October 1958.

'The Day We Didn't Go to War', *The Reporter*, 14 September 1954.

Robertson, Roland. 'Strategic Relations Between National Societies: A Sociological Analysis', *Journal of Conflict Resolution*, March 1968.

Robinson, James A. 'Crisis', in *International Encyclopedia of the Social Sciences*, vol. III. pp. 510–514.

Rosenau, James N. (ed.). *International Politics and Foreign Policy: A Reader in Research and Theory* (New York: Free Press, 1961 and 1969).

Rovere, Richard H. *Affairs of State: The Eisenhower Years* (New York: Farrar, Straus & Cudahy, 1956).

Senator Joe McCarthy (London: Methuen, 1960).

Rovere, Richard H. and Arthur M. Schlesinger, Jnr. *The General and the President and the Future of American Foreign Policy* (London: Heinemann, 1952).

Schelling, Thomas. *Arms and Influence* (New Haven, Conn.: Yale University Press, 1966).

The Strategy of Conflict (New York: Oxford University Press, 1963).

Schelling, Thomas and Morton H. Halperin. *Strategy and Arms Control* (New York: Twentieth Century Fund, 1961).

Schilling, Warner, Paul Hammond and Glenn Snyder. *Strategy, Politics and Defense Budgets* (New York: Columbia University Press, 1962).

Schnabel, James F. *Policy and Direction: The First Year* (Washington, D.C.: Department of the Army, Office of Chief of Military History, 1967).

Schram, Stuart. *Mao Tse-tung* (Harmondsworth, Middx.: Penguin, 1966).

The Political Thought of Mao Tse-tung (Harmondsworth, Middx.: Penguin, 1969).

Schram, Stuart and Hélène Carrère d'Encausse (eds.). *Le marxisme et l'Asie 1853–1964* (Paris: Colin, 1965).

Schurmann, Franz. *Ideology and Organization in Communist China*, 2nd edition, enlarged (Berkeley and Los Angeles: University of California Press, 1968).

Schwartz, Benjamin I. *Communism in China: Ideology in Flux* (Cambridge, Mass.: Harvard University Press, 1968).

Schwartz, David C. 'Decision Theories and Crisis Behavior: An Empirical Study of Nuclear Deterrence in International Political Crises', *Orbis*, Summer 1967.

Seabury, Paul. *The Rise and Decline of the Cold War* (New York and London: Basic Books, 1967).

Shaplen, Robert. *The Lost Revolution: The Story of Twenty Years of Neglected Opportunities in Vietnam and of America's Failure to Foster Democracy There* (New York: Harper, 1965).

Shepley, James. 'How Dulles Averted War', *Life*, 16 January 1956.

Singer, J. David (ed.). *Human Behavior and International Relations: Contributions from the Social-Psychological Sciences* (Chicago: Rand McNally, 1965).

Snow, Edgar. *Red Star Over China* (New York: Modern Library, 1944).

Snyder, Glenn H. *Deterrence and Defense: Toward a Theory of National Security* (Princeton: Princeton University Press, 1961).

Snyder, Richard C., H. W. Bruck, and Burton Sapin. *Foreign Policy Decision-Making: An Approach to the Study of International Politics* (New York: Free Press, 1962).

Snyder, Richard C. and Glenn D. Paige. 'The United States' Decision to Resist Aggression in Korea: The Application of an Analytical Scheme', in James N. Rosenau (ed.), *International Politics and Foreign Policy: A Reader in Research and Theory* (New York: Free Press, 1961).

Sokolovsky, V. D. (ed.). *Military Strategy: Soviet Doctrine and Concepts* (New York: Praeger, 1963).

Spanier, John W. *The Truman-MacArthur Controversy and the Korean War* (Cambridge, Mass.: Harvard University Press, 1959).

Stebbins, Richard P. *The United States in World Affairs, 1950* (New York: Harper, for the Council on Foreign Relations, 1951).

  The United States in World Affairs, 1954 (New York: Harper, for the Council on Foreign Relations, 1959).

  The United States in World Affairs, 1958 (New York: Harper, for the Council on Foreign Relations, 1959).

Steele, A. T. *The American People and China* (New York: McGraw-Hill, 1966).

Stein, Harold (ed.). *American Civil-Military Relations: A Book of Case Studies* (Birmingham: University of Alabama Press, 1963).

Stone, I. F. *The Hidden History of the Korean War* (London: Turnstile Press, 1952).

Sun Tzu. *The Art of War* (tr. by Lionel Giles) in Major Thomas R. Phillips (ed.), *Roots of Strategy: A Collection of Military Classics* (London: John Lane, 1943).

Tanham, George K. *Communist Revolutionary Warfare: The Viet-Minh in Indochina* (New York: Praeger, 1961).

Ten Glorious Years: 1949–1959 (Peking: Foreign Languages Press, 1960).

Thomas, John R. 'Soviet Behavior in the Quemoy Crisis', *Orbis*, Spring 1962.

Trager, Frank N. (ed.). *Marxism in Southeast Asia: A Study of Four Countries* (Stanford: Stanford University Press, 1959).

Truong Chinh. *Primer for Revolt: The Communist Takeover in Viet-Nam.* A facsimile edition of *The August Revolution* and *The Resistance Will Win.* Introduction and notes by Bernard B. Fall (New York: Praeger, 1963).

Tsou, Tang. *America's Failure in China 1941–1950* (Chicago: University of Chicago Press, 1963).

  (ed.). *China in Crisis* (Chicago: University of Chicago Press, 1968), vol. II: 'China's Policies in Asia and America's Alternatives'.

  The Embroilment over Quemoy, International Study Paper No. 2 (Salt Lake City, Utah: University of Utah Press, under the auspices of the Institute of International Studies, University of Utah, and the Center for the Study of American Foreign and Military Policy, University of Chicago, 1959).

  'Mao's Limited War in the Taiwan Strait', *Orbis*, Fall 1959.

  'The Quemoy Imbroglio: Chiang Kai-shek and the United States', *Western Political Quarterly*, December 1959.

Union Research Institute, *Communist China, 1949–1959*, Communist

China Problem Research Series EC25 (Kowloon, Hong Kong: Union Research Institute, 1961).

Communist China, 1955–1958, Communist China Problem Research Series EC15, 18, 20, 24 (Kowloon, Hong Kong: Union Research Institute annual, 1956–1959).

Communist China Today (Kowloon, Hong Kong: Union Research Institute annual, 1949–56).

Van Ness, Peter. *Revolution and Chinese Foreign Policy: Peking's Support for Wars of National Liberation* (Berkeley: University of California Press, 1971).

Vatcher, William H., Jnr. *Panmunjom, The Story of the Korean Military Armistice Negotiations* (New York: Praeger, 1958).

Whiting, Allen S. *China Crosses the Yalu, The Decision to Enter the Korean War* (New York: Macmillan, 1960).

Wiener, A. J. and Herman Kahn. *Crisis and Arms Control* (Harmon-on-Hudson, New York: Hudson Institute, 1962).

Wint, Guy. *What Happened in Korea?: A Study of Collective Security* (London: Batchworth, 1954).

Wohlstetter, Albert. 'The Delicate Balance of Terror', *Foreign Affairs,* January, 1959.

Wolfers, Arnold. *Discord and Collaboration: Essays on International Politics* (Baltimore, Md.: Johns Hopkins, 1962).

Wolff, Kurt H. (ed. and tr.). *The Sociology of Georg Simmel* (Glencoe, Ill.: Free Press, 1950).

Wright, Quincy. 'The Escalation of International Conflicts', *Journal of Conflict Resolution,* December 1965.

The Study of War (Chicago: University of Chicago Press, 1942), 2 volumes.

Yoo, Tae-ho. *The Korean War and the United Nations* (Louvain: Louvain University Press, 1965).

Young, Kenneth T. 'American Dealings with Peking', *Foreign Affairs,* October 1966.

Diplomacy and Power in Washington-Peking Dealings: 1953–1967 (Chicago: University of Chicago Press, for the Center for Policy Study, 1967).

Negotiating with the Chinese Communists: The United States Experience, 1953–1967 (New York: McGraw-Hill, for the Council on Foreign Relations, 1968).

Young, Oran R. *The Intermediaries: Third Parties in International Crises* (Princeton: Princeton University Press, 1967).

The Politics of Force: Bargaining during International Crises (Princeton: Princeton University Press, 1968).

Zagoria, Donald. *The Sino-Soviet Conflict, 1956–1961* (New York: Atheneum, 1967).

Index